Economics of the Product Markets of Agriculture

Economics
of the
Product Markets
of
Agriculture

HAROLD F. BREIMYER

Iowa State University Press
AMES, IOWA

HAROLD F. BREIMYER, Perry Foundation Professor of Agricultural Economics at the University of Missouri—Columbia, holds a joint appointment in teaching, research, and extension. His field is marketing and public policy. Ohio-reared and educated at Ohio State University, University of California, and American University, in 1936 he became an economist with the United States Department of Agriculture. After holding various government positions he joined the University of Missouri in 1966. He was President of the American Agricultural Economics Association in 1969, and in 1973 was named a Fellow of that organization.

ⓒ 1976 The Iowa State University Press
Ames, Iowa 50010. All rights reserved

Composed and printed by
The Iowa State University Press

First edition, 1976

_____

Library of Congress Cataloging in Publication Data

Breimyer, Harold F
    Economics of the product markets of agriculture.

    Includes bibliographical references.
    1. Farm produce—United States—Marketing.
2. Agriculture—Economic aspects—United States.
I. Title.
HD9006.B67   381'.41'0973   75–44220
ISBN 0–8138–1840–0

_____

CONTENTS

v

LIST OF ILLUSTRATIONS

LIST OF TABLES

PREFACE

TWO CONTRASTING FEATURES of marketing in agriculture as delineated in this book can be drawn on to describe the book itself. Marketing involves both bringing a degree of standardization to the natural diversity of farm products and undertaking imaginative efforts at differentiation. In like fashion, the ideas contained herein are designed to fit traditional courses in agricultural economics yet are also intended to lead the student into explorations that may be distinctive and in instances unconventional.

Titled to relate to product markets of agriculture, this study nevertheless draws heavily on principles of industrial marketing. More and more the techniques of marketing products of industry are being introduced into the markets associated with agriculture. On the other hand, the agricultural economy has not lost all identity; it retains certain features that are peculiarly its own. Particularly is the initial stage of farm product marketing not duplicated elsewhere. An attempt has been made throughout this book to distinguish between the principles in agricultural marketing that can be generalized from industrial markets and those that remain exclusively agricultural.

Like most contemporary textbooks on marketing in agriculture, descriptive data are kept subordinate to exposition of principles. Little commodity orientation will be found. Other sources are available on the marketing of cotton, wheat, or livestock.

Another point of view tacitly incorporated is that a text for upperclass or graduate instruction differs from an undergraduate one not so much in the addition of data as in the refinement of concepts. Especially are principles set forth more explicitly, terms defined more precisely. Just as a skyscraper is not built by adding more bricks to a bungalow, advanced concepts in the economics of marketing require a redesigning of the analytical structure.

Always some concepts and ideas previously learned become casualties. Not necessarily in error but unsuited to more advanced analysis, they are replaced.

On the other hand, the language is traditional—verbal, not mathematical.

As a final caveat, this book is truly written as a textbook and not as a compendium of essays. Basic ideas are presented in summary form and rapid order, without detailed elaboration. Most will justify further inquiry. For nearly all of them an extensive literature is available.

The conventional yet sincere expression of gratitude without accountability is due the several persons who reviewed portions of this book, as credited in footnotes to chapters, and to James W. McKinsey for helping to "shape up" the final draft. I owe appreciation to Mrs. Wendell Buckler for patience in transcribing countless earlier drafts and to a corps of secretaries for preparing the final one.

Though not stated elsewhere, I dedicate this book to the memory of my parents. To one parent goes credit for whatever literary quality it may have and to the other any analytical skill it may prove to reveal.

HAROLD F. BREIMYER

Columbia, Missouri

Economics of the Product Markets of Agriculture

CHAPTER ONE

MARKETING IN THE ECONOMIC SYSTEM

M A R K E T I N G is an integral part of the economic system. That system, reduced to basic elements, consists of purposeful recombination of resources involving two or more persons. This is a time-less, place-less, institution-less definition. Its only parameters are that activity be planned, normative, and interpersonal. Happenstance events are excluded, as is a home gardener's self-sufficiency.

An economic system so defined allows any degree of roundabout-ness—i.e., use of capital and training of people. It does not distinguish between private and public resources used or private and public goods produced. It does not even say that economic activity is invariably aimed at satisfying wants. Some of it, both private and public, goes for persuasion as to what the wants are; and a little serves to deny fulfillment of wants.

Usually postulated are a number (infinite or nearly so) of alternate combinations of resources that are technically possible, each with a unique outcome. These translate into alternate means to achieve any prespecified objective.

It follows that the first datum required for examining and evaluating an economic system is a set of technical coefficients in production and the counterparts that calibrate the capacity of goods and services to create or abate human wants.

If economics were limited to that, it would be a readily manageable field of inquiry, though of huge dimension.

But economics had its original taproot in political economy, and to this day it is concerned also with systems of motivation, regulation, communication, and command employed to set the production-consumption process in motion and keep it going.

Indeed, not a few economists would move the latter into the foreground. James Buchanan is one such: "Economists, as professional social scientists, should possess a comparative advantage . . . in their expertise in a particular sort of human behavior and in the institutions that emerge from that behavior." The behavior he refers to begins with the " 'propensity' " of man to " 'truck and barter' " that Adam Smith noted, and extends to the "theory of markets" which should be emphasized above the "theory of resource allocation." It

Credit is due William J. Staub for help in writing this chapter and to V. James Rhodes for critical review.

3

reaches "beyond these confines . . . to explore man's never-ending quest for more complex and elaborate forms of voluntary cooperation" and ends finally in study of "institutions of all kinds, including the political," and "collective decision-making."[1]

SYSTEMS OF ECONOMIC ORGANIZATION. If marketing of agricultural products is to be examined in the context of how it fits into the economic system, the various classifications of economic systems are worth a brief note. Boulding sets up three kinds of systems. These are exchange, threat, and integrative.[2] Exchange is decentralized and voluntary. Threat implies duress. An integrative system is more unified, more nearly all-encompassing. Boulding says it will work well if it is accompanied by benevolent ethical behavior.

Schmid and Shaffer focus on the exchange system, which they subdivide into *"status, administrative,* and *bargained."*[3] For them bargained exchange means individual negotiation. It does not extend to collective bargaining, which is a different system resembling Boulding's threat category.

The present author has chosen a matrix classification that separates the system for production from that for control. Three kinds of production systems are craft/agrarian, manorial, and industrial. The control system also has three categories: bargained commodity exchange, status, and contract. Combinations at opposite corners illustrate how the matrix can be applied to the marketing of farm products. Bargained exchange of the products of craft/agrarian production describes open market selling of livestock produced and sold by individual independent farmers. Industrial production under contract fits the production of oranges by Coca Cola or broilers by Allied Mills —internal arrangements of administrative rather than bargained-exchange nature.[4]

The notes above are made to call attention to the subject matter and to whet intellectual appetites. A substantial body of literature is available on the subject.

The United States System. Unfortunately for both academic and operating students of marketing, the economic system found in the United States in the 1970s almost defies classification. The customary language is to call it a price oriented market economy. This term is attractive to business spokesmen as defensive strategy as well as to economists who want to continue using their neoclassical analytical tools. Insofar as the economy can still be described in that way, it comes under Boulding's exchange category, Schmid and Shaffer's exchange by bargaining, and a combination, in Breimyer's classification, of bargained exchange of industrially produced commodities.

In reality the U.S. economy is highly mixed. Market pricing still prevails widely, though more is found in the marketing of farm than of industrial products. However, neither production goods nor consumer goods are any longer universally exposed to market valuation. Less and less does market determined price alone give directional control to the economy. In the Schmid-Shaffer language, some exchange is administered and a little is status. Boulding's threat and integrative systems are far from absent. In the Breimyer terminology it has proved difficult to make the contract system work well in large scale industrial production. We seem to be moving back to various kinds of status arrangements. Examples are private pension plans, the food stamp plan, direct payments to farmers, and even, in a sense, countless income tax concessions.

Some economists take a radically nontraditional view of the economy. The most publicized if not the most articulate is Galbraith. His thesis, as summed by Shaffer, is that "the market has lost its significance as a disciplining and allocating device in the highly industrialized sector of the economy."[5] Papandreou is equally positive: "The capitalist economy of today is *not* in fact a market economy. . . ."[6]

We need not accept so sweeping a judgment, yet we can acknowledge that the U.S. economy has indeed taken on a diverse character. More will be said on this subject, particularly as it relates to marketing, at the end of this chapter.

DEFINITIONS OF MARKETING. If the definition of economics is nebulous, that of marketing is scarcely easier to arrive at. To be sure, working definitions are found everywhere. Each author of a text relating to marketing presents a definition of personal choice, be it borrowed or coined.

Beyond doubt, any definition of marketing is conventional. Nothing in the generic definition of economics creates a neat niche for "marketing."

The Agricultural View. It may help to review various definitions that authors have used. At one extreme are the older, more established definitions pertaining to marketing of farm products, found mainly in texts written for undergraduates. Kohls and Downey, for instance, addressing themselves to marketing as viewed by persons "concerned with agriculturally related fields," call marketing *"the performance of all business activities involved in the flow of goods* *and services from the point of initial agricultural production until they are in the hands of the ultimate consumer."*[7]

Breimyer uses even plainer language to express the same idea. As the first of three definitional concepts paralleling those given here he refers to the "what happens" school of marketing. It includes as marketing "everything that happens" between the farm and consumer.[8]

The Industrial View. At the opposite pole are definitions borrowed from industrial marketing that put the emphasis on merchandising. A few authors make marketing almost synonymous with product development and advertising. Moreover, they look at marketing from the vantage point of the firm; it is something a firm does. That "something" is to cultivate the loyalty of consumers to the products of that firm. The products in turn are "developed" with that purpose in mind.

Although agricultural marketing has not yet been transformed that much, the industrial marketing image helps to refute the older agrarian notion that regards production of farm products as a primary, autonomous, farm-based activity and marketing as secondary, subservient, and nonfarm. Marketing has at least equal status. It may dominate production.

Marketing v. Production. It is even questionable whether marketing as a concept can be distinguished sharply from production. At each stage of marketing a recombination of resources takes place. This is production. Some authors, mindful of this conflict of terms, would sharply narrow the definition of marketing. One of them is Phillips of Australia, who would expunge such functions as storage and transport and essentially define marketing as information gathering and communication.[9] Bakken would go even further, confining marketing to exchange.[10] Although these more restrictive definitions are defensible, they do not entirely escape the production-marketing paradox, for communication and negotiation of exchange require productive resources, if only human labor.

THE STRUCTURAL APPROACH TO MARKETING. Neither the farm oriented definition expressed by Kohls and Downey nor the market development approach enjoys widest currency. Shaffer has especially objected to the former; he sees "the traditional definition of agricultural marketing as what happens to farm products from the farm gate to the consumer" as "inappropriate."[11]

The two definitions fall short when tested in the crucible of marketing as an instigating and coordinating force over economic processes. Agrarian and industrial definitions both stress the physical distribution role of marketing. The market development school only adds devices of merchandising and promotion. Neither explains how marketing contributes to allocation of resources, particularly at earlier stages of the marketing sequence.

Because of that shortcoming the majority of agricultural marketing economists have come to accept the structural approach. Shaffer sums the approach succinctly in calling marketing the "system of markets and related institutions which organize the economic activity of the food and fibre sector of the economy."[12]

The structural approach may appear almost self-justifying in view of the foregoing rationale, but it opens up a near morass of definitional boundaries of its own. Exchange and distribution of goods and services, and coordinative control over the economy, now are lodged in many institutional arrangements other than market-exchange pricing. There are a variety of integrative relationships, private group action of syndical nature, and a big role for government. All these extend far beyond using market price as the sole control mechanism. How far should marketing go, definitionally, to encompass all these?

Intrafirm "Marketing." No unequivocal stand will be taken on all these issues; it is enough to admit that differences of opinion exist. Intrafirm transfer of product is a case in point. It was noted above that some definitions of marketing are expressed in terms of the activities of a firm. Whether this is the best way to look at marketing is not so easily dismissed as it once was, for the old standard business firm has thrown mutants such as conglomerates that pull into a common genus various enterprises that formerly were separate and independent.

Does the economics of internal managerial decisions in giant firms belong in "marketing"? Shaffer, noting that "since the development of the large and complex vertically integrated and conglomerate firm, groups of transactions within the firm become similar to a market," chooses to regard "intra-firm interplant transactions" as "part of the subject matter of marketing economics."[13] Not all marketing economists would agree. But in any case intrafirm accounting practices have earned recognition as an important parameter in the conduct of firms. Terms such as transfer or shadow prices have entered the marketing lexicon.

Three Aspects of Organizational Structure. Without resolving all the boundary line issues, we can help keep ideas in order by distinguishing between organizational and competitive structure of the marketing system. The former is empirical and concrete. The latter, although empirically based, is abstract.

In considering how the system is constructed organizationally, three concepts are useful. Competitive structure is examined at length in later chapters, principally Chapter 4.

1. Specialization—Adam Smith based his *Wealth of Nations* on the principle of specialization in the economy. The principle is universal today. Specialization gives rise to exchange of goods and services and requires an accommodating institutional system. It is integral to the concept of marketing.
2. The sequential nature of the total marketing process—Specialized activities that service the marketing process are not random. They are organized sequentially.
3. The composite character of sequential activities in marketing—This aspect of marketing is probably the least recognized. It refers to the fact that as a product moves through successive stages various services are added to it yet are combined into a composite unit. They are not merely additive and detachable.

The value of the separate services likewise aggregates into a single valuation. The price of eggs at retail is a composite of the value added in sorting, shipping, cartoning, and all other services, plus original production.

SPECIALIZATION. Specialization is both vertical and horizontal. Issues arise as to how far the study of marketing should go in recognizing specialized activities. It will be pointed out in Chapter 6 that some studies of operating efficiency have extended to the minutiae of "therbligs" (the most elemental physical motions). In Chapter 4 the Mighell and Jones diagram of vertical-horizontal specialization is quoted favorably.

Horizontal specialization invariably leads to the quagmire of what is a separate versus a differentiated product. Where are lines to be drawn? The dilemma is made worse by the fact that the economist's analytical tools are best applied to standard product. The temptation is to assume a higher degree of standardization, and less differentiation, than is empirically justified.

Geographical specialization, sometimes called locational differentiation, is even more difficult to manage. Geography is probably the most important single differentiating factor in retailing. It is

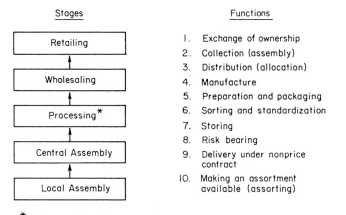

FIG. 1.1. Stages and functions in marketing farm products.

pointed out in Chapter 9 that the economics of location of enterprise is an underappreciated part of the economics of marketing. It is neglected too often. Among other effects, location bears on the competitive structure in marketing.

SEQUENTIAL PATTERN: STAGES AND FUNCTIONS. The sequential nature of marketing may be seen more clearly by referring to the simple diagram in Fig. 1.1. The diagram gives the familiar terminology of stages and functions. Farm products move in a continuous flow from farm to consumer, yet there are discernible interruption points, or stages, at which certain activities or processes—functions—are performed.

Figure 1.1 presents the simplest possible outline of stages, as they are confined to five. The sequence applies to the progression from farmer to family consumer. In reality, there are industrial consumers of products as well as family consumers. The terminology used here is that if an industrial consumer of a basic raw product transforms it into a distinctly new product, the marketing sequence is said to stop at processing. A new sequence then begins for the new (manufactured) product.

A stage, then, may be defined as a point of interruption in the sequential movement of a product from producer to consumer at which processes or services (functions) are performed.

Kohls and Downey define a function as "a major specialized

activity performed in accomplishing the marketing process." The functions are performed by "institutions."[14]

In Fig. 1.1 ten different functions are listed. Like the stages shown, the number and names are somewhat arbitrary. For example, some authors would make assorting a part of distribution. Even more debatable is calling delivery under nonprice contract a separate function. Is it not just another form of collection or assembly of products? It may be that. Yet it has been the usual practice to perform the collection function in connection with exchange of ownership. When broilers produced under contract are collected (assembled), ownership does not change. However, there is no need to bog down in debates on definition of functions.

It will be obvious that two or more functions are normally performed at each stage, but the particular combinations vary widely by product and indeed by individual marketing activities. It may be equally clear that stages may be telescoped. The most extreme case is a farmer's "peddling" his eggs or vegetables directly to consumers. On the other hand, it is necessary to remember that integration of stages need not eliminate functions. Retail food chains, for example, combine wholesaling and retailing stages but the functions associated with wholesaling continue to be performed.

COMPOSITE CHARACTER OF FINAL PRODUCTS. The distinctive feature of the marketing of farm products is that so many products retain their identity through many or all the sequential stages from farmer to consumer. Or at least family consumers, and the public generally, tend to think in those terms. They associate a great many of the foods they buy with the original farm product. Not only are original names retained for all fruits and vegetables but shoppers buy meats by generic names (pork, beef, broilers) and continue to distinguish between wheat ("white" or "whole") and rye bread. Among breakfast cereals they may choose corn flakes or rolled oats.

A few products do not move through to family consumers while holding their original identity. As just noted, some are transformed at the processing stage, whereupon a new marketing sequence commences. Few persons would deny that soybeans are manufactured into new products.

Phillips and Duncan adhere to the same distinction. They regard marketing as "including all the activities necessary to place tangible goods in the hands of household consumers and industrial users," and separate out "such activities as involve a significant change in the form of goods."[15]

There may be as much deep-rooted symbolism as economics in consumers' penchant to hold to agrarian language. It is nevertheless interesting and perhaps instructive that the Eastman Company did not have too much trouble coaching consumers to say "Kodak," nor Kimberly-Clark, "Kleenex." But the U.S. public still prefers to say "ham" rather than accept an advertiser's coinage for the name of a hog's leg.

Joint Product-Service: "Tie-in Sale." The economics of marketing farm products might be easier to understand if it had less sequential and composite character—if instead each stage turned out a new product. In that case marketing in agriculture could be confined to final merchandising, much like marketing in industry.

But when farm product marketing is addressed in the more traditional way, its composite feature introduces complexity. It means that each service added, each function performed, is incorporated into the basic product. These functions have no usefulness, indeed no identity, independent of the product to which they are attached. The consumer cannot buy bacon separately from packaging, or milk apart from homogenizing, pasteurizing, and refrigeration.

The closest analogy for what actually happens is a tie-in sale, such as the practice during World War II when a consumer was required to buy one shoddy item of merchandise to get a preferred but scarce one. Or it is like the one-cent sale in which, despite the child's request for the second item only (for a penny), it is necessary to buy the first one before the second can be had.

Consumers are offered some products with and without various attached services. Broilers can be bought whole or cut up, and potatoes fresh or processed. But it is impossible to go far to separate product and services. The possible combinations are almost infinite in number, and both the consumer's brain and the retailer's shelf have finite limits.

To this point there are many implications. One is that the consumer cannot really express a separate preference for each constituent service. Individual demand functions cannot be isolated. At best, demand for each service is expressed extremely vaguely. Therefore, the argument sometimes offered by apologists for a particular service that it "must be demanded, else it would not exist" is without validity.

Not consumer demand alone but competitive structure also must be taken into account in explaining the kinds of services that are provided in marketing.

In spite of the fact that the final product of marketing is joint, participants in the marketing process do not ordinarily see themselves as mere agents in a marketing sequence, doing their part in a mutual effort to get product efficiently from farm to consumer. On the contrary, each firm, its public relations brochures notwithstanding, is interested in selling *its* services. To the firm, the relation of those services to the total marketing sequence is incidental.

It is important to note this characteristic of market firms. So often the idea has been cultivated that those firms apply their services deferentially to the overall mission of getting products from farm to household consumer. They do not. They pursue their individual goals; and whether or not those goals are consistent with society's wishes for quick, efficient, and safe marketing of farm and food products is affected by (1) the internal economics of the firm, and (2) the competitive structure of the industry.

No implicit unity exists between the goals of the marketing firm and of the marketing system. It would be an error to assume otherwise. And the structure of the market goes far to determine whether unity prevails, case by case.

OTHER WAYS TO LOOK AT MARKETING. The preceding review has described the system for marketing farm products in comparatively prosaic language. It has adopted what Duddy and Revzan, in a standard text, term the "approach of the economic theorist."[16] It puts marketing into the framework of structural analysis.

Marketing nevertheless lends itself to a wide variety of approaches. Among the more familiar are:

1. Marketing institutions*—Business schools especially study how processors operate, as well as transporters and retailers.
2. Behavioral psychology, popular with advertisers—The exciting record of the psychologist John B. Watson will be noted in Chapter 2.
3. Decision making in the firm—This school divides into management design and analysis, and interpretive commentaries on the nature of the modern business firm such as those by Cyert and March (in *A Behaviorial Theory of the Firm*[17]), Boulding (in *The Organizational Revolution*[18]) and Galbraith (in *The New Industrial State*[19]).
4. Group organizational structure. "Consumerism" and group action by farmers, as in cooperatives and bargaining, fit in this category.

Esoteric Ideas. Marketing has not lacked for imaginative and articulate spokesmen. The following examples of esoteric thinking will

*This use of the word "institution" conforms to that of Kohls and Downey. It is a narrow definition. A broader definition embraces all the organizational system, including codes and laws, by which business is done.

provide reference points for the interested student, even though they are not a basic part of this text.

Often the various writings translate the workaday component of marketing into abstract conceptualizations of the marketing system. Bartels, in an enlightening 1968 article, first chronicles "explanations of marketing" beginning with traditional theory of the 1920s, continuing with Ralph Breyer's vision in the 1930s of the "marketing structure as circuits, or channels . . ." and extending to theories of marketing as "a type of behaviorism" and as "decision making of marketing managers." Most original is his recounting of a theory of "comparativism, or the relating of marketing practice to ecological factors in the cultural environment." He adds, "Primitive theory took environment as given. Environmentalism abstracts its essential characteristics and shows its causal relationship to marketing processes, systems, and practices."[20]

In a 1974 article Bartels elaborates his interpretation of the "evolution of the scope of marketing." He does so in acknowledging the tendency to broaden the scope, as he adds "marketing, as a social process . . as a societal process, . . . as a generic function applicable to both business and nonbusiness institutions."[21]

Bartels's preference is to avoid excessive broadening, but he depicts accurately the issues that run through marketing literature in the mid-1970s. He also observes wryly that if marketing be made too inclusive, subfields resembling earlier and simpler concepts will appear. An example is "the emergence of the field termed *logistics* or *physical distribution*." He concludes, "Perhaps marketing as originally conceived will reappear under another name."[22]

Contemporary disputes about how far marketing reaches, with advocates of reaching high, have their antecedents. Some years ago Peter Drucker, prolific writer on the philosophy and management of business, called marketing "a dynamic process of society through which business enterprise is integrated productively with society's purposes and human values." He soared higher:

> In an economy that is striving to break the age-old bondage of man to misery, want, and destitution, marketing is also the catalyst for the transmutation of latent resources into actual resources, of desires into accomplishments, and the development of responsible economic leaders and informed economic citizens.[23]

Writers in the early 1970s soared less but they wrestled responsibly with the extent to which social values should be brought into the marketing context. In a different probing they wondered how well the principles and terms developed in marketing could be applied to nonmarketing problems. Among sources worth pursuing are Lazer,[24] Kottler,[25] Tucker, [26] Shuptrine and Osmanski,[27] and Bagozzi.[28]

THE ALDERSON INSIGHTS. Any listing of esoteric views of marketing must pay deference to the late Wroe Alderson, in his lifetime the dean of marketing philosophers. Knowing no disciplinary bounds, Alderson started with cultural anthropology in laying the foundation for a theory of marketing. He set forth two opposite "types of equilibrating systems. One is the atomistic in which there is a tendency toward equilibrium among separate elements. . . . At the other extreme is the system regarded as an organic whole with structured components such as in the human body which are joined together in a fully determined and inflexible pattern." Midway between these he sketched "loosely coupled systems . . ." with which he identified the U.S. marketing system. "A marketing system, like an ecological group, can adapt to the environment. . . ."

Alderson followed through by linking "separate theoretical positions in marketing and economics" with each equilibrating system. "First is the atomistic model which has been well developed in classical economics. At the other extreme is the organismic model" which he associated with "the genuine institutionalists such as Marx and Veblen." The middle ground of an ecological model, which Alderson associated with functionalism, "can be observed in pseudo-institutionalists such as John R. Commons and J. B. Clark, and in pseudo-classicists such as J. M. Keynes." Functionalism is also the home ground for most contemporary writers on marketing theory.[29]

Bartels, Alderson, and a select few others must be credited with lifting theorizing about marketing out of the humdrumness in which it had previously rested. And if these flights of intellectual fancy seem to overcomplicate the business of getting an apple from the tree to a boy's mouth, let comfort be taken from still another quotation from the acute mind of Alderson, as he warned of "a counsel of despair telling us that we must know everything in order to learn anything."[30]

HISTORY OF MARKETING: AN INTERPRETATION. The historical record of marketing in agriculture helps to explain contemporary institutions, customs, and habits of thought. It aids in interpreting the marketing system of our day.

A preliminary word of caution is called for. The historical account is far from clear. Not until fairly recent times was evolutionary development of markets recorded reliably. We can suspect that the sketchiness of earlier accounts has tempted writers on marketing to substitute imagination for data. With this in mind, Bakken, for example, rebukes ". . . writers who believe implicitly in their ability to penetrate the heavy veil of time by the sheer power of their logic."[31] Robbins says that notions as to the origin of markets have as "the one thing in common" their "high degree of speculation unsupported by empirical data."[32]

Also complicating a historical review is the fact that marketing's evolutionary development was not a straight line. It progressed and regressed, detoured, and altogether took a wiggly course.

In an oversimplified scheme, the evolution of agricultural marketing can be traced through four epochs in economic development. Consistent with the central theme of this book, the outline that follows considers not only the collection-distribution side of marketing, but also how it may give direction or coordination to the economy.

More specifically stated, marketing may be viewed historically in terms of:

1. The nature of the participating unit—It will be seen that through much of history the unit was aggregative (except for royalty). The disaggregation that began in the Middle Ages is now being reversed into new aggregation and integration.
2. The economic role that marketing performs—Markets served to distribute products among consumers long before they acquired a reciprocal role in allocating resources in production.
3. The form of organization of the market—"Markets" that consist only of producers selling their finished products directly to consumers are rudimentary compared to those having intermediaries or "middlemen." The latter permit exchange between producers and consumers separated in time and space; and, in the interest of protection of all parties, they require a complex set of supporting services and rules that are absent in the former.

The four epochs are self-sufficiency, agrarian organization, agricultural organization, and commercial organization.

Self-sufficiency. Probably the earliest epoch in human existence involved no market exchange. This was the most primitive self-sufficiency. However, the self-sufficiency was attained within groups. The group could have been the extended family or tribe. Within the group there was specialization of activity and division of common product, but all was done by a combination of customary practice and administrative direction—often autocratic control by the family head, chieftain, or body of elders. Hicks believes that the traditional economy had much staying power, and the command element surged only in the presence of threat.[33] In the terminology of Schmid and Shaffer, this was status and administrative exchange (see page 4).

Marketing and exchange between groups doubtless came into being early. To large extent it involved luxury products for the ruling class; certain essential items for the populace, such as salt and medications; dyes; and in some parts of the world, human slaves. Miriam Beard, writing about the Mesopotamian merchant of 2500 B.C., reports that he "was forming trading companies for penetration into distant realms, he was trafficking in many kinds of wares, wool, spices, soda, silver, ointments and fair-skinned slaves. . . ." Moreover, ". . . he was seasoned in affairs, wary in drawing up contracts, stout in litigation."[34]

Attractive as are such accounts, and doubtless accurate, the warning given above should be reechoed. It is easy to exaggerate the amount of early market trading. Many of the early explorations into market trading were indeed venturesome. They were repeated with new participants in new places century after century. Nevertheless, a market *system* was not the basis on which ancient economies were organized.

Agrarian Organization. The second epoch in development was systematic sale and consumption of food and other necessities of life. During this epoch those products were the more or less accidental surpluses that producers accumulated.

Markets remained in this epoch during most of the Middle Ages. Local and regional markets or fairs grew during that era. They handled primarily consumer goods. Originally, producers sold directly to consumers, although the gradual entry of middlemen was a salient feature of market development during that time.

Markets of this kind help consumers to take advantage of available production, but they fall short of regulating economic activity in their interests. Not yet did a market system exert a recursive force to guide future production.

The medieval fairs were a richly promising progenitor of the sophisticated markets that followed, as well as a source of nursery rhymes.* But they too could easily be overglorified. During most of the Middle Ages the majority of ordinary people lived under the repression inherent in the feudal system. The manor retained the ancient structure of group self-sufficiency, with only a small fraction of the product sold into market exchange. Serfs were essentially denied a market's benefits and protections. A universal decentralized market system is inconsistent with a feudal society, and a market system of that kind could not come into being until the bonds of feudalism had been broken.

*There is sociological significance to the many marketing themes in nursery rhymes: "Simple Simon met a pieman, going to the fair . . ."; "To market, to market, to buy a fat pig . . ."; and many others.

Agricultural Organization. This third epoch in agricultural marketing differs from the preceding one not so much in how markets govern consumption, but in how they give direction to production. They serve to make production conform in some measure to the configuration of demand expressed by consumers. That is, demand enters into the equation alongside the economics of employment of available resources in order to determine what is produced.

This is the market system, and economic system, of classical economics and of older marketing textbooks.

Significantly, this model, like the preceding ones, still treats demand and productive resources as essentially exogenous. There is no place for using resources to influence demand, positively or negatively. On the production side, resources are typically regarded as fixed or given. Although intricate technology to develop resources is not logically excluded, it has not characterized the agricultural-organization epoch in history. Nor has negative development been taken into account, i.e., the social costs involved in destroying or polluting basic resources.

This is by all odds the most disintegrative of the four systems of organization. It has gradually given way since to reintegration, as will be depicted below.

As this epoch provided the historical setting for the highest development of a price oriented market economy, further review is in order.

HEROIC AGE OF MARKETS. A market system emerged during the Enlightenment period of Western Europe and came into fruition sometime around the middle of the Industrial Revolution. Scholars have debated the extent to which the market system was antecedent, cause, part of, or the result of cultural, technological, and institutional changes of that age in history. Thurnwald doubts that a market economy did "gradually evolve out of the commercial activities of the medieval bourgeoisie, as many historians believe. . . ." He asks if "the whole fabric of feudal society [had] to be broken by new methods of warfare, the rise of national states, the discoveries and the Reformation before modern capitalism could emerge."[35]

Certain it is that the market system had as prerequisites the institution of private property including rights as to its use and disposal, specialization in production, improvements in transport, a minimum level of literacy, and various legal protections. The market system was a sharp departure from the rigid feudal system built on status, a major element in a new kind of world.

A market system may be said to require also an economic order separate from a political order. According to Polanyi, "Normally the economic order is a function of the social order in which it is contained. Neither under tribal, nor feudal, nor mercantile conditions was there . . . a separate economic system in society."[36]

On the whole, there is reason to believe the emerging market system played an instrumental role. Writes Hotchkiss: "The idea that every person has a natural right to sell his products and services to the best advantage is of recent origin." "In England," he explains, "for at least six centuries after the Norman Conquest, the right to engage in either foreign or domestic trade was not a natural right but an acquired privilege. It was fought for or purchased, and then defended against new claimants."[37]

As the right to sell one's produce was extended, protective rules were needed and eventually granted. The authority to regulate its trade was one of the most cherished privileges that a town received from the Crown. Civil and ecclesiastical authorities accorded to medieval markets the privilege of sanctuary, that is, protection from brigands. Banks sprang up near markets. Market centers gave rise to growth of cities.

John R. Commons is one of the spokesmen for regarding marketing as giving a thrust to new legal institutions. He points out how briefly had a workable and enforceable system of contracts been attained when classical economists began their writing. Only in the 16th century did merchants gain enough political power to induce the courts to enforce their contracts. Not yet could contracts be sold to third parties. "It required not only the Seventeenth Century but all of the centuries following to invent ways of making this kind of promise [i.e., contracts in commerce] negotiable."[38]

A market economy probably reached its climax midway in the new industrial age. It was then that the doctrine of a self-regulating system in which economic units of modest size interact in a market mechanism, and the price of a product controls both its consumption and income to the producer, came closest to full expression.

It was then that the classical ideal was approached, as described by Polanyi:

A market economy [as] an economic system controlled, regulated, and directed by markets alone; order in the production and distribution of goods is entrusted to this self-regulating mechanism. An economy of this kind . . . assumes markets in which the supply of goods (including services) available at a definite price will equal the demand at that price. . . . Production will . . . be controlled by prices, for the profits of the goods also will depend upon prices, for prices form incomes, and it is with the help of these incomes that the goods produced are distributed amongst the members of society. . . . [There are] markets for all ele-

ments of industry, not only for goods . . . but also for labor, land, and
money. . . .[39]

Commercial Organization. We need not take time to question how
closely the markets of their heroic age conformed to the Polanyi ideal.
Scarcely had they approached it when a new epoch in the evolution
of markets began. It dates from perhaps a century ago.

It is always harder to encapsule current than historic events.
Even the term, "commercial organization," is less than a perfect choice
of words to describe developments in industrial marketing that com-
menced then and have since moved gradually to agricultural markets.

The key principle in commercial organization is reintegration.
This compromises or even eliminates the exogenous status of consumption and production—of demand and supply. No longer are
consumption and production separate and detached, to be coordinated
only by long distance communication in which exchange markets provide both the medium and the language.

Once this is said we should be guarded in our analysis. One
feature noted readily is the use of resources to influence demand. This
is absent in the first three epochs. But resources are used also to
develop resources. In the ultimate version of a capital-using economy
of the fourth epoch, in Joan Robinson's words, "there are no persistent
differences in factors of production."[40]

DIVISIBILITY AND MOBILITY OF RESOURCES. It may help toward clarifying
the significance of this fourth epoch if one more theoretical concept is
introduced. The concept will be referred to repeatedly throughout this
book. It may be expressed in terms of the divisibility and mobility of
resources.

Resources exist in wide variety, though certain ones are more
plentiful than others. Human beings have likewise an almost unlimited number of wants—before or after being swayed by promotion—
and each human being presents a unique combination of them. Yet
certain wants are more common and more powerful than others.

Ideally, there exists a unique combination of resources that best
fulfills each person's unique combination of wants.

If resources were infinitely divisible and perfectly mobile, an
economic system could in fact tailor all products to the precise specification of each consumer. There would be a perfect matching up of
resources and wants. Everything would be custom-made; all services
would be personalized. It is not farfetched to regard this as the ideal
situation toward which we hope to guide the actual economic system.

Manifestly, it is impossible to reach that ideal. Yet it serves as an adequate base point for examining our economic system in action.

We begin by observing that resources in their native state (including untrained human beings as workers) are capable of satisfying very few human wants. Thereupon a process begins for bringing production capability and consumption closer together. Paradoxically, it involves two quite different kinds of activity. These are as follows:

1. To tool resources, including training of people, so as to minimize their indivisibility and immobility—that is, to make them capable of highly varied uses. In that way they can come closer to matching consumers' demands.
2. To use the arts of persuasion to induce consumers to want what is easiest (and most profitable) to produce.

The first involves intricate technology and high training of people. It results in a wide array of diversified products.

The second course, sharply different from the first, introduces philosophical questions about the human psyche and individual will, and at its extreme it presents scare warnings of a totally pliable, propaganda-conditioned populace.

CONTEMPORARY U.S. SCENE. In brief restatement, the fourth epoch in marketing is distinguished by making both consumption and production subject to management or development, and in principle it offers a spectrum of choices between primarily developing resources versus primarily influencing or manipulating demand.

United States marketing in the 1970s has many marks of this fourth epoch. Yet it has entered only partially and imperfectly into that epoch. It has gone farther in that direction in industrial than in agricultural marketing.

The expositional scheme of setting forth successive epochs in development might imply progressive improvement. Such an implication is a snare if not a delusion. Not only is the concept of epochs in development normatively neutral, but the actual implementation at each epoch can take a wide variety of forms with an equally wide range of outcomes.

It nevertheless is undeniably true that the fourth epoch broadens the marketing role, giving it more scope and tools and therefore more power. It makes marketing operational. It endows marketing with motive force and almost, it would seem, with human personality. Marketing thus has more capacity to perform well, by society's standards, or to perform badly.

In preceding epochs, marketing was weakly subordinate to the economic forces of basic production and final consumption. Even in the third epoch which exalted the market as an economic institution, prevailing thinking gave it little independent status. If conditions were proper (good information, no monopoly, etc.) the system would be self-regulating and the behavior of firms virtually circumscribed.

The neoclassicists were the intellectual savants of the third epoch of marketing. They harmonized the concepts of diminishing marginal utility in consumption, credited to the Austrian school, with those of diminishing marginal utility in production, which had older classical roots. Marketing was the innocent harmonizing instrument.

The fourth epoch grants individual firms more decision-making options. Their range of options is the "conduct" that Bain puts into his trilogy of structure-conduct-performance. (The Bainsian analytical scheme is discussed in Chapter 4.) As conduct is not foreordained by structure, the quality of performance is not predetermined.

In the United States, firms have moved notably toward larger size. They have grown large horizontally and have integrated vertically and merged conglomerately.* They have thereby eliminated big chunks of the market exchange that typifies the third epoch in marketing. There is aggregation in consumption too—not only the intra-firm consumption of primary and intermediate goods but, in the final stage, consumption of social goods and institutionalized consumption (as in school lunches and the food stamp plan).

In a real sense modern business firms have taken on such a capacity for power, and they are being countervailed by so many other forms of organization ranging from organized labor groups to the ever-extending role of government, that institutional organization becomes an important separate subject. In some respects this is still the most elusive aspect of the modern marketing system. At the least must it be recognized that the Engine-Charlie Wilson syndrome does *not* apply: there is no necessary identity between interests of large firms and society.† The same idea is cast in language of a respected writer on marketing. McCarthy has written that marketing shall operate so as to "satisfy consumers and accomplish the company's objectives."[41] He presupposes an identity of interests that cannot in fact be assumed to exist.

Not least among attributes of marketing today is its vocabulary. A distinctive lexicon has come into use. Control and planning and strategy; models and simulation; systems analysis; feedback; and a

---

*A question may properly be raised as to whether firms of the fourth epoch necessarily are large. Perhaps not. In the U.S. experience they certainly have tended toward bigness, and the suspicion is that the immense advantage accruing to the firm from successful persuasion of consumers induces bigness. John Kenneth Galbraith (*The New Industrial State*) among others insists that economy not of production but of market development underlies the giant firm of recent (and present) decades.

†During hearings for his confirmation as Secretary of Defense Mr. Wilson, President of General Motors, declared in response to a question that what was good for General Motors was good for the country. His added comment, "and vice versa," was lost in press accounts.

host of other words and phrases fill the pages of journals and the air of marketing meetings.

The prolix, telescoped, versatile but power-laden market system that, for better or for worse, joins production and consumption closer together lends itself to a variety of characterizations. Galbraith's and Papandreou's negative comments were noted early in this chapter. David McCord Wright stresses the elevated status of consumption. "The demand for the produce of the upper stages of production is no longer uniquely linked to the output or even the expected output of the lower stages."[42] McCarthy calls the U.S. system one of market orientation, and he separates "market-oriented independent firms" from "market-oriented integrated firms."[43] The latter, of course, have increasingly come to the fore.

It remains for Duddy and Revzan to sound the alarm of challenge to all the collected understanding and wisdom that has heretofore marked the third epoch of marketing and even, it may be said, U.S. ideology about the economic system. "Marketing includes elements of strategy of control that are repugnant to the economic theorist for whom the market is free, open, and competitive—a place where information is accessible to buyers and sellers, where rational judgments prevail, and where buyers exercise complete freedom of choice."[44]

The fourth epoch of marketing is indeed a long way removed from the third.

IN PERSPECTIVE. Marketing not only is an integral part of the economy, but goes far to shape its character.

The economy has become more and more a consciously managed economy and less and less a way of adjusting to the whims of nature. We no longer separate marketing from the process of production as though production were a different world. We do not say that a one-way delivery line between production and consumption defines marketing. We recognize the directional control powers present at all stages in marketing. Modern marketing accords volition to its various actors.

If all this versatility offers opportunity for using marketing to do good, as is Drucker's vision, it offers equal chance of failing to do so, or doing harm. There falls then to the processes of collective decision, not only volition but an obligation to evaluate and if necessary to regulate the structure and the conduct of the marketing system.

In the final analysis, more than in any other epoch marketing in the fourth epoch puts a heavy burden upon the instruments of public policy.

CHAPTER TWO

WELFARE GOALS IN MARKETING

E V E R Y   U N I T in a production and marketing system, at every level of aggregation from the individual worker and the individual consumer to the national economy, pursues one or more goals.

It is impossible to examine and evaluate the operation of that system, or the agricultural marketing part of it, without first setting forth as accurately as possible what those goals are. The next step, obviously, is to design ways to appraise performance relative to the goals.

Goals are many, mixed, and inconsistent. Yet the greater problem lies not in the first step of identifying them but in the second of judging how well the economy performs toward meeting them. The latter plagues all observers. It shakes up producers, marketers, and consumers—and economists and policy makers as well.

For example, it is almost a ritual to say, "Marketing costs too much." Perhaps it does. Or perhaps it does not. But the two-step problem arises. How can a desirable or even acceptable cost of marketing be decided? And then, how can actual costs be measured?

ELUSIVENESS OF GOAL-PERFORMANCE ANALYSIS. Everyone concurs on the importance of goal-and-performance analysis of marketing, and countless practical men and scholars have tried to do it, yet it remains slippery, elusive, hard to pin down.

Volumes of data are collected on the marketing system, with the U.S. Department of Agriculture in the lead. Selected series of descriptive data are presented in Chapter 5. Distinguished groups, such as the National Commission on Food Marketing of 1964–66, have probed in depth.

Performance testing in marketing is only an extension, or branch, of the field of inquiry known as the Economics of Welfare. Hence the title to this chapter. Eminent scholars have written at length on the subject, although not entirely conclusively. Among them are Scitovsky, Bator, Mishan, Arrow, and Hicks.* Selected quotations

*Economics of Welfare is the term coined by economic theorists. Writers on industrial marketing have used language such as societal values in marketing (compare notes on later trends in marketing analysis in Chapter 1). The two lines of inquiry, although almost without intercommunication, are closely related.

will be presented in this chapter. Yet this part of the economics of marketing is still the least satisfactory of all.

This chapter offers little more than a road map to help guide through the spotty terrain. The first part tells more about difficulties and problems than about solid solutions. Later in the discussion, welfare goals for consumers and the goals of the business firm are commented on at more length.

The Individual's Pleasure-Pain Calculus. Probably the best starting point is the old idea of a pleasure-pain calculus for each producer-consumer. This applies only to persons who hold both roles. It will not fit recipients of transfer payments. In this thesis, each individual performs economic enterprise *(work)*, and consumes the product of his labor (directly or via exchange) up to the point where the displeasure of further effort exactly equals the pleasure of consumption resulting from that effort. This is self-revealing as equating at the margin. It is the most elementary exhibition of marginal analysis.

PROBLEM 1: NONMEASURABILITY. The pleasure-pain calculus as so set forth is unchallengeably valid and yet deceitfully oversimplified. Human beings do indeed make some rough judgments between kind and length of work relative to rewards received. But that simple formulation does not take us far along the path to understanding the welfare economics of marketing.

The first problem is that pleasure and pain are subjective psychic concepts. They are quantitative, for they involve intensity, but they are nonquantifiable. No "hedometer" has been invented by which to measure the degree of pleasure or of pain an individual may experience.

Moreover, the utilitarian pleasure-pain equation seems to rest mainly on physical sensuality. By all counts human appreciations, positive or negative, are more complex than that. A simple example, far short of the issue of artistic appreciation, is attitude toward safety and security. How can work-safety be introduced into the estimating of effort in production? How much satisfaction value is there to a consumer in knowing that clothes are not inflammable, or drinking water not polluted?

At this point a precaution against despair may be strategic. It would be tempting, and almost excusable, to drop the whole goals-and-performance subject on grounds of nonquantifiability. Indeed, studies in the economics of welfare were all but abandoned for a decade for just that reason. Particularly rejected were judgments about the worth of social programs affecting individual welfare, because, in the language of the rationale, it is impossible to make "interpersonal comparisons of utility." To be sure, without a measuring device the intensity of satisfaction (or dissatisfaction) felt by two or more consumers cannot be compared accurately. Yet such comparisons are involved in a host of public policies ranging from graduating the income tax (a $100 tax supposedly pains a rich man less than a poor man) to providing free food to the poor and hungry. This subject is considered further in later pages of this chapter.

For now, the point to be made is that the whole marketing system operates according to private and public decisions that are quantitative in nature but cannot be quantified with high accuracy. If we lose faith because of limits to measurability we disavow all capacity to interpret, direct, and improve the functioning of the system. Conceptual ideas and statistical approximations will often have to substitute for solid, low-error data.

PROBLEM 2: PERSONAL UTILITY IN A SOCIAL CONTEXT. The calculus of individual utility is fundamental but encounters even more objection from its second problem than the first. The pleasure-pain equation of utility is totally atomistic: it puts each person on his Crusoe island, to calculate the margin between work and consumption.

In reality, every person makes any such calculation in a social context. Much meaning can be drawn from the social dimension of utility judgments. With regard to utility in consumption, the notion of pleasure or satisfaction is not confined to physical sensation in the isolated individual. A contemporary author puts it that "universal needs" are for "food, clothing, shelter, *and political security*," (italics added) but the "value of abundance is the diversity of experience, life-style, social role and expression it provides."[1] John Brewster puts near the pinnacle in human motivation the "striving for significance or worth." He explains, "Men the world over strive for an ever finer image of themselves in their own eyes and the eyes of others. . . ." And this "status hunger" is more than "the mere desire for popularity. . . ." It includes favorable valuation in one's own eyes.[2]

These are doubtless admirable kinds of satisfaction. Carrying the idea further, however, can lead to Veblen's disparaging commentary about conspicuous consumption.[3] Does the jet-set jet about the world as much for display as for exotic delights? Marketers and economists can join in raising societal value questions about social display in the psychology of consumption.

PROBLEM 3: WELFARE CALCULUS OF CAPITAL-USING PRODUCTION. The simplest version of pleasure-pain is applied more easily to a craft/

agrarian economy than a capital-using one. Handicraft production of
goods to-order at least allows an approximation to direct comparison
of pain-cost and pleasure-reward.

A handicraft economy comes closest to the conceptual ideal
sketched in Chapter 1 of infinite divisibility and perfect mobility of
resources. In such an economy each consumer's wishes can be met
precisely and without any extra cost.

Manifestly, our industrial economy is far removed from that
state. Handicraft production has all but disappeared. The production processes are capital-using, and the products are standardized to
considerable degree.

Various writers on the economics of welfare have noted how crucial the principle of divisibility-mobility is to any analysis of performance of the economy. They stress divisibility more than mobility, although the two are essentially the same. Mishan, for example, reminds
early in his incisive book that for exact application of theory of welfare, divisibility as well as homogeneity must be assumed.[4] Baumol
goes the opposite direction. Acknowledging indivisibility, he seeks
ways to accommodate it.[5]

A first characteristic of a capital-using industrial economy is that
it is highly organized. It is orderly. It has work rules. Each person
employed in it is obliged to conform to the rules. He is denied the
flexibility implicit in the pleasure-pain equation. Rare is the em-
ployee who can equate marginal discomfort and reward on a daily
basis. Few are free to work when and where they wish, governed only
by whims derived from spontaneous matching of pleasure of consumption and pain of effort.

This is the first example of how capital-based production inter-
feres with the simplest version of a welfare calculus.

The second instance is much more weighty. It gets to the heart
of capital-using production. At this point it is necessary to shift to
the commonplace language of cost. (True economic cost essentially
only reflects human effort, for it has not been U.S. policy to build a
reservation value into raw material resources.) Thereupon is introduced the devastating principle that *cost* of a *capital* good cannot be
translated directly into cost of the consumer goods produced from it.

The distinguishing feature of capital-using production is that
the capital factor can produce one or more units of a good or service
without reducing its capacity to produce more such units, or at least
without reducing that capacity proportionately.

If some calculation now is sought of the "cost" of the consumer
good obtained from the capital-using production, the dilemma is en-
countered that the cost depends on how many items are to be produced.

This is the dilemma underlying the whole body of neoclassical
economic thought that began to flower at the end of the 19th cen-

tury. The ingenious device then coined was to apply to capital-using production the same marginality principle that is expressed in the pleasure-pain utility calculus. The principle has also been implanted in some of the most pervasive Western mores, as that each factor of production, including human labor, shall be rewarded according to its productivity. But marginal productivity of each factor depends on how intensively it is employed—and in what combination with other factors. It is not possible, no matter what the intellectual heroics, to treat capital-using production as only a more elaborate form of a handicraft system. It is so much different that any similarities striven for are highly artificial.

The Counterpart in Consumption. The indeterminacy of production cost just described has its counterpart in consumption of consumers' goods that are not consumed at a single time or in a discrete process, like food at dinner time. This phenomenon takes two forms. One is durable consumers' goods, as a home or automobile. Perhaps some consumers can anticipate the pattern of use, and make cost and value estimates accordingly, but by and large this remains an area of high uncertainty.

Some other consumers' goods and services are social or collective in nature. These yield satisfaction to a number of individuals without reducing their capacity to yield equal satisfaction to one or more additional individuals. Frequently the rule holds true only up to a critical maximum. Examples are public parks, purification of the town water supply, or even public schools and roads. Consumption of these services is variously called consumption of public, or collective, or social goods.*

The Meaning to Technique of Analysis. An inference or two may be drawn in anticipation of arguments that are put forward in later chapters.

With regard to the economics of production as applied to the marketing system, there is good reason to reject marginal analysis, particularly at processing and retailing. Not only it is of doubtful applicability, but business managers do not follow marginal principles at all closely when they make managerial decisions. This subject is examined in depth in Chapter 4. A whole school of theorists now downplays marginal analysis. Their argument and several sources in literature are cited in Harold F. Breimyer.[7] A literate piece of apostasy is Brady's:

> Of all the jejune ideas that have muscled into the painful discourse of economics surely that of the "marginal efficiency of capital" has struck a new low. No folly, no waste, no rendering to the just or unjust, no

*Baumol and others examine the indivisibility of social goods at length.[6]

crisis, no debacle up to and including the ruination of the country's natural resources, or pitching the nation into war, or even the total erosion
of competition—not to mention impact of business practices upon de-
mocracy or constitutional government—can be caught in the net, or
weighed and appraised by the "tools" of this cock-sure calculus by way of
which the professional economist gives unsought for advice to those who
do not need it, the entrepreneurs. . . . [8]

But the idea that much of the price-and-reward system in our economy is more conventional than determined by marginal valuation was
advanced by Frank H. Knight a generation ago—and by John Stuart
Mill more than a century ago.

The economics of pricing product for consumption introduces
entrenched ethical rules that are virtually folklore, such as that only
uniform (nondiscriminatory) pricing of a product is "democratic."
If capital-using production cannot associate value of product directly
with cost, why should uniform pricing—the same price to all buyers—
be regarded as the only ethical system?

PROBLEM 4: WELFARE GOALS AT SUCCESSIVE LEVELS OF AGGREGATION.
Years ago, when the economics of marketing farm products received
more analytical attention than it has since, a workshop produced a
useful analysis of how the goals of the participants in marketing vary
at successive levels of aggregation.[9] The initial point was not the
firm, but processes within the firm. For processes there are time and
motion standards. The firm has its own goals. They may be dominated by profit but are not confined to it.

Competing firms obviously have some conflicting goals, as each
strives to outpace the other. At the industry level there are many
goals, including growth and a preferred composition and distribution
of output.

At the society-as-a-whole level of aggregation noneconomic goals
are prominent. Among these are security, stability, and freedom. But
also at that level arises a problem as to what sort of national goal for
productivity is to be selected. In the mid-1970s it is a source of frustration and even anxiety. Uncertainty has replaced the confidence of
a decade earlier, when the acknowledged macro-goal for the economy
was epitomized in Gross National Product. The GNP was to be
big, and to keep growing.

The first doubts centered on whether Gross Product for the nation, like sensual pleasure for the individual, truly captures our as-
pirations. An eloquent denunciation is that of the late Robert Kennedy:

The gross national product of the United States . . . counts air pollution and cigarette advertising—and ambulances to clear our highways of

carnage. It counts special locks for our doors and jails for the people who break them. It includes the destruction of the redwoods and armored cars for the police to fight riots in our cities. It counts Whitman's rifle and Speck's knife and television programs which glorify violence—the better to sell toys to our children.

The gross national product does not allow for the health of our youth—the quality of their education—the joy of their play. It does not include the beauty of our poetry—or the strength of our marriages—the intelligence of our public debate, or the integrity of our public officials. It measures neither our wit nor our courage, neither our wisdom nor our learning; neither our compassion nor our devotion to country. It measures everything about Americans except why we are proud to be Americans.[10]

Later, as our nation's raw material resources became shorter and a focus of fretful concern, conservation of those resources along with expansion of employment and restraint of inflation superseded gross productiveness as a national goal.

At higher levels of aggregation another phenomenon has risen to prominence, or to notoriety. It is called externalities. These are consequences, desirable or undesirable, of the production process that escape the cost-and-value calculations—the welfare economics—of the individual firms. Familiar examples are pollution of air or water by an industrial plant, or, on the favorable side, the growth of enough small businesses in a rural community to bring in community-serving services of medical facilities, schools, or transportation. These interfere seriously with calculations matching benefits against cost, for the reason that some of the benefit or of the cost, or both, lies outside the business unit or industry for which data are obtainable. The very word, externality, suggests correctly that it is hard to encompass in analyses.

Other Complications. A few other complications in welfare analysis will be listed, mainly as a catalog.

One is the preexisting distribution of income. The highly uneven distribution of wealth and income that exists at a given time does not invalidate theoretical concepts of goals and performance in marketing. However, it makes it difficult to apply them. The wealthy classes can use their wealth, if they see fit, to influence current production, current consumption, or both in ways that can depart from a desirable or even a meaningful balance between production and consumption. Papandreou affirms that "the pattern of factor supplies is directly dependent upon the initial distribution of wealth." He adds, ". . . to each initial distribution of wealth there corresponds, in general, a different equilibrium set of prices and a different collection of commodities."[11]

Scitovsky deals with the knotty problem of wealth distribution by separating a concept of economic efficiency from that of equity. Efficiency accepts the existing distribution of wealth and is often regarded as begging the basic question.[12]

A similar kind of complication, though often originating among the poor rather than the rich, is transfer payments. Retirement payments alone account for a sizable part of current purchasing power. The payments made at a given time need not equate at all closely with collections received.

Still another difficulty in goal-and-performance analysis comes to the fore whenever resources are unemployed. Scitovsky observes trenchantly that an efficiency test of an economic system makes sense only if resources are fully employed. "Efficiency in the use of underemployed scarce resources is as irrelevant as it is in the administration of free resources . . ."[13] Also, "Only in a fully employed economy does allocation become an economic problem."[14]

The final difficulty to be noted is that the neoclassical welfare economics analysis of comparing resource use with consumer utility is frustrated when resources are employed to alter the parameters of consumer satisfaction. To quote Scitovsky further, "It would be meaningless to apply the criterion of economic efficiency to a measure aimed deliberately at changing the consumer's preferences or influencing his market behavior."[15]

This enumeration of problems is enough to discourage further investigation of the subject, as was suggested earlier. No complete analysis will be essayed. Only certain aspects on which literature is available will be developed.

CONSUMER MOTIVATION AND BEHAVIOR. Classical economics was virtually an economics of privation. Providing the basic necessities was the overriding economic concern and value was associated mainly with their production.

Bentham and the utilitarians came along to introduce the pleasure-pain nexus into an economics of production and consumption. But it remained for the Austrian school to set up a calculus of utility of consumption, which we identify with the principle of diminishing marginal utility in consumption. Gray gives a good summary:

> Firstly, as against all cost-of-production theories of value, [the Austrians] held that value essentially springs from utility, that it reflects the mind of a person who finds something useful; secondly, that this value is determined at the "margin," that is to say, that successive portions of a good having diminishing utility, the crucial use which determines value is the least important use to which the good, having regard to the amount available, can be put; and thirdly, that value is reflected back

from things consumed to the agents which produce these commodities, that is to say, that value sanctions costs and is not caused by costs.[16]

That a rational consumer makes subjective judgments on the worth to him of individual goods and services is universally attested to. Even though the human body is unequipped with a pleasure-pain hedometer, the concept of magnitude is applicable. There are degrees of satisfaction. Further, in some crude fashion human beings weigh the relative satisfaction value of various kinds of consumption.* The idea of equating satisfaction at the margin is solidly based in human psychology.

At this stage in exposition of the economics of consumption almost every text introduces the twin concepts of cardinal and ordinal utility. The former is correctly called the more imponderable. Because of difficulties in dealing with it an ingenious array of techniques in ordinal analysis, such as rank order preference, revealed preference, and indifference equations, has been devised. It is notable that when Houthakker commented on the battery of demonstrations of choice (from Fisher and Pareto to Samuelson, Hicks, and Allen) he observed that they "showed . . . not that utility cannot be cardinal, but merely that appeal to its cardinal properties is not necessary for deriving a number of fundamental conclusions on demand functions in general."[17]

The ordinal utility approach has proved to have its own hazards. It is now employed with more sophistication than when Baumol glibly had consumers expressing an indifference between cummerbund and zabaglione.[18] Consumers do not in fact match up satisfaction values of (marginal) consumption for the hundreds of items they select from among the thousands available to them.

A summary statement by Hendrik Houthakker puts it well:

> It has been increasingly realized that utility theory should make some allowance for the fact that some commodities appear to be more closely related than others, and the specific items can often be meaningfully grouped into larger categories. . . . There is a closer connection between oranges and bananas than between oranges and overcoats, and oranges belong under the heading "food" and overcoats under the heading "clothing."[19]

Gordon King extends this idea: "It is possible to aggregate commodities into groups if, for example, the relative prices of a subset remain constant." He notes that analytical studies have "developed conditions under which it is possible to analyze these subaggregates,

---

*They also are capable of weighing work vs. leisure, but the standardization of work hours previously referred to has interfered with expressing this equation at all freely.

involving the concept of 'separably additive' utility functions." His article is an excellent reference.[20]

It seems, then, that consumer choice and the indifference calculus approach to studying it relate best to successive groupings of consumption goods and services. The indifference idea probably is most applicable to quality distinctions of a given product; and secondly to closely substituted products. Choice and indifference can also be fitted to a bundle of goods and services—matching bundle versus bundle.

The student of this subject will want to be familiar with standard demonstrations such as indifference curves for complements and substitutes, income effect and substitution effect, "standard of life" line for a rich man's good vs. a poor man's good, and even, mainly as a curiosity, Giffen's paradox.

Economics-of-the-Firm Analogy. Preference and indifference functions, though enlightening and manipulable, do not contradict the idea that consumer satisfaction is a phenomenon of magnitude. Several investigators have found it helpful to treat individual consumption economics in a manner paralleling the economics of the firm. Ferber credits Margaret Reid as a pioneer in regarding the household as a producer. His review article on consumer economics will long serve as a base work.[21]

The family is the managerial unit. Input is of a good or service. Output is consumer satisfaction or utility expressed in the coined term, utils. A util is a unit of want satisfaction.

As an input—a particular good or service—is consumed in increasing quantities, total output of utils from it rises to a peak and then decreases. In the example shown in Fig. 2.1, marginal utility rises briefly then falls off. Whether the stage of increasing marginal utility, so common to expositions of economics of the firm, truly fits consumption is open to question. But the principle of diminishing marginal utility is unchallengeable.

In the usual demonstration, each util is valued at a certain amount of money. Thereby the number of utils of satisfaction value can be converted to marginal value of utility. The valuation (five cents per util in the illustration) derives from the aggregate income-expenditure-satisfaction value equation for the individual. If the item consumed were a sizable part of a person's consumption, an unchanging marginal utility of money and a constant value of each util could not be assumed. In this demonstration the marginal value of utility is comparable to marginal revenue of product in the economics of the firm. And as in the economics of the firm, if the cost of the input be known the solution can be read. The cost must intersect the mar-

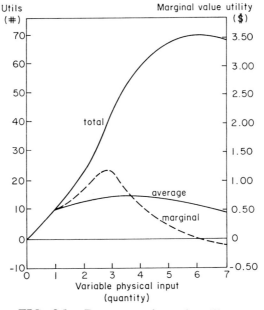

FIG. 2.1. Demonstration of utility as a "product" of consumption.

ginal value curve at some point to the right of the intersection of average and marginal value curves.

Psychic and Social Influences on Consumer Behavior. Maximization of satisfaction value in almost mechanical fashion may be a way of depicting consumer behavior that pleases analytical economists. Less mechanistic concepts have long underlain the science and art of merchandising including advertising and promotion. They start from drives, and various kinds of rational and emotional influences on actual buying behavior, and the role that individuals play.

John B. Watson, a founder of behaviorist psychology, left the academic world for advertising. In his new venture he made a small fortune by applying principles of habituation in buying.[22]

Wroe Alderson provides a good index to psychological approaches to consumer buying behavior. The following subjects covered in his exposition illustrate:

Consumer buying as an operation—rational problem solving vs. habit and impulse vs. instinctive drives.

Consumer as purchasing agent—rational behavior vs. habit and impulse vs. problem solving.

Behavior as ends and means—congenial behavior vs. instrumental
behavior vs. symptomatic behavior.

Coordination and compatability in households; shopping behavior
and problem solving; children and adults in the household structure.

Individual psychology and marketing—[ideas of] Locke and Leibnitz;
self-image; self and perception; symbolism; phenomenal self and
learning; introjection; individual psychology and organized behavior systems.[23]

THE ROLE CONCEPT. Schmid and Shaffer prefer to view the behavior of
individuals in any marketing activity in terms of their role. To them
role is "a patterned sequence of prescribed, expected or actual actions
relating the behavior of individuals to a social position."[24] The idea
of role shows up in so simple a distinction as a person's serving as a
purchasing agent for a client, vs. buying for himself. If an individual fails to act "in accordance with a prescribed role" he can normally expect to feel the effect of sanctions, which the authors classify
as social, political, economic, and religious.[25]

VALUES, MORES, MASS PSYCHOLOGY. Still another system of analysis di-
rects attention to the winds of change in the national temper, to
which all persons are subject in some degree and which modify consumer behavior in some manner.

As an illustrative example, in a 1971 study Daniel Yankelovich
isolated several categories of trends in national attitudes and values.
The first category is "traceable to the effects of the 'psychology of af-
fluence' " which causes consumers to feel free enough from economic
insecurity to "seek the fulfillment of other needs." This includes
trends toward physical self-enhancement, personalization, personal
health and well-being, new forms of materialism, social and cultural
self-expression, personal creativity, meaningful work. A second category reflects a "quest for excitement, sensation, stimulation, and meaning to counteract the practical and mundane routines of everyday
life." Embraced are trends toward the "New Romanticism," novelty
and change, adding beauty to one's daily surroundings, sensuousness,
mysticism, introspection. Trends reflecting a reaction "against the complexity of modern life" are those toward life simplification, return to
nature, increased ethnicity, increased community involvement, greater
reliance on technology, away from bigness.[26] In 1975 Yankelovich
and two coauthors reported that 50 percent of persons interviewed

agreed with a statement which was labeled, "the psychology of entitle-ment." These are explosive words applying to an attitude at odds with the U.S. tradition.[27]

Thus, in the ways sketched here and in many other ways do the actions of consumers attract the scrutiny of both economists using their tools, and sociologists and psychologists employing theirs. The lenses differ sharply. And the differences lead to, and account for, variations in techniques of analysis of consumer behavior, in merchan-dising practices to cultivate or exploit consumer responses, and in at-titudes toward public policy.

THE GOALS OF THE MARKETING FIRM. The two contrasting descriptions of the economics of consumer behavior just reviewed find close parallels in delineation of the goals and motivations of the busi-ness firm.

The first standard approach is directed toward profit. Much eco-nomic analysis of the business firm has telescoped goals into maximiza-tion of some kind of profit. Due, for example, in his standard inter-mediate text declares, while noting "significant exceptions," that "from all indications, the primary goal which is pursued is that of profit maximization."[28]

The first question concerns the kind of profit that is to be max-imized, particularly with regard to length of time. This alone is a puzzle. Any manager looks to the annual report he is due to present to stockholders and will be influenced by pressures to make it look good. Yet a firm's owners and managers alike presumably seek lon-gevity as much in their business operations as in their persons. The customary judgment puts an average level of profits over a consider-able period of time ahead of the strictly short run as the time zone for profit maximization.

But there are other side issues. Among Due's "exceptions" are those arising from the well-publicized separation of management from ownership. Professor Due believes managers seek profit levels that will promise most security for managers. This may call for avoiding "full exploitation of all the temporary situations which might allow very high profits." Further, "more than anything else, those in the man-agement group are interested in the continued operation of the firm and maintenance of their own position. . . ." When this goal con-flicts with maximum profits, "security of position is likely to take precedence over greater profits."[29]

Herbert Simon qualifies the profit maximization goal in other language. As paraphrased by Torgerson, Simon

. . . suggests that profit maximization is an unreasonable assumption under conditions of imperfect competition. . . . Simon postulates that a
more reasonable assumption would be one of "satisficing." Accordingly,
firms will aim at attaining certain profit levels or maintaining certain
market shares instead of pursuing the goal of profit maximization.[30]

Baumol advances the idea that firm managers are motivated to
maximize total revenue subject to a certain profit constraint. This
amounts to an emphasis on growth of volume of business as more important than winning the largest possible profits—provided profits
reach a certain acceptable minimum.[31] This viewpoint deserves much
credence, at least if the reports to stockholders that corporation presi-
dents make each year are to be taken at face value. Often, in those
reports, growth of size of the firm is stressed ahead of earnings ratios.

Nielson and Sorenson, in describing goals, quote McDonald as
saying that "businessmen are torn between the desire for control,
power, or prestige." The authors are impressed with how inconstant
goals may be. "Not only may firms have a multiplicity of complementary and competing goals, but the goals themselves are subject to
change from time to time."[32]

Is there a consensus among these ideas? Probably the closest approximation is that during periods of prosperity there is a two-level
projection of goals: long run stability and growth are earnestly sought
provided a minimum level of profits—Baumol's profit constraint—is
attained concurrently. During times of depression, survival alone may
take precedence. For further delineation of goals we must look at
the structure of the market in which firms operate. Structure affects
both what is sought and what is attainable. In chapters that follow,
this will be expressed in terms of managerial options or, in Bainsian
language, the conduct variable.

CONSUMERS' WELFARE: AGGREGATION OF UTILITIES.
The subject matter considered thus far is comparatively easy.
Granted, it is difficult to know just what motivates individual consumers and individual business firms. But the really big imponderable is how to establish goals at successively higher levels of aggregation.
This problem was alluded to earlier. It will now be considered in
more detail. The problem cannot be avoided if the marketing system
is to be subject to appraisal, and public policy to examination.

Interpersonal Comparison of Utility. A rational consumer equates
marginal utility of all forms of consumption. This equating tells us
nothing about equating among persons.

Distinguished economists have declared contradictorily that (1) some kind of interpersonal comparison of utility is essential to an economics of general welfare, and (2) interpersonal comparisons of utility cannot be made. Regarding the first, Due observes that marginal consumption of any product by each consumer, that is, one consumer relative to another, ought to yield equal satisfaction value. "If this position is not attained, an increase in total satisfaction will result from shifting income from those for whom the marginal utilities of their purchases are relatively low to those for whom the marginal utilities are relatively high.[33] Due deals with some of the problems of this thesis by coining a concept of "marginal social costs" of producing goods.[34]

Boulding declares that "the total utility of society is a maximum . . . when the marginal utilities of all persons' incomes are equal."[35]

The celebrated Alfred Marshall not only posed the same issue but postulated that "it would naturally be assumed that a shilling's worth of gratification to one Englishman might be taken as equivalent with a shilling's worth to another . . . until cause to the contrary were shown.[36]

Two groups of critics have taken up the cudgels. Social activists shout that those egalitarian conditions are violated to extreme degree. A legion of theoreticians have tush-tushed that it is impossible to make interpersonal comparisons of utility. The early Samuelson was among them. Evasive routes were sought and various coinages introduced.[37] Paretian and other optima were devised.

In a gem of a comment of two decades ago, Brekke and Zellner discuss interpersonal utility in the language of "commensurability." They are scornful of the idea that we cannot use interpersonal comparisons of utility in consumption for policy purposes, when we freely advocate changes in allocation of resources in production, among them labor and management. The latter surely involve an interpersonal productivity comparison. The human input in any productivity is effort with its disutility quotient.[38]

Mishan makes the same point in emphatic language: if we are unwilling to make interpersonal comparisons of utility, *"the logic of choice impels us to be indifferent as between 'good' and 'bad' allocations of resources."*[39]

A distinguished putting of economists' feet to the welfare fire is that of Georgescu-Roegen:

> The dogma of the interpersonal noncomparability of utility has . . .
> been strongly advocated. But if this dogma is accepted, economics must
> reconcile itself to being a science . . . unable to recognize at least a
> modicum of standards in the phenomenal domain which it purports to
> study. Fortunately, the dogma flies in the face of two irresistible forces:

the faculty of man called empathy, without which there really is no game we can play at all . . . ; and the hierarchy of wants. . . . It can hardly be denied that it makes objective economic sense to help starving people by taxing those who spend their summers at luxurious resorts.[40]

It is worth noting in conclusion that Samuelson, the early apostate, finally demonstrated (according to Bator) "that a 'welfare function' denoting an ethic was needed after all."[41]

A Summary Position. The summary that follows starts from the proposition that interpersonal comparisons of utility are made every day. However imperfectly fallible human beings do it, they take comparative utilities into account in public policy.

In economic affairs, many decisions are made and acted on that are quantitative in nature but not measurable.

In the words of Little, another student of the economics of welfare, "Value judgments . . . in particular those about distribution, cannot be avoided in welfare economics."[42]

It will be helpful to recall the analytical theme presented in Chapter 1. If resources were perfectly divisible and mobile (and, we should add here, each person were free to choose his hours of work), it would be possible to match production with consumption perfectly.

But this condition does not exist. Capital-using production is based on limited divisibility of resources. It makes the economy more productive but introduces the perplexing issues of efficiency and equity that are at the heart of the economics of welfare.

Also implicitly involved is the question of the ethics of equal (or unequal) pricing. This can apply to pricing of either factors or products but it will be applied here to product pricing. This ethic, a legacy of Calvinism if not earlier theologies, calls for treating all people alike even though the consequence may be marked inequality in consumer utility.

If, empirically, the marginal level of utility (satisfaction) varies widely among individual consumers, a persuasive case can be made that well-chosen discriminatory pricing can reduce inequality and enhance aggregate welfare.

Repeating, this issue becomes relevant in a capital-using production system. As a down-to-earth illustration, if a piece of equipment can turn out 10,000 plastic raincoats for a total cost only slightly greater than for 1,000, is there a compelling reason why the coats must be priced the same to all potential customers?*

*If 1,000 raincoats were being produced by 1,000 different individuals each working alone, the moral reason for equal pricing would be much more convincing.

Irrespective of how theoretical economists view these matters, it is abundantly clear that the public is not inhibited. It makes interpersonal judgments of utility, and acts on those judgments.

Economists, weighed down by their need for sophistication, can lag behind the public understanding.

This is not to suggest that the utility scales of all persons are regarded as identical. Few persons believe that. But neither do many believe that each individual is able to equate his disutility of effort exactly with utility of consumption. As an extreme case, a person might be so unproductive due to limited endowment of skills that even if opportunities were unlimited he would be unable to earn enough money for medical care. Yet a broken bone would bring pain as racking to him as to Madame Gottrocks.

This opens up an engaging question that once set economists off on philosophical forays. Do we want, from a moral standpoint, to allow or require all individuals to live with the largess or deficiencies, as the case may be, of their natural gifts? That is to say, ought the gifted pay society some rent? The question gains cogency from the obvious fact that so much of the opportunity to take advantage of native skills is provided by society. Bob Hope would hardly command his astronomical income if radio, television, and the cinema had been still uninvented in his time. James Hunter could not earn his big salary for throwing a baseball were it not for the attractiveness of Yankee stadium.

Apparently, the American populace has made up its mind. It grants that wealthy persons have a differential capacity to enjoy certain kinds of consumer goods, among them perhaps opera concerts and Rembrandt paintings; or, as another possibility, it regards those items as so inconsequential that a skewed distribution of their consumption is not worth fretting about.

Not so with certain basic consumption items. For food, housing, medical service, and education through high school, the hedometer measuring utility is believed to show only narrow differences. We accept not only the idea of commensurability but an approximation toward equality. Accordingly, public policy has concentrated on meeting minimum needs in those four categories.

This is the kind of dichotomy in public attitudes that John Maurice Clark, while aiming a dart at economists, summed up in these words:

> . . . resources [are] allocated between different uses by the actions of persons, no one of whom needs to be aiming at, or even conceiving, the whole economy-wide resultant. The resulting allocation does not have to be the one best possible. The only persons likely to worry about that

are theoretical economists, overly impressed with the burden of hypothetical omniscience which they bear. Even theoretical "welfare economics" seems nowadays to be foregoing the concept of a definable single best allocation, largely as a result of its view that the utilities of different individuals are incommensurable. On the other hand, an idea of rough commensurability, in terms of some kind of "social minimum," seems to underlie social policy.[43]

CHAPTER THREE

ECONOMICS OF THE MARKETING FIRM

CONSUMPTION is singular but production is plural. This axiom is not airtight but it helps to focus on a basic feature of our economy: that virtually all production takes place in organizational units of some size.

Business firms of various kinds dominate the marketing of farm products. A few country traders in livestock remain, and a handful of farmers peddle their own produce. These are rare instances. The business firm is all but universal.

Texts in economics once gave short shrift to the nature and behavioral characteristics of the commercial business firm. It long was regarded as virtually neutral, a mechanical link in the production-consumption process. More recently the neglect has been corrected. Now a large literature is being built up, examining the behavioral characteristics of business firms of various types.

Older definitions of a firm need detain us only briefly. Leftwich, in his standard text, says only that a firm is "an individual business concern."[1] McConnell begins by noting a plant as a "physical unit of production . . . a physical establishment . . ." whereas a firm is "the business organization which owns and operates these plants."[2] Due is more inventive in that he separates factor-owners from the business firm, which latter "actually conducts production activity."[3] And Lipsey and Steiner observe that a firm is a "unit that makes decisions regarding the employment of factors of production and the production of goods and services."[4]

No harbor will be given in this chapter to the more blandly mechanistic interpretations of the firm. It will not be proposed that the modern business firm, a vital and vibrant creature of the law, has no more id than a rag doll. On the contrary, full respect will be accorded the volitional aspects of a firm operating in imperfect competition.

The imperfectly competitive structure of marketing puts the firm in the limelight. In perfect competition the industry is of first concern, and the behavior of the firm is circumscribed. But in imperfect competition the firm takes on an instrumental character.

How shall a firm be described? What uniquely identifies it?

P. J. D. Wiles notes that a firm can be appraised in terms (among others) of its possession and exercise of sovereignty and enterprise.

41

Moreover, enterprise involves "the thinking up of policy for the sovereign to lay down, and the exercise of delegated command."[5]

Certainly a firm has a near human quality of drive, motivation. It almost seems to possess libido. Enterprise may in fact be the single best term for it. Calling management a factor of production falls flat; it does not convey the message.

Possibly a part of this characterization must be that a firm has unity of purpose. This does not mean singularity of purpose, nor internal homogeneity. It only means that to the surrounding business world, and probably also to the public policy world, it presents a single pose. Therewith have arisen codes of internal behavior, sometimes called "ethics," such as that a sales representative does not tear down his firm's name, however tongue-in-cheek he finds it necessary to be. Managers of firms are not expected to sidetrade to the firm's disadvantage. When an official of a large motor firm was caught doing that a few years ago, his demise was quick and summary.

SHORTCOMINGS OF NEOCLASSICAL ECONOMIC ANALYSIS.

Classical or neoclassical economic analysis has proved increasingly unadapted to explaining the operations of the large business firm.

Years ago Paul Nelson, patterning after Frank H. Knight, reminded us that the classical model of a firm explicitly set forth these qualities: small size, homogeneous product, no restrictions upon new firms seeking to enter business or older firms to leave, "price and profits as the major criteria for policy formulation," good knowledge, and profit maximization as the goal to be sought. It was postulated that "successful performance of such firms . . . will automatically assure an optimum allocation of resources. . . ."

Moreover, wrote Nelson, implicit assumptions made the firm act as though it were a proprietorship grown large, so that decisions were arrived at straightforwardly and implemented directly. Most costs were for production, and they were neatly divisible between fixed and variable; it was almost unthinkable that total costs could be constant. Possibly the most drastic assumption of all was that maximizing profit in the short run would result in maximizing profit in the long run.[6]

Nielson and Sorenson use different language to list assumptions in "static economic theory" that violate today's reality: constant production functions, fixed utility functions, fixed institutional framework among motivational forces, rational behavior of the firm toward maximization of profits, and perfect knowledge and foresight.[7]

Cyert and Hedrick choose still other terminology, as they describe the "hypothetical construct" of the classical firm as having a "single decision criterion" that responds to "information received from the market." They add, in denunciation, "None of the problems of real firms can find a home within this special construct. There are no organizational problems nor is there any room for analysis of the internal-decision-making process."[8]

Their survey of literature led them to classify into five categories the recent studies of the economics of the firm, namely, those using:

Unmodified neoclassical approach
Simple extensions of the neoclassical approach
Modifications of the objective function ("an attempt to utilize empirical knowledge about the goals of the microeconomic units")
Generalized maximization techniques (these "arise in an attempt to extend neoclassical models to cases where there is uncertainty.")
Nonmaximizing models[9]

THE TYPICAL MARKETING FIRM. With some license, perhaps the following attributes can be said to delineate the typical firm in the marketing system for farm products. These particularly apply to firms at stages past initial assembly. They fit processing and retailing notably well:

1. The firm is a corporation.
2. Its management is professional. Nearly all the "family owner" clan have departed the scene.
3. Although the major stockholders retain some of the traditional policy-making power, their influence has been watered down as professional managers provide continuity of leadership in most policy decisions.
4. The firm is multiplant.
5. It is also multiproduct, and there is enough diversity among products to give some characteristics of a conglomerate.
6. The firm is large enough that its actions have independent force in supply or outlet markets or both.
7. Management practices have some element of what is known as "technocracy." That is, the simple notion of direct lines of communication and command up and down a hierarchy is unrealistic. Instead, command relationships are labyrinthine, and various management divisions or units enjoy a considerable degree of autonomy—covertly if not overtly.
8. The mechanics of internal management are best tagged as those

of bureaucracy. They involve codified rules and regulations; organization charts and flow charts; committees and task forces that cut across those charts or junk them entirely; a layer-by-layer specification ("decomposition") of performance objectives, both qualitative and quantitative; infinite reliance on fast communication and voluminous record keeping, the latter based on electronic data processing; a constant internal propaganda effort at building up firm loyalty, using house organs, recognition ceremonies, and other devices; and finally, in the largest firms a separate investigatory operation that clandestinely or openly checks up on how well the farflung parts of the firm carry out central policy.

9. Elaborate systems of "transfer prices" or "shadow prices" accompany transfer of commodity or services among divisions of the firm. (See page 7.)

10. Product development and merchandising loom large in management policy. Establishing an identified output (as by brand name) is seen as the anchor to the firm's continuing success. Moreover, in order to protect and exploit any such advantage, vertical mergers, liaisons, franchising, and other devices are entered into.

11. Prices of product are "administered." The firm is a "price maker."

12. Long range goals take precedence over shorter term ones. Survival alone is a primary goal, and survival as an independent entity is usually ranked higher than survival as a unit of a larger firm. Growth is sought, of and for itself. High profit ratios are a desideratum, but even the shorter term objectives are much more complex than mere maximization of profit.

Other characteristics could be named, some whimsical. For example, a well-run larger firm provides for self-criticism and self-improvement. In addition to internal evaluation units, outside consultants are engaged. They parade in and out of business offices like a drum and bugle corps. Fledgling managers, key technicians, and others are dispatched to short courses and seminars and enrolled in "refresher" courses.

The modern business firm has its singularly identifying characteristics.

Applicability of Production Economics. In spite of the iconoclastic tone of the above introduction, conventional tools will not be abandoned. Even the most prolix managerial entity applies principles of the economics of production. Resources are combined. New product is produced. There is regularity between the relationships of input to output. Invariably one input is held fixed as another varies. Even in the longest run it is hardly possible to conceive of all factors as infinitely expansible. If nothing else, the management factor runs into limits of extensibility.

Models of production economics applicable to the modern business firm are necessarily complicated by virtue of characteristics of the firm—such as that it produces multiple products; that many costs are common to several products; that it is big enough that prices of some inputs will not be perfect (i.e., price will differ according to volume purchased); likewise, that it sells into a market that is imperfect due either to differentiation of product or oligopoly conditions; and that it employs nonprice methods of merchandising.

The analysis to be presented in this chapter will build around three themes, all of which will become clearer as the chapter progresses. The first is that management decisions are exercises in successive categories of futurity. The longer range is the lodestar, and shorter range decisions conform to the longer goal, or depart from it, according to the intensity of current pressures. Secondly, decisions as to kind, volume, and price of product mix, and merchandising tactics to be used, are made simultaneously, with strategy vis-à-vis close competitors an additional consideration. And thirdly, pricing practices are more accurately described by the concept of "full cost pricing" than in any other way.

CIRCUMSTANCES THAT CAN OR CANNOT BE CHANGED. If the management of a firm juggles not less than five major variables and does so within the precarious framework of importunate short run pressures and inviolable long run goals, it is very important to know how long the time period is ("length of run") within which various management variables can be changed.

Students have long chanted, "In the long run everything is variable." Actually, this is not strictly correct if infinite survival of the firm be sought. But more to the point is the obvious fact that there are big differences in the length of run for each variable. The listing in Table 3.1 is more illustrative than indicative. It does call to mind the differences among a number of familiar factors in management of a firm.

We need not be concerned with how long a "short," "medium," or "long" run may be. It is enough to recognize that there are discernible differences.

TABLE 3.1. Alterability of Factors Affecting Firm Management.[a]

Item	Alterable in		
	Short run	Medium run	Long run
Plant	no	no	yes
Machinery	no	yes	yes
Technical skills	no	yes	yes
Technical knowledge	no	no	yes
Finance capital funds	no	yes	yes
Distribution system	no	no	yes
Patents, trade marks	no	no	(Depends on market structure[b])
Good will	no	(Depends on market structure[b])	(Depends on market structure[b])
Managerial skill	no	no	yes
Consumer demand curve in sale to household consumers	no	no	(Depends on market structure[b])
Consumer demand curve in sale to other firms	no	no	possibly
Reaction of competitors	no	no	no

[a] Factors that underlie output, price, and merchandising practice decisions.
[b] E.g., may be inapplicable in perfect competition.

CATEGORIES OF COST. Variability of cost items is more familiar ground. Every economic analyst recognizes a distinction between fixed and variable costs. In an overall sense, the distinction is valid. Some costs do in fact vary directly in line with variable output. Some do not.

The apparent simplicity is nevertheless deceiving. As one complication, the financial relationship between cost items and output need not be the same as the physical relationship. Recognizing a difference between fiscal and physical variable costs, Wiles developed a nomenclature such as of direct costs, and marginal cost with partial adaptation or total adaptation.[10] His language will not be used here, however.

Among more obvious examples of variable physical costs (i.e., use of resources) that cannot be varied financially are the wearing out of machinery according to its use even though the investment, once made, is not readily recoverable; and union wage rules that call for full salary of workers irrespective of whether work is performed.

When production analysis is looked at from the standpoint of managerial decision making, interest in variable costs is confined to those that are financially controllable. In the analysis that follows, "controllable variable" will be one category of costs. These costs, to repeat, vary directly and immediately with output of a given product in not only a physical but a financial sense.

A large part of the cost structure of a modern business firm is not controllably variable. Much is common cost covering two or more joint products,* but the more weighty feature is that it cannot be varied directly with short-term output.

It is tempting to set up several categories of cost other than controllable variable, but in a simplification that may be acceptable for our purposes all such costs will be lumped as overhead and then subdivided only into those that are specific to a product or product line and those that are not. A specific overhead cost is a cost item that can be associated with a single product but cannot be varied in the short run. An example is the cost of a specialized piece of machinery —or, for that matter, of a person or a technical staff that has a single kind of output. General overhead obviously covers all other overhead expenditures.

In recapitulation, the three categories of cost to be employed in this chapter are:

Costs that can be varied with short-term output—*controllable variable*
Costs that cannot be varied with short-term output
    Confined to a product or product line—*specific overhead*
    Not confined to a product or product line—*general overhead*

On the whole, in today's organization of business the bulk of costs are overhead, and many are general overhead. Trends in both technology and business practices have the effect of throwing an increasing proportion of costs into the overhead category. A smaller share of all costs than formerly fluctuate in line with—and can actually be varied with—output of a particular good or service.†

Moreover, there is increasing evidence that controllable variable costs do not have as much relevance as has been assumed in many textbooks on economics. Technical considerations often govern the level of operation of a plant. The only watertight generalization is that once the rated capacity of a machine or a plant is passed, variable costs rise rapidly.

---

*Where two or more joint products are turned out in fixed proportion, cost analysis is simplified. The situation is not very common in food processing and distribution.

†An interesting commentary is that the kind of expense that can actually be varied approximately with output of a particular product is less likely to be production expense than merchandising expense. This situation may help to account for the growth in merchandising activity.

TABLE 3.2. Illustrative Calculation of Controllable Variable Cost in Loading of Trucks.

No. trucks per day	Number men	Controllable Variable Cost at $50/Day Wage		
		Total	Per truck	
			Average	Marginal
10	1	$ 50	$5.00	$ 5.00
20	1.8	90	4.50	4.00
30	2.4	120	4.00	3.00
40	2.9	145	3.62	2.50
50	3.4	170	3.40	2.50
60	4.0	200	3.33	3.00
70	6.0	300	4.28	10.00

Controllable Variable Cost. It is nevertheless instructive to begin with the basic economics of controllable variable cost. The data that follow are a simple demonstration. They apply to the loading of trucks. The usual phenomenon of increasing and decreasing returns applies.

Number men employed	1	2	3	4	5	6	7
Number trucks loaded	10	24	44	60	68	70	68

It might be observed that the data are the same as were used to illustrate utility of consumption in Chapter 2.

If we next apply a wage rate for labor we can compute data on controllable variable cost per truck. As is usually done, the easiest possible assumption will be made, namely, that the supply price for labor is constant. Let us take a figure of $50 per day. See Table 3.2.

The data yield conventional figures as to average and marginal controllable variable cost. If only that category of cost need be met, the firm could load trucks so long as the price received were as much as $3.33. (Actually, it could be slightly less: where marginal and average costs intersect.) In the graph of Fig. 3.2, page 52, a horizontal line for this or any higher price for loading trucks intersecting with marginal cost would give the output solution. This is the conventional analysis, and under the usual assumptions it is, of course, correct.

Can a firm afford to cover only controllable variable costs? In the very shortest run, it can. Under the most gripping short run circumstances, it may be forced to do so.

A more realistic view of things would tell us that any rational manager of a firm will ordinarily be under pressure if not duress to cover more than controllable variable costs.

How much more?

There is no general rule that tells us how much more cost a firm will feel itself necessary to cover. Least of all can we make a routine arithmetic calculation apportioning the overhead cost among various possible levels of output. In direct if undiplomatic words, the exercises so often presented are irrelevant, and they convey an inaccurate picture of how costing is done.

The best general description of reality is that each firm calculates an amount of cost that it regards as the minimum it must recover if it is to continue to produce the commodity or service. Having established the minimum, it then proceeds to estimate how much above the minimum it can hope to recover. In other words, it takes a careful reading on the state of the market when it decides on the actual price policy.

This is worth repeating in a slightly different way. The price and output and associated decisions of a firm can be described as having two steps. The first is to calculate a minimum level of costs that must be repaid. Unless those costs can in fact be paid, production will be discontinued. Obviously, this means that it must be possible to charge and get a price that, at the predicted volume of sales, yields a revenue at least equal to the minimum costs that are to be met. But no manager will be satisfied just to recover minimum costs if it is possible to do better. The manager will also set goals for each product's contribution to the total overhead expenditure of the firm, including a profit.

This is the basic skeleton of how price decisions are approached in a contemporary business firm. Obviously, it applies to firms that set or "administer" the prices of their products, and not to those that sell in open-market auction.

Manifestly, there are three interrelated elements in this basic skeleton: category of costs, time, and the degree of urgency or mandate in a pricing decision.

Specific Overhead Cost. In a broad approximation, the three categories of cost are related directly to the three lengths of time period: the short, intermediate, and long run.

A realistic picture of business practices today can be presented as follows (see Fig. 3.1). In the very shortest run, the minimum costs that must be recovered are only the controllable variable costs (except in times of price wars or when a new product is first merchandised).

As the intermediate run is approached, the level of minimum costs that must be met moves higher. At that length of run it becomes necessary to repay some of the overhead costs. Although it is difficult to put a finger on exactly what kinds of costs become a man-

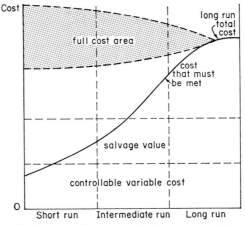

FIG. 3.1.   Cost calculations for pricing, by length of
run.

dated minimum in the intermediate run, they come close to fitting
the category of specific overhead. But the minimum that must be
met is only the portion which can in fact be saved by discontinuing
operations. This concept is often called salvage value.

Almost always, some portion of the cost associated with a specialized overhead investment or unit can be saved by selling the
equipment or transferring or dismissing the employees. Seldom will
a firm take such a step in the short run. It will often do so in the
intermediate run. By this logic, and this observation of how business
is done, we get the principle of salvage value applied to specific overhead costs. The principle resembles the idea of opportunity cost that
once was so popular in economic writings.

In the illustration of truck loading, the specific overhead costs
associated with the operation doubtless include specialized mechanical equipment. One or more clerical personnel may be assigned
exclusively to record keeping for the operation. On the other hand,
as the firm is assumed to do other things in addition to loading trucks,
much of the central office overhead applies to the firm's business generally and is not a cost assignable to truck loading.

The term salvage value misleads a bit inasmuch as neither equipment nor assigned personnel need be thrown on the dump heap if
production of a given product or service is terminated. Yet in the
technological and business system now prevailing almost invariably
some loss occurs when a machine or man must be turned aside from
its or his established employment. And some machinery, if sale is
forced, brings a low price.

TABLE 3.3. Illustrative Calculation of Costs, Including Full Costs, for Pricing a Product.

(1)	(2)	(3)	(4)	(5)	(6)	(7)	(8)	(9)	(10)	(11)	(12)	(13)	(14)
Number trucks loaded per day	Number men	Controllable Variable Cost @ $50 Wage			Salvage value equivalent (per day)	Controllable Variable Cost Plus Salvage Value		Apportioned Overhead Cost (per day)[a]		Full Cost Calculations			
		Per truck								A		B	
		Total	Av.	Marg.		Total	Av./truck	A	B	Total	Av./truck	Total	Av./truck
10	1	$ 50	$5.00	$ 5.00	$60	$110	$11.00	$ 80	$ 60	$130	$13.00	$110	$11.00
20	1.8	90	4.50	4.00	60	150	7.50	110	90	200	10.00	180	9.00
30	2.4	120	4.00	3.00	60	180	6.00	140	120	260	8.67	240	8.00
40	2.9	145	3.62	2.50	60	205	5.12	170	165	315	7.87	310	7.75
50	3.4	170	3.40	2.50	60	230	4.60	200	220	370	7.40	390	7.80
60	4.0	200	3.33	3.00	60	260	4.33	230	280	430	7.17	480	8.00
70	6.0	300	4.28	10.00	60	360	5.14	260	345	560	8.00	645	9.21

[a] This is an arbitrary cost accounting decision. It includes salvage value. Actual data are arrived at by a firm after many factors are taken into account. The two examples used here are illustrative only of policies that (1) apportion *less* overhead per unit at higher than intermediate volumes, and (2) that apportion *more* at the higher volumes.

Shiftability of resources relates to length of time. There may be labor contracts guaranteeing employment for a specified time, and within that period the cost of labor may be an unavoidable expense whereas over time it can be adjusted. Likewise, cost of physical facilities can be depreciated fully over time. For these reasons, the salvage value concept is usually regarded as appropriate to an intermediate period of time.

To anticipate the argument that will be advanced later, the costs a firm incurs in the (very) long run are treated differently in management policy than the two kinds of cost that set minimum levels of cost recoverability in the short and intermediate run. Those two costs will now be examined further.

The simple mathematics of short- and intermediate-run cost calculations for minimum level of pricing are shown in columns 4, 5, and 8 of Table 3.3 and Fig. 3.2. A salvage value of $60 per day (equivalent) in the trucking operation is arbitrarily assumed. This value must be recovered irrespective of whether one truck is loaded or 101. It can thus be apportioned in inverse ratio to volume. It traces the familiar rectangular hyperbola. It is the only kind of cost of which this can be said.

Adding a salvage value to average controllable variable cost produces a higher curve and one of considerably different slope. In the illustration, the lowest price at which trucks would be loaded is increased to approximately $4.33. Other data can be read, as that at a price of $6.00 about 64 trucks would be loaded.

At a $6.00 price a rent, or quasi-rent, would be received. It

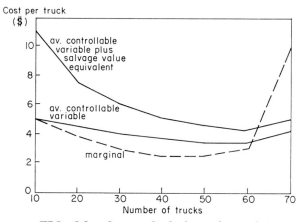

FIG. 3.2.   Cost calculations for minimum pricing
for short and intermediate run.

would be about $1.30 per truck over controllable variable cost plus salvage value, or about $2.30 over controllable variable cost alone.

In these simple calculations, a "perfect" market for input and output is assumed. In any big operation in an oligopolistic (or oligopsonistic) firm, this may be an unrealistic assumption. This issue does not affect the mechanics of internal cost calculations, however. (But see below regarding actual pricing decisions.)

Minimum Costs and Price Strategy. An exceedingly important explanation or *caveat* must be inserted. It is a warning in interpreting the exercise presented thus far as providing price and output "solutions." The data do not do that. They serve only to establish price minima as arrived at under the conditions set forth.

Further, this explanation accommodates the principle of quasi-rent. It says that once the minimum costs have been equalled or exceeded, the manager of a firm casts his eye on quasi-rent, and he tries to realize a substantial amount of it. For he knows that all other costs (overhead) must be paid from some source.

FULL COST PRICING. The quasi-rent principle is nevertheless too nebulous. It is so indeterminate as to be unrealistic.

In business operations, cost calculations for arriving at target prices are much more elaborate than the demonstration just given. The term that has come to be applied to them is full costing, or full cost pricing. Full cost calculations carry the salvage value idea one giant step further. In them, a firm apportions all its overhead costs to individual products, in order to establish base points or guidelines for its pricing decisions.

Full cost data do not become directly binding upon price and other decisions. As base data they provide useful information to management, but not exact, determinate solutions.

The salvage value concept is in fact one leg of full costing. It helps to set the lower limit. Full cost can hardly be lower than the combined salvage value and controllable variable cost.

How does management arrive at full costs? Day by day, full costing is calculated by established accounting formulas. But in a longer view the formulas are arrived at within the context of the prevailing competitive situation.

Full costing has a triple personality. First, it reflects arbitrarily chosen accounting rules, mechanically applied. Second, those rules carry a "what the traffic will bear" label, and they are changed as the competitive situation changes. Third, full cost data provide guidelines and are not necessarily controlling. Because it has such a mixed nature, full costing is variously defined and sometimes misunderstood.

Full costing makes most sense for multiple product firms having sizable overhead costs. If a firm's several products are sold into markets of similar competitive fabric, the full costing may be based on simple measures such as weight or volume. But if some of a firm's products go into a highly price-competitive market while others enter a market of sleepy competition, the chances are high that the firm will edge downward its apportionment of overhead to the former, and upward to the latter.

Full cost may be regarded as a substitute for the "fixed cost" that often inhabits textbooks. The notion that a firm sets up a single fixed cost that must be recovered year in and year out, irrespective of fluctuations in demand, is totally unrealistic. Salvage value may approach that concept, but in seeking to recover overhead costs above the salvage level any rationally managed firm will establish a higher target figure for a good sales year than a bad one.

In other words, the full cost apportioned to a product is not a lump sum to be applied to varying volume. It may be nearly the opposite—a constant figure per unit. But practices differ (note illustrations below).

John Maurice Clark, who has developed the full cost pricing principle more perhaps than any other person, insists that "the full-cost price is one that will cover costs under normal conditions of operation, disregarding minor fluctuations."

He adds, "This means that it does not espouse the anomaly of raising the price if a downward fluctuation of demand reduces the operating rate and raises unit cost by spreading the overhead over a smaller number of units." Instead, ordinarily some estimate of "standard costs" is used, and " 'full-cost' may accordingly be construed as covering standard accounting costs, plus some conception of a normal return on investment."[11] For the full cost idea Clark credits two men at Oxford, Hall and Hitch, who coined it following their analysis of responses business firms gave to their inquiry as to how pricing actually was done.[12]

In an attempt to illustrate these principles, data have been entered in Table 3.3 for two apportionments of overhead cost, preparatory to calculating full cost data. It is difficult to know how realistic the two series are. At the least, they show the sharp contrast with conventional fixed cost data. One series is so drawn that the overhead per truck is slightly less at the 60 to 70 truck level than 30 or 40; the other has a higher per truck figure for the larger volumes. (Per truck calculations are not shown.) The difference between the two series could be compromised by taking a flat rate per truck, as suggested above, and that might not be too far removed from actual business practices.

For full cost data, only average cost per unit is calculated. Marginal cost data for such a concept are meaningless. What is the significance of a marginal cost datum that is calculated from a purely arbitrary apportionment of overhead? Furthermore, the only true marginal costs are confined to controllable variable expense items. They are shown in column 5 of Table 3.3.

One consequence of the full cost calculations of Table 3.3 is striking: the average full cost, for either A or B series, is much higher than the marginal cost shown for all truck loadings through 60 per day. This is not a rarity. In the organization of contemporary multiproduct business firms, the average full cost is significantly higher than the marginal operating cost at anything close to normal volume of operations.

To be sure, extending the volumes in Table 3.3 to 70 trucks carries marginal costs above the level of average full costs. This happens when a plant is pushed to or above the limit of rated capacity. In the illustrative data, 70 is the maximum truck loading capacity. Most business firms do not expect to operate constantly at full capacity, and both their planning and the economics of the industry usually lead to operations at something less than rated capacity.

And at the normal less-than-capacity operations, average full cost per unit is not adjusted much according to volume. This is the picture shown in Table 3.3 for loadings in the 40–60 per day range, particularly for series B. Thus is exemplified the principle that Clark argued for in the quotation above.

Full Costing and Time Period. Full costing is an arbitrary accounting device, yet it is not quixotic. It is solidly based on a firm's operating data and its competitive situation. It applies to the short or intermediate run. It is not a long-run concept in the usual textbook sense of the term.

For these reasons the area of full cost pricing is shown in Fig. 3.1 as a triangle that narrows with the increasing length of time period. In the very long run, total cost governs.

The matter of time period can be illustrated by considering the retail pricing of fresh meat. A supermarket chain may have a standard markup above wholesale cost—a full cost device—that it uses as a starting point in pricing. It probably does not reconsider the accuracy of that markup more often than once or twice a year. Hence, its full cost formula is retained a number of months.

With regard to actual prices, though, the firm may price its processed meats close to the formula week in and week out, but for some fresh meats it may depart from the formula frequently. It certainly resists changing the posted price for fresh meat as often as wholesale values change. On an upswing in wholesale prices it will hesitate to be the first retailer to jump its retail price. On a downswing it may resist being the first to reduce. When pricing, the firm will always keep an eye on its competitors. And yet, meat managers will hold the markup formula in mind, will often apply it directly, and will tend to return to it following short-run departures.

Long-run cost calculations, both conceptually and in practice, are a world apart from all short- and medium-run cost calculations and price decisions. Long-run total cost has reference value, and in a sense full cost calculations not only blanket it (Fig. 3.1) but converge with it.

Full Costing Intrafirm Transfers. All the above remarks are pitched at the pricing of a firm's salable product. In large firms today there can exist a sizable volume of transfer of product among operating divisions. It can be raw material, semifinished products, capital goods, or even salable consumer goods that are used internally. Much has been written about transfer prices or shadow prices that are attached for internal management or accounting purposes. In a sense these are versions of full cost prices. And the full cost pricing of the final product may be affected by practices employed in transfer or shadow pricing.

Full Costing and Price Theory. Full cost pricing does not conform to the marginal pricing that has been stock in trade of much price theory. Some leading theorists now accept the validity of the full cost approach, in defiance of conventional wisdom. As a selected illustration, Baumol and Bradford examine the "paradox" which they blithely call, *"The Purloined Proposition or The Mystery of the Mislaid Maxim,"* but then put in straight language as the "proposition . . . that, *generally, prices which deviate in a systematic manner from marginal costs will be required for an optimal allocation of resources, even in the absence of externalities."* Nor do they confine the circumstances to those where "the revenue yielded by marginal cost pricing will fall short of the total costs of the firm." They explain that "in practice revenue requirements of the firm are often based on historical accounting cost figures which management feels it must recover."[13]

Full Costing and Business Strategy. The case for the full cost approach must be made on grounds of how well it explains business practices, not by its standing in the literature of price theory. But the terms of the argument change as actual practices are considered, because pricing decisions are usually made not separately but as a part of overall business strategy.

To recapitulate, most large business firms operate in a setting of (1) producing multiple products, (2) a cost structure in which relatively few costs are strictly variable ones that can be controlled according to the volume of output of a particular product and (3) a market structure that is imperfectly competitive. Moreover, such costs as are truly controllable-variable for a product are likely to be nearly constant over a rather wide range of output, only to increase sharply as plant capacity is approached. The firm operates as what Wiles calls a "price maker."[14] That is, it uses administered prices, so that price is established first and the volume sold is an endogenous datum.

But only in the shortest run is price arrived at as a separate decision. Over any length of time, price is only one of several managerial variables that include the characteristics of the product itself, any ancillary services that may be attached to it, the kind of promotion to be employed, and business strategy as such vis-à-vis competitors.

In this setting, simplified models of cost- and price-determination are at best of limited help toward understanding business practices. If trusted implicitly, they mislead. Critics are now numerous. Among the more vocal is Shubik, who first quotes Vickrey as warning the student "that 'the gradual development of the modern corporation has made the entrepreneur of classical economic theory a somewhat unreal figure in a part of the typical modern industrial economy.' " Shubik then adds, "In a world with large complicated corporations, selling thousands of goods and services . . . , the way we stick to our simple models . . . is ludicrous." Further,

> The power of a firm in one market may depend delicately upon its price control; in another, upon product variation; in yet another, upon its retailing and distribution setup. The important strategic variables of a firm may be advertising, control of resources, financial strength, advantages in production processes, or dozens of others, depending upon economic circumstances. There is no Royal Road.[15]

Yet business firms must employ cost calculations as guides.* As one business writer puts it,

> Setting fair prices is a problem. . . . Although accountants can neither set prices nor provide a formula so the marketing department can set them, they nevertheless can provide much assistance to management in the search for a fair price.

*A brief review of business oriented pricing literature is found in Oxenfeldt (17).

Costs are a starting point, and accountants can provide information that will produce a clear understanding of the effect of pricing decisions.[16]

The cost data as starting point are controllable variable costs plus an allocation of overhead arrived at by accounting formulas that take into account the prevailing competitive situation in which the product is sold. This is full costing.

The manager is confident that if it proves possible to hold actual prices close to their full-cost level the firm will be profitable and be able to maintain its plant and perhaps expand it.* He hopes to hold that level on the average year in and year out, for all products generally, even while knowing that he can expect to recover less than full costs for some products at some times, and more than full costs for other products at other times.

When the situation for any product turns particularly rocky and price cuts are inescapable, the intention is still to recover enough revenue to cover salvage value for the equipment and people specifically allocated to a product.

It is an exercise in averages and futurity.

Costing of Basic v. Modified Products. A number of inferences about how firms behave can be drawn from the above account.

As one example, the flexibility allowed a multiproduct firm as to its costing and pricing becomes important when some products consistently yield a good revenue. The firm can then, if it wishes, price other products at closer to controllable variable cost plus salvage value. It may have various reasons for wanting to do this. It may believe it desirable to "offer a full line" even though some items may not find an active market. Or it may wish to minimum-price a product in order to push its way into a new market.

Perhaps a more important application of the idea of orchestrating the allocation of overhead in a multiproduct firm relates to adding modifications to—differentiating—a basic product. Often, those modifications can be produced without great added variable cost. If in addition it is decided to go easy on assigning overhead cost, the result is to create a cost and price situation for that product that no competing single-product firm can match.

An illustration is the ability of an automobile manufacturer to add new models. If Ford Motor Company is geared up to turn out a basic Ford sedan, it can add modifications without excessive cost. Particularly if the basic Ford sells well and carries a large share of overhead costs, a special model can be sold at a comparatively low

---

* This raises the question of whether full-cost formulae include excess profits. See Clark, *Competition as a Dynamic Process*, pp. 369–72.

price. A competing firm producing only a direct competitor of the model is then at a disadvantage. To use established if slightly inaccurate language, Ford can marginal-cost-price the variant model, but a competitor producing only a similar car would have to average-cost-price it.

Full Costing as an Aid to Price Leadership. It is sometimes alleged that full cost pricing as an accounting exercise can readily be converted to a device for leadership or tacit collusion in pricing. The argument is that if an industry is oligopolistic so that each firm is highly sensitive to the actions of other firms, the mutual advantages of muted price competition are self-evident. If, then, standard cost accounting practices become established, all firms routinely arrive at almost identical full-cost price data. The incentive to price according to those data may be strong.

Full Costing and Business Cycles. Some economists suggest that the cost structure and management practices described here help to explain how the business cycle comes into being and persists.

One point of view relates to the tendency of business firms to reduce volume of operations during a recession while at the same time they maintain prices. Full cost practices may make it easier to hold prices up. Objection is raised that the recession itself would be nipped if instead firms maintained volume and cut prices. Perhaps so.

A better connection to the business cycle may be that full costing provides a signal system to managers that affects their investment decisions and therefore contributes to an investment cycle. Whenever a firm's business falls short of the expectations set for it, and quasi-rent decreases, the tendency is to postpone or reduce planned new investment. When demand is brisk and revenues (quasi-rent) exceed expectations, interest stirs in expansion of operations. To the extent such happenings take place in many firms at the same time, reflecting industrywide market factors, investment cycles can be generated.

Full Costing and Plant Size. Everything written thus far in this chapter relates to utilization of plant and not to choice of the size of a new plant.

The economics of plant utilization and of new plant construction are two different phenomena. They should never be confused.

The economics of the choice of size of a new plant relates to economies of scale. And this, in turn, in language introduced in this text, derives from the economics of divisibility of resources. It is usually thought that as ever larger sizes of plant are projected more specialization is possible, and therefore more economy of scale is achieved. The one obstacle is divisibility in management. The management function may become more complex and frustrate further specialization. The result is to offset any other economies.

The overall outcome is a generalized point of view that for almost all plants, a point is reached in curves of scale economy past which the slope is very nearly horizontal.

These prevailing interpretations are believed correct. Nevertheless, the analysis presented in this chapter raises some further questions. The first and most nagging one concerns the degree of utilization of a plant at which comparisons of scale economy are to be made.

That is, for each size of plant, the actual operating costs vary according to the percentage to which capacity is utilized. In the familiar envelope curve, a minimum cost is established for the least-cost plant. Often that cost is not further defined. According to the analysis just advanced, there is no objectively determinate minimum cost at which product will be produced and priced—in the least-cost plant or any other. Furthermore, if there were such a minimum, management would not expect to operate at that minimum, month in and month out. No firm's business is that stable.

Hence there is a substantial arbitrary element in any comparison of the economics of alternate size of plants. In principle, some standard percent-of-capacity figure could be chosen for making plant size comparisons. It might or might not be realistic.

In these brief comments a perfect market continues to be assumed for input and output of a plant. At relatively large volumes the likelihood increases that some markets will be imperfect—that prices of items bought or product sold will be affected by the quantities involved. However, this is a separate consideration in the economics of size.

This last observation relates further to the often-heard dictum that physical economy of size is confined to the individual plant but merchandising economies may be realized in a multiplant firm. This may be true; but the odds are high that oligopoly or oligopsony power is involved in savings such as those of advertising. The water becomes murky.*

---

*In no sense has this brief review done justice to the important topic of economy of size or scale. Nothing is said about definitional confusion regarding the two words, *size* and *scale*. Nor have genuine external economies or diseconomies been mentioned (genuine, and not disguised oligopolistic or oligopsonistic power).

Full Costing and Output Decisions. According to the preceding explanation of full costing as a decision-making technique, managers choose a full-cost accounting formula but they may depart from it as they intermix all the decision variables. It is a highly indeterminate, nonobjective process.

Even the presentation here falls short of the many variations and complexities—and the shortcuts that managers may take. As an illustrative example, Lynn has written about how, in circumstances that are not rare, high unit volume is the best objective to be pursued in choosing pricing policies. Lynn especially warns that "short-run restraint on profits and pricing will often be consistent with the attainment of favorable long-run profits." He explains further: "The sale of more product units and perhaps the raising of market share will serve as a broader base for profits as well as provide a measure of security in periods of trouble."[18]

Full costing for decision-making typically results in production at less than the full capacity of a plant. Thus, production very often is not extended to the point where marginal revenue equals marginal controllable variable cost. Marginal analysis is rejected in the argument that has been advanced here. A further explanation may be called for.

The first explanation is that both revenue and cost are subject, to some degree, to internal decisions of the firm. We are not working with strictly objective "market" data.

Second, the marginal revenue-cost solution may be at very near full capacity. A firm expects to operate at capacity part of the time. In the normal course of events it cannot sustain such a peak continuously; demand is too variable.

Third, the configuration of cost and revenue may be such that not enough overhead cost will be recovered if the volume is determined by equating marginal revenue with marginal controllable cost. This is only an application of the decreasing-cost-industry conundrum.

Fourth and most important, very often the firm's cost and output dilemma is magnified because it operates in oligopoly and its decisions are not made in disregard of response by other firms. Moreover, in such a setting most firms expect to use full capacity only at peak periods. Therefore, if any one firm were to try to adjust its prices and promotion fluidly so as to keep its own capacity fully utilized at all times, it would have to reckon with similar defensive moves by its competitors. Firms operating in such a setting almost invariably adopt the full cost procedure described in this chapter in place of marginal analysis. Their technique, though defensible, does not escape tests of welfare.

INGENIOUS RECOURSE. A common tactic by which a firm's management tries to keep volume high while avoiding sharp competition with direct competitors is to multiple price its product. It may attach some form of nominal differentiation to facilitate doing so. If unused capacity can be employed to produce for a separate market that is insulated from the firm's main market, that capacity will be diverted into the additional production, joyfully. This is the explanation for drug firms' selling pharmaceutical products at sharp discounts in foreign markets. It is also the explanation for the bargain prices that food processors have often quoted to the U.S. Department of Agriculture when that agency asked for bids on food for school lunch or other programs. The processing firms know that the school lunch market is effectively separated from their commercial outlets.

Full Costing and the General Welfare. Several of the issues just touched on have welfare implications. Price and output decisions in large firms operating in imperfect competition involve a substantial zone for arbitrary choice. The analysis presented in this chapter is somewhat defensive of decision-making practices, inasmuch as they fit the kind of cost structure and competition that prevail widely today. This admission is double-pronged, however. Actual decisions made in particular instances might meet welfare tests, but they also might not. Where business decisions are not made entirely by objective data but partly subjectively, they stand open to scrutiny; and no general judgment, pro or con, can be declared.

CHAPTER FOUR

COMPETITIVE STRUCTURE OF THE MARKET

IF THE MARKETING ECONOMIST seeks to reduce, not the year as in Omar Khayam's case, but the economy to better reckoning, the choice of a structural framework is all-important.

This is not an idle cliché. The economy is so huge and heterogeneous that some simplifying device is essential to bring it within the capacity of the human mind.

Selection of a framework or "model" is not a neutral process. The telescoping device chosen affects the relevance and accuracy of judgments arrived at: judgments of prediction, judgments of private decision making, judgments of policy action.

Much of the debate on economic issues, especially those involving public policy, turns on the choice of model. Often, once the model is agreed upon, the contest, whether substantive or ideological, is won (or lost). Certain implications tend to follow from particular models.

In Chapter 1 the subject is opened up briefly. In a very loose way it is suggested that the U.S. marketing economy of the 1970s combines the third and fourth evolutionary epochs, and shows an increasing tendency toward the latter. Other chapters have necessarily anticipated the inquiry into market structure to be presented in this one. This is particularly true of Chapter 3 on the economics of the firm. In fact, it is an engaging question as to how the economics of the firm and the structure of the market are interconnected. The conventional rule has been that market structure strongly influences the behavior of firms, or at least sets certain metes and bounds for that behavior. It is equally plausible that certain characteristics of the production and marketing process within firms help to account for the structure of the market. The familiar, almost hackneyed, example is a decreasing cost structure that leads to oligopoly. Equally relevant is the example offered near the end of Chapter 3, in which other features of cost structure are shown to encourage producing several variations on a basic product—that is, product differentiation.

The idea of a reciprocal relationship between the firm and market structure is suggested even by ambiguities in defining such terms as "firm" and "industry." These in turn give an excuse for putting the whole matter into an historical setting.

The classicists, as is well known, thought in terms of only two competitive models, perfect (or pure)* competition, and monopoly. Even neoclassicists such as Marshall stopped short of adding new models. The classicists were not as naive as might be supposed. True, their perfect competition involved only standard products, so that the producers of each such product comprised an industry. The industry was the entity subjected to analysis, and the appropriate analytical tool was numerology. How many firms and how large?—this was the structural question. It is a question we still use, or try to.

We may suppose that most such products were the basic necessities of life. Where production of those products remained monopolized, the monopoly was the creation of the crown, a system to which the classicists objected. This was almost the substance of their argument. On the other hand, production of luxury goods lent itself less well to competitive forces. We may infer that classical writers were not so indignant over crown dispensed monopolies for luxury goods and services, which went mainly to the nobility in any case. Their conscience was more sensitive to noncompetitiveness in providing necessities to ordinary people.

A structural consequence of the perfectly competitive model is to make the distinction sharp and clear between the firm and the industry. Furthermore, the analysis is thereby simplified. Economic forces extend their sway through the industry. Cyert and Hedrick, who are referred to in Chapter 3, explain that within the firm in the classical competitive model "there are no organizational problems nor is there any room for analysis of the internal decision-making process." Moreover, they add, "All of the empirical content" of even the neoclassical economic analysis lay "in the description of the environment within which the firm must operate. . . ."[1]

Manifestly, the firms of modern industry which typically produce a number of differentiated products do not fit in the neat classical or neoclassical mold. In a manner of speaking each such firm *is* the industry. This is the clear case in pure or absolute monopoly, as of public transport.

The classical firm and industry are horizontal categories. They relate to a single stage in the marketing sequence. Clearly, modern firms violate this condition profusely. Not only does vertical integration abound, but conglomeration introduces cross-industry combinations that extend to various stages.

In spite of this melange of structural types among firms as now found, we hold tight to the concept of the industry. It remains basic to structural analysis, including that of this chapter. The U.S. Department of Commerce and the Federal Trade Commission pour out

*For easier exposition, the terms perfect and pure competition will be used interchangeably in this discussion. Although the distinction between them is genuine, it is not basic to the argument of this chapter. Further, it is a convenience simply to contrast perfect and imperfect competition.

streams of business data arranged according to industrial classification schemes of usually three- or four-digit categories. The limited reality of the data is illustrated by the failure (at this writing) to compel conglomerate firms to report operating data separately by industrial categories.

What we do, obviously, when we identify industries is recognize that there are varying degrees of difference among products and therefore among firms. We separate industries at the widest gaps. Popular usage is our guideline: automobiles divide from airplanes, and meat from leather goods.

LIMITED DIVISIBILITY, MOBILITY OF RESOURCES. The firm-versus-industry puzzle may be interpreted in terms of the principle of limited divisibility and mobility of resources which was discussed earlier. If all resources were infinitely divisible and perfectly mobile, all production would be custom designed to individual consumers' wishes (see Chapter 1). No effort would be made to persuade, as there would be no need for it. Each firm would be a tiny monopoly and a miniscule industry, the ultimate in differentiation of product. As no mass production would be carried on, valuation would be free of the complexities associated with capital goods. Also, incidentally, the system would yield no producers' or consumers' surplus, and no rent or quasi-rent.

The production and marketing system as it exists obviously departs far from perfect divisibility and mobility. Yet the elaborate differentiation of product that is so visible goes part way in that direction. And one way of looking at the existing structure is to distinguish between the economy of mass production of a standard product, which caters less to consumers' individual tastes but saves them money, versus the more costly differentiation which does cater to preferences. The choice—the balance—is affected in turn by (1) the production economics of the firm, and (2) the substitutability of demand (native or induced), as is explained below.

All this relates too to the popular but slightly demagogic idea of consumer sovereignty. Only under perfect divisibility-mobility could the consumer be truly sovereign. Short of that elysian state the consumer is forced to share sovereignty with producers. The analysis of this chapter helps to reveal the terms of sharing, and the outcome.

COMPETITIVE MODELS. Although the divisibility-mobility theme is weaved in, the principal framework for studying market structure used here is the familiar competitive models. Primary emphasis is on

TABLE 4.1. Abbreviated Classification of Competitive Models.

Category of Product	Number of Sellers		
	Many	Few	One
Standard (homogeneous)	Perfect competition	Homogeneous oligopoly[a]	Single-firm monopoly[a]
Differentiated	Monopolistic competition	Differentiated oligopoly[a]	

[a] Matching terms of oligopsony and monopsony are not shown.

the relationship between those models and the decision options of the firm. Performance judgments then follow.

Among conventional classifications, the following is typical. As applied to organization of sellers, it is as shown in Table 4.1.

Conditions associated with these models usually begin with ease of entry and exit. Perfect competition offers easy in-and-out movement, and monopoly forecloses any new entry.

But conditions of entry and category of product are not themselves accidental. They reflect interrelations between the nature of resources employed and the characteristics of demand for products produced. Moverover, we are interested in knowing how the several models affect the behavior options of each firm—what Bain calls the conduct variable. One approach is to consider the extent to which each firm is subject to, or shielded from, the decisions made by other firms.*

With these several questions in mind, the outline presented in Table 4.2 was drawn up. The table employs the competitive models and begins (in the stub) with customary criteria such as number of firms, size distribution, and ease of entry.

The more difficult concepts arise with factors which help to account for the presence, or prevalence, of each model. Why does a particular model exist?

The table repeats the pairing of the characteristics of resources and demand. In the limiting case of monopoly, resources are rigid and demand resists substitution. Where either condition is relaxed appreciably, monopoly is not possible. For all other models, however, not resources alone nor the character of demand alone is model-determining. The two interact, and there can be trade-off between them.

In the modern economy, which is partway into the fourth evolutionary epoch, the characteristics of resources and of demand are not

*This revealing interpretation was presented by the author's professor of many years ago, Alfred Sherrard.

TABLE 4.2. Models of Industrial Organization.[a]

Item	Perfect competition	Imperfect Competition			
		Monopolistic competition	Oligopoly Homogeneous	Oligopoly Differentiated	Monopoly[b]
Number of firms in industry[c]	Many	Many	Several	Several	One
Size distribution of firms	No domination	No domination	May be domination	May be domination	...
Ease of entry	Very easy	Fairly easy	Difficult	Difficult	Nearly impossible
Model-determining conditions[d]					
Divisibility-mobility of resources[e]	Moderate	Moderate	Low	Low	Almost none
Substitutability among products	Moderate	Moderate	Low	Rather Low	None
Conditions affecting firm's conduct					
Sensitivity of sales quantity to firm's own actions					
Price actions	Infinitely elastic	Moderately elastic	Indeterminate[g]	Moderately inelastic	Infinitely inelastic[h]
Nonprice actions	None	Small	None	Moderate	None
Sensitivity of sales quantity to competitors' actions					
Price actions	None	Small	High	Moderate	...
Nonprice actions	None	Small	None	Moderate	...
Determinateness of price-quantity decisions[f]	Determinate	Indeterminate	Indeterminate	Indeterminate	Determinate

[a] Classified according to organization of sellers. The model refers to the *industry*.

[b] A hypothetical model, with no cross-elasticity of demand for products. Therefore a "no competition" model.

[c] As "industry" is usually regarded. In the narrowest interpretation, each firm in monopolistic competition and differentiated oligopoly is an industry.

[d] The balance (with tradeoff) between these conditions affects the kind of model that prevails.

[e] This may be natural or institutional: patents, access to communication, and other institutional factors can limit divisibility-mobility—and often do.

[f] Assuming objective data available on price-quantity relationships in demand, but not on response to nonprice competition nor on the consequences of strategic rivalry.

[g] Indeterminate depending on excess capacity in the industry, but indeterminate also because leadership or tacit collusion is highly likely.

[h] Therefore regulated.

wholly exogenous. Regarding resources, we take measures both to improve and to impede divisibility-mobility. Efficient transport and the patent system are examples—the former to improve, the latter to restrain. All promotional persuasion of consumers can be interpreted in terms of how it affects substitutability.

Surely the consequences of each model to the range (and kind) of decision options open to each firm are just about the most important inference to be drawn from the table. Here as in many instances, perfect competition and "perfect" monopoly are the clear-cut examples. The three intermediate models are not so accommodating to the analyst—or to the decision-making businessman. The entries for oligopoly anticipate a theme of this chaper, namely, that conscious rivalry and deliberate strategy are seldom absent among the larger firms in oligopolistic industries.

The several uncertainties are summed in the last row of entries in terms of how determinate are the price-quantity solutions for each model. In the present state of empirical knowledge, only the first and last models make determinate solutions possible. As data are known for neither the response of demand to nonprice competitive actions nor the reaction of competing firms to oligopolistic strategy, the middle three models are indeterminate.

Welfare Judgments. It is timely to touch on the topic of general welfare once again. We focus first on the firm but we are concerned also for macro-outcome, which Bain calls performance. In the final analysis a social judgment is passed.

Provisionally we can draw some inferences but also issue warnings. The warning is to be slow about jumping to conclusions. As only in perfect competition and monopoly are price-quantity outcomes determinate, only for them can welfare judgments be made explicitly. For the other models of indeterminate performance, no *a priori* evaluation is possible. To the extent the form of prevailing industrial organization (homogeneous oligopoly, for instance) reflects basic characteristics of resources or demand or both, we should not be surprised at its existence. On the other hand, the three intermediate models offer much opportunity for arbitrary decisions by managers. There is no reason to take for granted that they will be in the public interest—or against the public interest. Those three models properly raise empirical questions as to whether conduct, as judged by the performance that results, is acceptable.

THE ECONOMICS OF IMPERFECT COMPETITION. Nearly all the discussion that follows relates to imperfect competition:

monopolistic competition, homogeneous oligopoly, and differentiated oligopoly. Perfect competition and monopoly will be referred to occasionally for pedagogical purposes.

Most of the economy operates in some variety of imperfect competition. Says Hotelling, "Between the perfect competition and monopoly of theory lie the actual cases."[2] Nor is the situation much different in agricultural marketing. Marketing of agricultural products takes place primarily in a vast turbulent sea of imperfect competition. Only a few quiet bays of nearly perfect competition are to be found. Slaughter of hogs and cattle in the Corn Belt may approximate that model. But imperfect competition is the general rule.

As a second reason for omitting perfect competition, the model offers no analytical challenge. Expositions on it are available from many sources.

Imperfect competition comes about principally because of (1) the basic economics of the typical firm, particularly the economy of scale that results from limited divisibility-mobility of resources and (2) the limited substitutability among products in consumer demand. We therefore have big firms using large installations of fixed capital generating an equivalent overhead cost. The productive plant can usually be used for many combinations of a huge output of a few standard products and smaller quantities of a sizable number of differentiated products. The decisions and the allocation of overhead cost are somewhat arbitrary, dooming marginal cost pricing as an analytical device and leading to the practice of full costing as a basis for pricing (see Chapter 3).

But those are only part of the range of opportunities that are opened up—though the particular opportunities available to an individual firm depend on its immediate circumstances. Frequently there is a possibility of using advertising and other nonprice competition to influence demand. Fairly ofen, some form of stratified pricing is feasible. And the whole gamut of interrelated decisions by the firm, which in the aggregate characterize an industry, is overlain with the possibility of an interdependence—an interaction vector among firms—that brings firm-versus-firm strategy into consideration.

These are the primary decision variables around which further analysis of the several models will turn.

Product Differentiation. Differentiation of product as a competitive practice has intrigued economists since it was first publicized in the 1930s. The idea is simple, and in a logical sense it merely reflects the fact that some members of a family of products are more nearly alike than others. When a small firm produces a product that carries just enough distinctiveness to avoid stereotype, this kind of differentiation describes the competitive model of monopolistic competition. That model is interesting but not complicated.

Differentiation by large multiple-product firms is another matter. Where a large but flexible productive plant is involved, a fascinating scenario comes into view. It is often—in fact, usually—possible for such a firm to design differentiated products as variants upon basic products (or other differentiated ones). Extra costs of production are not excessive. Dodge Brothers can add a Dart to their line at a cost much less than would be required for a new company to produce the same vehicle from scratch. In the modern economy, economy of size or scale has more meaning in the capacity to diversify (differentiate) products readily than in high-volume production of a standard product.

A close parallel is found in merchandising. Once a large firm has promoted a brand name and built up loyalty, under that rubric it can create and introduce newly differentiated versions of its basic products.

Nevertheless, differentiation involves some cost. At least a moderate volume of output is sought for a new product, be it an economy automobile, two percent milk, or a new sausage. Thereupon arises the calculus between fineness of differentiation as a way to tap existing consumer demand, and advertising and other promotion as a means to lure consumers to the fewer, less differentiated and therefore higher volume products.

Differentiation by a multiproduct firm also takes advantage of any differences in quality of competition in the markets for the various products. This reintroduces the idea of full-cost allocation of overhead so that products which encounter weak competition bear a heavy overhead-cost load in the firm's accounting and pricing, and those entering a tighter market bear less.

DIFFERENTIATION AS MARKET STRATIFICATION. Orchestration of products has a vertical component too. Very often, products are differentiated not just as lateral modifications, as brown shoes and black shoes or white bread and brown bread, but as vertical market stratification. The "line" of differentiated products is chosen so as to cater to various cultural, occupational, ethnic, or income levels of the population.

Sometimes the stratification is openly admitted. The Dodge Dart is advertised accurately to be less luxurious than the Coronet. Swift publicizes the quality differences in its brands of processed meat.

A second form of stratification is more subtle. In it, physical differences in products are small but one variety is glamorized so as to capture a particular stratum of the market, usually that of high income. This nominal differentiation often has snob appeal and may be accompanied by aggressive advertising.

A third category of stratification is fiat, contrived, or simply false. Two products may differ only in the label, yet one is promoted as superior to the other. This raises perplexing questions. If a dairy firm sells its canned condensed milk (from the same vat) to two firms, one of which attaches a premium label and the other a less prestigious one, is the milk the same? The answer is not just academic. It can enter into some trade practice regulations.

Clearly, the various forms of market stratification have significance not only for decision-making conduct by firms but also for general welfare judgments on performance.

MAXIMUM VERSUS MINIMUM DIFFERENTIATION. Another aspect of differentiation, which has some of the gamesmanship of chess, is the issue of whether it is better for a firm to choose maximum or minimum differentiation. The reflex response may be to suggest maximum. It could be sharply distinguished, visible. Hotelling has demonstrated that minimum differentiation may be the more promising of substantial volume. Using geographical differentiation for his illustration, he argues that if one firm is already centrally located in an area, any new firm can gain a protective geographical shelter (allowing it to charge a higher price) only if it retreats to a remote spot and accepts a limited zone and small volume. If the new firm wants to fight for a large volume it will snuggle up close to the existing firm and contest for sales in the entire area. And if the original firm had not found the exact center, the new one will hasten to locate there; or it will otherwise seek some central locational advantage, however slight. Hotelling extends the principle to small differentiations in type, style, or quality of product, noting "the tendency to make only slight deviations in order to have for the new commodity as many buyers of the old as possible."[3]

This principle of degree of differentiation has a host of applications. Political parties that differentiate sharply stay small. The two major parties have usually presented minimum differences; and when one has not, it has lost.

Do universities differentiate their instructional product? They usually pretend they do not, as they try to keep students from showing preferences among professors. But students are not fooled. Neither is the public, and especially public interest groups seeking to tap the scholarly skills and reputations of university staff in support of their enterprises. The late Jacob Viner was a cynic. He commented on "the emergence of a variety of kinds of economists, so that no layman needed to be at a loss in finding some school of economics which provided him with professional justification for whatever policies he was attached to."[4]

Market Stratification. Stratification of the market via differentiation of product is only one application of the broad principle of dividing the market into strata, usually those oriented to income of consumers. As suggested earlier, differentiation can often fulfill the two requirements (or preconditions) for stratification. These are that the demand curve have a different slope at one market stratum than another, and that the two or more markets be separable, with no backflow possible. Differentiation meets the second requirement with the help, frequently, of trademark laws. It is illegal to sell Swift's second grade brand of ham as the first. It is impossible to pass off a Dodge Dart as a Coronet.

Stratification nevertheless is usually thought of as division of the market for a standard product. On the production side, stratification becomes attractive because of the characteristic of modern production that has already been referred to repeatedly, namely, the limited divisibility-mobility of resources that underlies economy of size or scale. When costs have a sizable component of overhead, stratification may be profitable to the firm. It is likewise so to an industry under cartelization or government program—as in market-order pricing of fluid milk or the time-dishonored practice of export dumping.

Stratification has often carried moral connotations. Some instances, as of higher medical fees charged wealthy patients, frequently find general acceptance. Other applications are more likely to encounter skepticism or disapproval. As is pointed out in Chapter 2, this may not be justified. In any event it is necessary to describe stratification for what it is.

A common and rather clever scheme for graphing stratification for a standard product between two markets is the unbalanced teepee chart of Fig. 4.1.

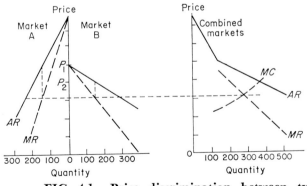

FIG. 4.1. Price discrimination between two markets.

In the chart, the demand curves for the two markets are combined for comparison with the (single) cost curve. The marginal-cost, marginal-revenue solution is then carried back to the individual markets, where the price solutions are P_1 and P_2.

Moral qualms about stratification of the market for a standard product may be altered by a demonstration of how stratification by a monopolist yields results that in important respects resemble perfect competition. At constant cost quantity is the same, as is price to lowest income consumers.

This is only the familiar demonstration of discriminatory pricing by a monopolist. It is relevant to imperfect competition in the market system for agricultural products, because all imperfect competition contains some element of firm monopoly. Although mathematical (algebraic) demonstration is simple, the graphics help to draw conclusions.

Assume that demand and cost data for a product are as follows:

1st 5,000 consumers would pay	$1.50
2nd 5,000 consumers would pay	1.20
3rd 5,000 consumers would pay	1.00
average and marginal cost per unit	.95

By the simplest arithmetic it will be seen that the solution for the nondiscriminating monopolist is to produce only 5,000 units, where his profit is $2,750. At 10,000 units his profit drops to $2,500, and at 15,000 units to $750.

Figure 4.2 pictures this solution in terms of how a monopolist fac-

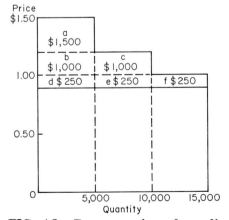

FIG. 4.2.   Demonstration of nondiscriminatory versus discriminatory monopoly pricing.

ing a demand curve as assumed here finds it unprofitable to increase output. This may be viewed in terms of his losing revenue from well-heeled consumers as he expands to accommodate consumers of more modest income. When he moves from $1.50 to $1.20 he loses the net revenue of box a, or $1,500, and gains only that of boxes c and e or $1,250. If he were to go one step further, to a $1.00 price, he would lose boxes b and c or $2,000 and gain only box f or $250.

The discriminating monopolist would retain the revenue of boxes a, b, and c and would hold d, e, and f as he sold at three different prices. (For simplicity, it is assumed that the next price stratum is $0.90, below the cost of production; hence the "solution.") This is of course the same quantity solution as under perfect competition.

The demonstration is unrealistic in its constant cost curve, though even that is not farfetched in the zone of normally produced quantities, as Chapter 3 points out. It is accurate in its implication that discriminatory pricing realizes the same quantity of output as perfect competition does. The big difference shows up in what happens to consumers' surplus. In discriminatory pricing the monopolist gets it (he keeps what would have been consumers' surplus). In perfect competition consumers get it. In nondiscriminatory pricing by a monopolist, consumers may retain a little surplus, but the potential value is reduced by virtue of reduced volume.

Another way of looking at it is that nondiscriminatory pricing by a monopolist denies to marginal consumers the product for which they are willing to pay the marginal cost. In discriminatory pricing the higher income consumers pay a bounty to the monopolist and allow the marginal consumers to buy at marginal cost.

It is interesting to extend the illustration to producers' surplus—and to raise a policy question about matching up high cost producers with high income consumers. To some extent this is accomplished in stratified differentiation.

Various inferences are intriguing yet important. Mishan pointed out in 1960 that "a situation in which price equals marginal cost in all lines" is as much "a corollary of perfectly discriminating monopoly . . . as of perfect competition."[5]

CHARACTERISTICS OF THE MODELS. Although it is simplifying to think in terms of three models of imperfect competition, a more accurate viewpoint is to regard all imperfect competition as a single entity containing many combinations and gradations. Figure 4.3 is intended to help present such a picture. The usual variables of number of firms in an industry and degree of differentiation are the two axes. Three models are discretely delineated: monopoly, duopoly,

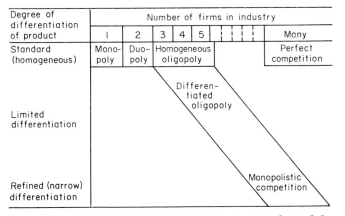

Degree of differentiation of product	Number of firms in industry									
	1	2	3	4	5					Many
Standard (homogeneous)	Mono-poly	Duo-poly	Homogeneous oligopoly							Perfect competition
Limited differentiation				Differen-tiated oligopoly						
Refined (narrow) differentiation								Monopolistic competition		

FIG. 4.3. Schematic arrangement of models of industrial organization.

and perfect competition. Duopoly is included because three firms are a practical minimum for oligopoly. Homogeneous oliogopoly is conceptually pure but probably empirically nonexistent. Even the most homogeneous product is usually accompanied by some special services. But there are enough industries that approach homogeneity to make the model useful.

The numerology of an industry is somewhat misleading, not only because size distribution is not of numbers as such but because firms operate in an awareness of an interaction vector—of interdependence. This is the distinction Doll, Rhodes and West make between large group and small group. In a small group each firm is aware of firm-to-firm interdependence and acts accordingly. In a large group no firm fears direct retaliation to actions it may take. "The key concept of the large group is the lack of interdependence between any pair of firms."[6]

Monopolistic Competition. The large group includes perfect and monopolistic competition.

Monopolistic competition, the latest model to be created in economists' minds, is the most interesting. It is a paradoxical model. At its extreme it approaches perfect competition. The firm is free of the power and the power struggles that mark oligopoly. There is a slope to the firm's demand curve, yet market development and non-price competition in general usually overshadow price policy. In more technical language, the demand curve may usually be regarded as having more shiftability than slope.

Among merits customarily cited for monopolistic competition is the somewhat negative, lesser-of-several-evils one that it is better than oligopoly and may be a counter-irritant to it. The second is a little more positive in that monopolistic competition by its nature can cater to individual preferences better than any other model.

This second feature has its complications. As one, a good deal of the differentiation in monopolistic competition is differentiated stratification. It can cater to prestige-conscious consumers, and lightly relieve them of the consumers' surplus they would retain in a more nearly perfectly competitive model.

The more questionable or negative aspects of monopolistic competition fall into three categories:

1. *Consumer knowledgeability.* It is alleged, with good reason, that profuse differentiation escalates the number of separate products put on the market to the point that it is impossible for the household consumer to be knowledgeable. It is not a happenstance that most of the targets of the consumer movement, calling for inspection for safety, labeling, and similar services, have been differentiated products.

2. *Cost of excessive market development efforts.* There is a cost to altering the demand curve for a firm—to shift it to the right and/or to steepen it. (In monopolistic competition the former is usually the more feasible.)

Market development costs take myriad forms, partly because immense promotional campaigns are not available as a base. The latter fit oligopoly, not monopolistic competition. Rent for locational advantage is a common and sizable cost to the firm in monopolistic competition. Advertising, giveaways, and a host of small services can aggregate into a tidy sum.

In this regard we introduce the phenomenon of "cost-escalating imitation." Independently reported by Beem and Oxenfeldt[7] and the present author,[8] it applies to "extra added attractions" that may be attached to a basic product. These may be personal services, or trading stamps, or lengthened hours of remaining open, or coupon games. So long as it has excess capacity and the services attract buyers, the innovating firm may be able to bear all costs without increasing prices. When competitors offer exact or approximate equivalents ("imitations"), the initial advantage is lost. The process tends to build in costs. Also, it is not symmetrically reversible, as firms only reluctantly withdraw the bonuses they had previously added.

3. *Pricing policy.* Firms in monopolistic competition do not have as much latitude for a pricing policy as those in oligopoly. Yet price policy choices can be made.

In general, it is believed that firms in monopolistic competition cannot increase prices a great deal compared with those in perfect competition. Nor will the quantity produced and sold be reduced very much. But there are two other schools of thought. One is that promotional activities can be so elaborate and costly as to build in a sizable increase in price. The other is defensive: it is that successful promotion will kick economy of scale into gear, yielding a net price saving to consumers. It is a casual use of the idea of economy of size or scale.

The actual quantity-and-price outcome under monopolistic competition probably varies widely according to circumstances. There is reason to believe that three combinations are possible. The following are the three comparisons that might be found with perfect competition. They apply best to the relatively short run:

> smaller quantity, higher price
> larger quantity, lower price
> larger quantity, higher price

Only one combination is highly unlikely. It is smaller quantity and lower price.

QUANTITY-PRICE RESPONSES TO ADVERTISING. It is difficult to make convincing algebraic or graphic comparisons between imperfect and perfect competition. A different kind of comparison can be made readily. It is instructive. It demonstrates the several outcomes of varying intensities and effectiveness of advertising and promotion. When confined to the zone where marginal cost can be asumed to be decreasing, it reveals the same three quantity-price combinations as are listed above for comparing monopolistic and perfect competition. In fact, the demonstration that follows gives some basis for the general judgments just offered about monopolistic and perfect competition.

The demonstration in Fig. 4.4 shows alternate quantity and price responses when a firm in imperfect competition advertises. The demonstration is an elementary one of a single product firm, and does not fit the analysis of a large multiple product firm given in Chapter 3. It is rather short run and is confined to a situation where marginal cost is decreasing.

The initial position is the marginal cost and average revenue curves MC_1 and AR_1 (the latter yields MR_1). The initial solution is P_1, Q_1. To this is added two levels of advertising and two responses in demand, which give four possible combinations. When the high MC_2 is matched against the modest demand response AR_2, the price is increased and quantity reduced. When the small extra cost MC_3 yields the sharply shifting AR_3, quantity is increased and price actually decreases slightly. When the same small extra cost is assumed to bring only a modest dividend in increased demand, the solution is P_4, Q_4,

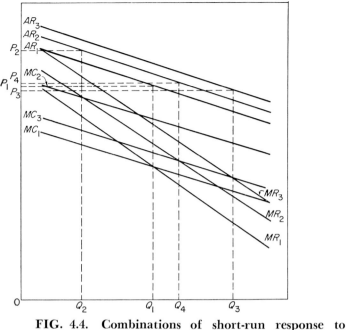

FIG. 4.4. Combinations of short-run response to advertising.

which is a bigger quantity and higher price. The chart does not show a combination of large extra cost and small return in demand; it would be a second case of smaller quantity and higher price.

The example will not allow heroic passing of judgment. It only serves to illustrate one point: that even when the firm-versus-firm strategy of oligopoly is absent, quantity and price performance of firms in imperfect competition can vary widely. Throughout this book, readers will be admonished not to leap to sweeping conclusions about what happens in imperfect competition.

Nevertheless, the illustration does not deny the prevailing judgment about monopolistic competition. Insofar as firms in monopolistic competition tend to restrain their advertising and promotional effort, and seldom reap great windfalls, the likelihood is that price will be higher and quantity smaller than might be expected under perfect competition, but the differences are usually not great.

PRICING PRACTICES IN MONOPOLISTIC COMPETITION. Firms in monopolistic competition that handle a variety of products engage in their own version of full cost pricing. This especially applies to retailing, where it takes the form of variable markups. It is the traditional wisdom in food retailing that some products are more customer-attracting. than others. These usually carry relatively low markups. Others are priced relatively higher and contribute more to overhead costs of the firm. Nelson and Preston have given to this practice of orchestrating prices the term "variable price merchandising."[9]

This common practice has two aggressive offshoots. One is temporary price specialing. Weekend or all-the-week specials are chosen for their customer-drawing effect. The second is price wars. Firms in monopolistic competition, unlike those in oligopoly, do not often deliberately engage in predatory competition. But when beset by excess capacity and struggling to survive, they can drift into price wars.

Oligopoly. Homogeneous oligopoly presents a simpler case. Here there may be production economy but also raw power. Prices are likely to be higher than they would be under perfect competition, and quantity lower. Life is nevertheless hard for the manager because firm-versus-firm strategy is a daily fact of life, notwithstanding the fact that price leadership and other tacit devices short of collusion soften the edge of rivalry. (Some critics would say they dull it.) Stratified pricing not infrequently is found attractive. Competitive practices naturally lead to excess capacity and weak price competition. The story has been told often.

The irony of it all, as is suggested in Chapter 3, is that this kind of conduct and performance is the logical outcome of the structure. The opposite extreme, price wars, is neither practicable nor desirable. And when they come usually they are predatory.

The conduct zone in homogeneous oligopoly is wide. Conduct decisions can range from contempt for the public interest to beneficial public service.

DIFFERENTIATED OLIGOPOLY. Differentiated oligopoly is more ambiguous than homogeneous oligopoly and even more far-ranging in its potential behavior. It has features of both homogeneous oligopoly and monopolistic competition. Its relation is closer to the former, however, owing to the recognized interdependence among firms.

Differentiated oligopoly that borders on monopolistic competition can share with it both the positive and negative features of that model. On the plus side, its differentiation can cater to individual preferences of consumers. Negatively, its cost and complexity must be taken fully into account.

Price and output decisions in differentiated oligopoly can, in principle, relate to perfect competition in the same way as was sketched above for imperfect competition in general. But because differentiated oligopoly stands close to homogeneous oligopoly, the odds are always high that it yields higher prices than either perfect or monopolistic competition.

Firms in differentiated oligopoly vary widely as to how much they rely on promotional activities. One pattern that is seen rather often is for firms with clearly differentiated and established products to maintain their position without any great outpouring of advertising or new product development. On the other hand, where competing firms produce products of very similar nature, developmental activities may be aggressive and costly. It is expensive to convince the consumer that two products are different when he knows them to be essentially alike.

It follows that the conduct variable, already wide in homogeneous oligopoly, scarcely has any bounds in differentiated oligopoly.

INDETERMINACY OF PRICE/OUTPUT. For reasons that are obvious by now, price-quantity solutions in all oligopoly are indeterminate. Literature on the subject of behavioral patterns has taken many forms. Several imaginative graphic demonstrations have been devised. One is the well-known duopoly illustration. If firm A takes such-and-such an action, firm B will respond with its own action. Thereupon firm A revises its plans, firm B likewise, and so on. Is equilibrium reached? Probably not.

George Stigler won a wide audience for his kinked demand curve.[10]

Various authors have tried to classify patterns of response. Siegel and Fouraker did so some years ago. They not only recognized differences in numbers of firms but considered whether firms are primarily price adjusters or quantity adjusters, and so on.[11] Stigler described a particular pattern in his "A Theory of Oligopoly."[12]

Game theory is both a challenging and an appropriate tool for analyzing the conduct of oligopoly. It is appropriate provided its limitations be respected.

STRUCTURE-CONDUCT-PERFORMANCE. Some years ago Bain devised and publicized the simple terminology of structure, conduct, and performance as an aid in interpreting industrial organization.[13] Bain attracted a school of followers. Even those who reject his language and disagree with conclusions he draws from his empirical studies find themselves treading similar linguistic paths.

Clodius and Mueller, Paul Nelson, Sosnick and a number of others have elaborated the Bain analysis in relation to agricultural products. Clodius and Mueller capsule the central theme accurately: "All aspects of market structure analysis rest on the basic assumption that market structure determines, in large part, the competitive conduct of firms in a market which in turn generates certain forms of industrial performance."[14]

The key elements in this statement are the words of ambiguity, "in large part," and "the . . . conduct of *firms*" (italics added). The conduct variable is the novel and significant member of the structure-conduct-performance family. The *structure* of the *market* influences but does not absolutely control the *conduct* of *firms*.

Obviously, the formulation is aimed at imperfect competition. In perfect competition (and in absolute monopoly) structure forecloses conduct options and leads directly to performance.

In imperfect competition structure is thus not all-controlling. Foregoing pages have dealt primarily with the kind of conduct that is possible and even probable under various structural models.

By its nature the Bainsian system is nondeterminate—nondeterminate as to conduct and therefore as to performance. No given performance follows determinately from structure.

The spotlight is thrown on conduct as the instrumental variable, and on performance. How shall performance be judged? Can the system be of any use in arriving at public policy?

One route taken is to coin nondeterminate criteria for evaluation. The idea of workable or effective competition has gained some acceptance. This avoids the once-popular prescription that industrial behavior should be judged by how closely it approximates what would happen under perfect competition. Workable or effective competition applies to performance that is practically attainable and socially desirable. Sosnick has named 12 or more criteria for arriving at a judgment. Far from being quantitative, they employ adverbs of degree. They are axiomatic in nature.[15,16,17]

In a nondeterminate marketing system there is no escape from applying nondeterminate criteria judgmentally.

VERTICAL RELATIONSHIPS. All that has been written thus far has been oriented horizontally. So it is in most economic literature. The implied thesis has been that when firms at each horizontal stratum or stage function well, product will move smoothly and efficiently through successive stages to the final consumer, be that consumer a household, an industry, or an institution.

Furthermore, the preponderance of the literature is focussed on a single horizontal stratum and not its relationship to other strata. The competitive structure of the neighboring stage or stratum to which product is sold or from which it is bought is not usually considered as such. The implicit assumption apparently is that the contiguous stratum is atomistic or nearly so.

The assumption is not valid. A great amount of trading is done between two strata, each of which is characterized by considerable concentration. In his landmark study of the structure of the agricultural industries, Nicholls went to considerable length to discuss oligopoly-oligopsony and bilateral monopoly.[18] His contemporary, Hoffman, referred to "bilateral or successive monopoly," by which he had oligopoly-oligopsony in mind.[19]

Galbraith's dalliance with the notion of countervailing power was directed toward a contrived balance between degrees of concentration at successive stages in the marketing sequence.[20] Galbraith dropped his advocacy, presumably because of evidence that firms which countervail relative to each other may jointly exploit still other less concentrated sectors, notably consumers. Rhodes's examination of this point echoes Hoffman's teaching of many years earlier, when he declares that oligopoly-oligopsony contests are so destructive of the public interest that "paradoxically . . . the public would probably be helped rather than injured" by a conspiracy rather than a contest among them.[21]

A Knutson study of "bilateral oligopoly" in milk distribution serves as surrogate for various inquiries into the fabric of competition between bigs and the nature of big-versus-big competition in the distribution chain. Knutson accords the milk distributor buyers considerable market power, and he notes the strategic devices used, including bluffing.[22]

Individual large firms nevertheless often try to avoid head-to-head competition. In food processing and retailing, the evidence is that the larger firms at one stage try to avoid doing business with the larger firms at the other stage.[23] This observation was anticipated many years earlier by Nicholls: "According to my limited observation . . . there is a tendency for . . . large buyers and sellers not to deal with each other. . . . They tend either to integrate . . . or to deal with the smaller independent competitors. . . ."[24]

Vertical Integration. Vertical relationships are established not only in market exchange between successive stages in marketing but also by integration of those stages. Mighell and Jones have written the already-classic introduction to vertical integration in the production and marketing of farm products. They begin from the elements of atomistic structure, delineating units that individually describe a process that could produce a product for sale. These units are organized in a checkerboard for each industry.

The geometry of how the units are actually combined within individual firms indicates the industrial structure of an industry. If each unit were a separate firm (and not itself of giant size) the structure would be atomistic—and the competition "perfect." If many units are combined horizontally into single firms, the industry is concentrated. If they are combined vertically, vertical integration prevails.[25]

To shift the idiom, Mighell and Jones declare that the production-marketing sequence must be vertically coordinated in some fashion. If the units are vertically independent, coordination is by market exchange. If they are vertically linked, coordination is attained within vertical integration.

We now revert to our concept of stages in the marketing system that are more comprehensive than Mighell and Jones's atomic units—stages such as local assembly, central assembly, and processing. We can adopt Trifon's definition of vertical integration as ". . . the ownership or control by one company of enterprises in different stages of production or distribution, where each stage yields a salable commodity."[26] The definition is usually narrowed to confine it to contiguous stages.

The principle of control set forth by Trifon implies that the managerial authority exercised, and not the legal form per se, defines vertical integration. Among contracts in agriculture, a distinction that is accepted rather widely separates production contracts from marketing contracts. The former classify as vertical integration, the latter do not.

Some authors distinguish between forward and backward integration. Supposedly, leadership and control tend to be centered in one of the linked stages, and not shared equally, democratically, between them. But this need not be the case. Perhaps integration is forward or backward depending only on the position of the observer.

The Mighell and Jones checkerboard implicitly presupposes a homogeneous product. Where products of an industry are differentiated, some of the units in the checkerboard diagram must be separated a slight distance. Figure 4.5 illustrates how the organization of the marketing system for the food products of agriculture might be visualized. The chart begins from the same sequence of vertical stages as was presented in Fig. 1.1. It then presents several kinds of horizontal composition. In a roughly realistic replication of the real world, the firms at local assembly are shown as atomistic. Those at central assembly have some horizontal concentration. Wholesaling and retailing are composed primarily of horizontally concentrated firms. (The labels of kinds of retailers can be disregarded here, as they anticipate a later discussion.)

More significant are the alternate systems of vertical coordination

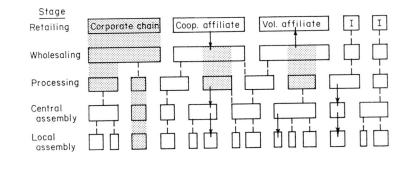

Ownership integration. ↕ Contractual integration. ┊ Buying and selling. I Independent retailer.

FIG. 4.5. **Illustrative sketch of food marketing structure as related to four kinds of retailers.**

that are shown. The chart distinguishes among market exchange, ownership integration, and contractual integration as three systems. By the direction of arrows it indicates forward and backward integration.

Integration in agricultural marketing shows up among retail food chains that process some of their own products, food processors that contract for their supplies (as in broilers and fruits), livestock slaughterers that feed their own cattle, and in many other instances.

ORIGIN OF VERTICAL INTEGRATION. Why does vertical integration take place? What are the consequences?

A simple but valid distinction is between integration that results from inefficiency or inadequacy of market exchange as a coordinating mechanism and that which arises in contest for market power. The latter involves aggression and as a rule is the more likely to violate standards of general welfare.

Wherever the market exchange system does not work well, integrated relationships come into consideration. The market for a product may be inefficient operationally. Livestock slaughterers who find it expensive to keep buyers scouring the countryside may turn to contracts. Or the market system may be loaded down with promotional costs: feed dealers found it more attractive to distribute poultry feed on contract than to fight for markets via advertising and costly salesmanship. That was the origin of contractual integration in broilers.

A market system works best for standard products. Where products are differentiated, both the processor-buyer and the farmer-seller are more likely to enter into integrated relationships. Or the product may not be so distinctive but the whole production-marketing sequence may be confined to narrow channels, and so make integration somewhat attractive. This last situation also fits broilers, for although broilers are a standard product, the specialized productive facilities (house, feeders, etc.) are not readily shifted to other uses and the dressed broilers go into narrowly restricted distribution. The channel is much narrower for broilers than for field corn, for example.

Another imperfection of the market that induces integration is concentration. If a firm finds that the industry from which it buys or into which it sells is excessively concentrated, leading to high prices it must pay or low prices it can receive, it will consider integrating into that industry as a recourse. Some fruit processors manufacture their own cans to detour the can manufacturing industry. Farmer cooperatives sometimes integrate forward into processing and distribution to avoid what they allege to be excessive concentration among private firms in those industries.

Veritably, imperfection in the structure of the marketing system for farm products breeds more imperfection.

The more aggressive type of vertical integration comes about when a firm that possesses size and power in an industry believes it can increase its power by integrating forward or backward. This is a vertical extension of horizontally based power (which is derived in turn from a high degree of differentiation or high concentration). Vertical integration has a power dimension, in fact, only when it can be linked into some degree of horizontal power. A farmer selling his produce at roadside is vertically integrated, for he combines several stages in marketing in his own operation. He is never accused of possessing oligopoly power.

The greatest opportunity for power-motivated vertical integration arises when a firm can thereby deny or obstruct its competitors' access to raw materials or to markets.

In the now-celebrated Brown Shoe Case the Court declared that if a firm which is large at one stage in marketing were to integrate with a sizable firm at another stage, the horizontal-vertical combination would magnify the effects on competitive structure of the distribution system.[27]*

Conglomerate Structure. Modern business does not merely concentrate and integrate. It also conglomerates. The largest firms extend

*Among other references on vertical integration in agriculture are: Marshall Harris and Dean T. Massey, *Vertical Coordination via Contract Farming*, U.S. Dept. of Agr., Econ Res. Serv., Misc. Publ. 1073, 1968, and Harold F. Breimyer, "First Case Study: Vertical Integration in Broilers," in *Individual Freedom and the Economic Organization of Agriculture* (Urbana: Univ. of Illinois Press, 1965), pp. 205–24.

their operations and control in myriad directions, creating a vast network of control.

The forces underlying the conglomerate movement are not clearly understood. High operating efficiency, in the usual sense of the word, is seldom claimed. There may be economies in communication and promotion and even in political influence.

One school of thought accounts for the conglomerate movement in terms of financial advantages to the instigator. These arise out of accounting practices, including those affecting taxes. Hoffman and others speak of "financial legerdemain."[28]

Or the attraction may be relentless pursuit of economic power. This may employ the "deep purse principle," otherwise known as cross-subsidization. According to it, a conglomerate firm has such great financial resources that it can selectively practice predatory competition. In that way it can eliminate existing firms and win a place for itself.

Conglomerate business is still something of a newcomer and is not fully understood. It may be as much a political as an economic entity, a fact accounting for its imponderability to economists.[29]

Evaluation of Vertical and Conglomerate Structures. A summary judgment on vertical integration is not arrived at readily. From the standpoint of the individual integrating firm, in many instances the decision to integrate is defensive rather than aggressive and therefore, in a micro sense, defensible. The argument about oligopoly-oligopsony carries weight: perhaps it is better to have bigs integrate than remain independent and victimize others in their contests against each other. But this may be only a less-bad-of-two-evils rationalization.

There is lots of room for skepticism as to how well vertical integration functions and the desirability of its outcomes. Vertical integration offers instances of efficiency in operations and in reducing costs of the nonprice competition that would otherwise be conducted by an integrated firm's constituent units. However, this argument cannot be carried too far. There are numerous examples of a firm's adding auxiliary services, as of transportation or printing, that proved uneconomical. The parent firm was not skilled in the auxiliary field and the scale of operations was not optimal.

The most generalized and most trenchant observation about vertical integration is that it replaces the market exchange pricing system as the mechanism for giving coordination to the economy. Market exchange pricing is not without weakness but it exposes economic processes and valuations to view. Vertical integration hides them.

Furthermore, any contest between vertical integration and market exchange as systems of vertical coordination is not neutral. Once vertical integration becomes extensive, efficient markets are difficult to sustain. This was the manifest experience in the U.S. broiler industry.

Integration by firms that are already horizontally large introduces a consideration that is absent when only small firms combine vertically. The admission made above that sometimes oligopolists and oligopsonists may as well integrate is really a snare, for it only deals with a situation that already is fraught with violation of general welfare. Vertical integration by bigs can increase their power position. This is an almost incontestable conclusion.

The most binding instances of vertical integration are often those that establish a satellite relationship between the integrator and integratee. In industry this may be seen in small service enterprises that are virtually captive to the larger firm. In agriculture a similar charge has been leveled at integration in broilers. J. M. Clark, remarking on satellite arrangements, warned that "the situation contains elements of potential arbitrariness. . . . Such a status is feudal rather than competitive."[30]

The conglomerate structure needs little further explanation. Although the conglomerate is not free of the shackles imposed by the competitive situation in each industry in which it operates, it has potentially great power. Among behavioral patterns revealed by conglomerate firms are those of reciprocity, dual distribution, and "mutual forbearance," in addition to the cross-subsidization referred to above. As a hybrid, it may possess the potential for combining the less desirable attributes of both horizontal concentration and vertical integration.

CHAPTER FIVE

DIMENSIONS AND STRUCTURE OF THE MARKETING SYSTEM FOR FARM PRODUCTS IN THE UNITED STATES

THE FIRST four chapters of this book have been primarily conceptual. Chapter 5 is essentially empirical. It describes the marketing system for farm products. An introductory review that draws on published statistical data will be followed by a more detailed examination of the stages of retailing, processing, and assembly from the farm.

In principle the marketing system could readily be described and measured. In reality there are many handicaps. As always, the choice of terms and technique affects the kind of picture that is pieced together.

The simplest method, still widely employed, is to sketch the gross magnitudes of the system and its major components. For this there are statistics of the "marketing bill" and various estimates of factor costs entering that "bill." The data are almost always confined to food, however. Similar statistics for fibers and tobacco are sketchy.

Aggregate marketing information of this kind provides a useful statistical profile of the industry.

A manifest weakness of broadly descriptive data is that they do not help us to evaluate efficiency of performance. Empirical description seldom converts directly to evaluation. On the other hand, data can be set up in a fashion that makes it easier to attempt evaluative judgment.

Gross data on the marketing system, largely obtained from the U.S. Department of Agriculture, are designed to accommodate structural analysis. Data from other sources cited later are even more structurally based. Certainly all data on concentration and ease of entry/exit rest on the concept of an industry. In this sense the "industrial kingdom" is classified in a manner analogous to the animal kingdom. At a given level in the classification scheme there is assumed to be a family of firms producing comparable products. Some

Gratitude for reviewing this chapter and providing material is expressed to my colleague V. James Rhodes and to William Manley, Levi Powell, Donn Reimund, Harry Harp, and Andrew Weiser of the Economic Research Service, U.S. Department of Agriculture.

differentiation is of course accepted but it cannot reach such extreme proportion as to erase all internal "familyness." Where it does so the firm becomes, in effect, a separate industry.

The similar products of an industry normally carry a generic name. Manufacture of dairy products, for example, is definable as an industry even though a host of products are turned out, nearly all of which have proprietary brand labels in addition to the product names.

In principle, structural concepts in industrial organization remain sound. The problem that arises is that a number of marketing firms, notably integrated and conglomerate ones, do not conform to structural lines of distinction—between industries or between stages in the marketing sequence.

With this problem in mind the National Commission on Food Marketing recommended that integrated and conglomerate firms be required to publish information about the volume of their operations *"in each field of operations in which the annual value of shipments is larger than a given minimum."*[1]

Recent trends toward vertical systems of organization in farm product marketing and toward conglomerate mergers almost escape measurement. Very few data on vertical integration are presented herein.*

Thus do developments in our time threaten to outrun our competence to observe and appraise them.

OVERALL DIMENSIONS. For many years the Department of Agriculture has compiled elaborate data on the overall dimensions of the marketing system for farm products. Basic data have been supplemented from time to time by special studies, such as those undertaken or commissioned by the National Commission on Food Marketing.

The Food Marketing Bill. One such basic statistic is the aggregate "marketing bill" for U.S. farm food products. This is the total value added in the marketing system to the foodstuffs U.S. farmers produce. It is basically the difference between what consumers pay for all the U.S.-produced food they buy, and what farmers receive. The data are then separately disaggregated into the major commodity groups, and into major cost items.

*In recent years, however, the U.S. Department of Agriculture has compiled and published considerable information on contractual integration in the marketing of farm products.

TABLE 5.1. **Consumer Expenditures, Marketing Bill, and Farm Value of Domestic Farm-Food Products Bought by Civilians, 1947–74.**

Year	Expenditures[a]	Marketing Bill	Farm Value[b]
		(bil)	
1947	$ 41.9	$22.6	$19.3
1948	44.8	24.9	19.9
1949	43.4	26.0	17.4
1950	44.0	26.0	18.0
1951	49.2	28.7	20.5
1952	50.9	30.5	20.4
1953	51.0	31.5	19.5
1954	51.1	32.3	18.8
1955	53.1	34.4	18.7
1956	55.5	36.3	19.2
1957	58.3	37.9	20.4
1958	61.0	39.5	21.4
1959	63.6	42.4	21.2
1960	66.9	44.6	22.3
1961	68.7	45.7	23.0
1962	71.3	47.7	23.7
1963	74.0	49.9	24.1
1964	77.5	52.6	24.9
1965	81.1	54.0	27.1
1966	86.9	57.2	29.8
1967	89.2	60.4	28.8
1968	94.0	63.6	30.4
1969	98.9	65.2	33.7
1970	105.9	71.1	34.8
1971	110.7	75.4	35.3
1972	116.6	77.9	38.7
1973	132.0	82.0	50.0
1974[c]	147.6	92.0	55.5

Source: Terry L. Crawford and Andrew Weiser, "The Bill for Marketing Farm-Food Products," *Marketing and Transportation Situation,* U.S. Dept. of Agr., Econ. Res. Service, Aug. 1975, p. 18; and previous August issues.

[a] Consumer expenditures for domestic farm food products. Imported foods and fish are excluded. Foods are valued at retail store prices except food sold in the form of meals and those sold at less than retail prices, which are valued at the point of sale.

[b] The farm value is the gross return to farmers for products equivalent to those sold to consumers. Value of inedible by-products, nonfood products, and exports are not included.

[c] Preliminary.

Marketing bill data thus are both a summation of factor cost and a distribution of consumers' expenditures. In the words of Economic Research Service authors, "The marketing bill is an estimate of the total charges by marketing firms for transporting, processing, and distributing U.S. farm originated foods purchased by or for civilian consumers in the United States. It is the difference between civilian expenditures and the farm value."

They explain further:

> Civilian expenditures for farm foods . . . [include] expenditures for food served in restaurants and other away-from-home eating establishments and bought directly from farmers, processors, and wholesalers. Also included is the value of food served by schools, hospitals, and other institutions, and of food furnished by employers to civilian employees. Sales taxes and tips are also included. Excluded are expenditures for imported foods, for fish and other foods not originating on U.S. farms, and for alcoholic beverages; the value of food consumed on farms where it is produced is also excluded.[2]

Data on civilian expenditures for U.S. farm foods and on the marketing bill and net farm value are presented in Table 5.1 and Fig. 5.1.

Similar data on expenditures, marketing bill, and net farm value by major commodities for recent years are presented in Table 5.2.

The Economic Research Service also makes estimates of the gross values of the major cost components of the marketing bill. Data for 1974 are shown in Fig. 5.2.[3]

Similar aggregate data for nonfood products of agriculture, principally the fibers and tobacco, are manifestly more difficult to compute. From time to time the Economic Research Service attempts to

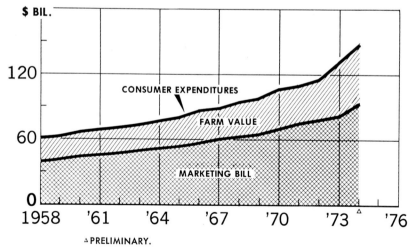

FIG. 5.1. Farm-food marketing bill and consumer food expenditures (for domestic farm foods purchased by U.S. civilian consumers for consumption both at home and away from home). (USDA-ERS)

TABLE 5.2.   Consumer Expenditures, Marketing Bill, and Farm Value of Farm Foods, by Commodity Group, 1970–74.

Year	All Farm Foods			Fruits and Vegetables		
	Expenditures	Marketing bill	Farm value	Expenditures	Marketing bill	Farm value
	(bil)					
1970	$105.9	$71.1	$34.8	$21.8	$16.7	$5.0
1971	110.7	75.4	35.3	23.0	17.7	5.2
1972	116.6	77.9	38.7	22.8	17.3	5.5
1973	132.0	82.0	50.0	28.0	20.7	7.2
1974[a]	147.6	92.0	55.5	31.6	23.1	8.5
	Meat products			Grain mill products		
1970	32.3	18.2	14.1	3.2	2.7	0.6
1971	33.3	19.0	14.3	3.2	2.7	0.6
1972	37.8	20.7	17.1	3.3	2.7	0.6
1973	42.2	21.2	21.0	4.1	3.2	0.9
1974[a]	42.9	23.3	19.6	5.2	3.9	1.3
	Dairy products			Bakery products		
1970	16.1	9.3	6.8	9.6	8.3	1.4
1971	16.7	9.9	6.8	11.2	9.6	1.6
1972	17.7	10.4	7.3	11.6	9.9	1.7
1973	18.9	10.8	8.1	12.7	10.0	2.7
1974[a]	21.1	11.9	9.2	15.6	11.9	3.6
	Poultry and eggs			Miscellaneous		
1970	8.7	4.8	3.9	14.2	11.2	3.0
1971	8.4	4.7	3.6	15.0	11.7	3.3
1972	7.6	4.5	3.1	15.9	12.4	3.4
1973	10.3	5.1	5.2	15.8	11.0	4.8
1974[a]	8.6	4.3	4.3	22.6	13.6	9.0

Source: Terry L. Crawford and Andrew Weiser, "The Bill for Marketing Farm-food Products," *Marketing and Transportation Situation,* U.S. Dept. of Agr., Econ. Res. Service, Aug. 1975, pp. 18–19.

[a]Preliminary.

make rough estimates of the aggregate bill for marketing nonfoods, but these data are not published regularly.

THE MARKETING BILL, AT HOME VS. AWAY FROM HOME, BY AGENCY. Data have been compiled on value of food consumed at home and away from home, and on the marketing bill by agencies. Table 5.3 pre-presents summary data on the former breakdown. Detail by seven commodity groups is available from the source cited. Figure 5.3 gives marketing bill data by four kinds of marketing institutions or "agencies."

Data have been compiled on the value of food going to and through the food service industry. A summary sentence from the

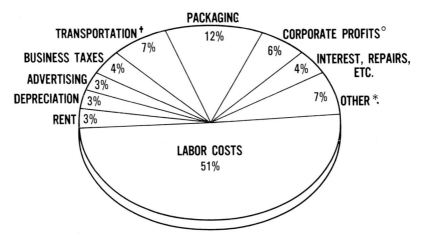

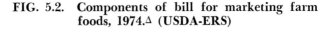

* RESIDUAL INCLUDES SUCH COSTS AS UTILITIES, FUEL, PROMOTION, LOCAL FOR-HIRE TRANSPORTATION, INSURANCE.
° BEFORE TAXES.   † INTERCITY RAIL AND TRUCK.   Δ PRELIMINARY DATA.

FIG. 5.2.   Components of bill for marketing farm foods, 1974.Δ (USDA-ERS)

most complete report reads: "Retail value of food and nonalcoholic beverages moving through all outlets making up the market for food served away from home was estimated at $35 billion in 1969, up from $28 billion during 1966."[4]

Productivity Data. The Economic Research Service also makes analyses of certain of the cost items in the aggregate marketing bill. One example is productivity of labor. For this study, estimates of the output of food marketing services are compared with data on man-hours

TABLE 5.3.   Consumer Expenditures, Marketing Bill, and Farm Value for At-home and Away-from-home Consumption of U.S. Farm Foods, 1974.

	Consumer Expenditures	Marketing Bill	Farm Value
		(bil)	
At home	$106.4	$60.9	$45.5
Away from home			
Public eating places	32.3	24.3	8.0
Institutions	8.9	6.9	2.0
	147.6	92.0	55.5

Source: Terry L. Crawford and Andrew Weiser, "The Bill for Marketing Farm-Food Products," *Marketing and Transportation Situation*, U.S. Dept. of Agr., Econ. Res. Service, Aug. 1975, p. 34.

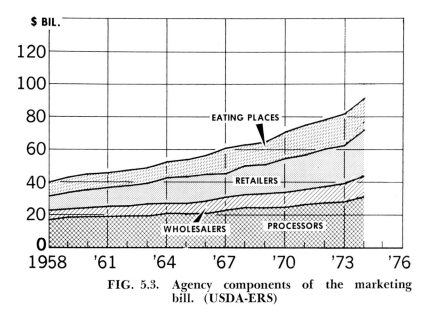

FIG. 5.3. Agency components of the marketing bill. (USDA-ERS)

employed, yielding a time series of indexes of man-hours per unit of farm food marketed.

Data indicate that man-hours per unit decreased steadily from the late 1940s to the mid-1960s. Since 1967 no further improvement has occurred. During the years since 1967, productivity has decreased in distribution compared with processing. "Because of automation, processing now [in 1974] takes 17 percent less labor per unit of farm foods marketed than in 1967. But more labor is now required for distribution."[5]

Unit labor cost in marketing farm foods reflects changes in both productivity and wage rates. Hourly wages increased only gradually until the mid-1960s, then more rapidly. The unit labor cost in marketing increased only about a sixth from 1959 to 1967, but 62 percent from 1967 to 1974.[6]

Separate studies have been made of costs such as transportation.[7] Also, data on profit ratios are published from time to time.[8]

MEANING OF DATA. It might be expected that aggregate statistics as just sketched would be the magic key unlocking answers to questions as to how the marketing system functions and how well it meets performance norms. The irony of the matter is that the data answer almost all questions except the crucial ones.

It is commendable, for instance, that output per man-hour has generally increased in food processing. But partial analysis in which each cost factor is viewed in isolation can be misleading. For example, it is highly likely that as labor productivity rose, capital investment per worker also increased—and in fact helped to make the higher labor productivity possible. Hence relatively less labor was used in operating the processing machinery, but more was used in constructing it. Unless the cost of the additional machinery is taken into account or the labor hours for machinery construction are added in, few reliable judgments can be made.

Furthermore, labor productivity has risen throughout the economy. It is important to know whether productivity gains in food processing have led or lagged behind those in the economy generally. There is reason to believe they have lagged. And there is good reason to suspect that the productivity record in food marketing as a whole is not very favorable.

Finally, data on resources used in marketing tell us nothing about whether the marketing services that were performed were actually worth being performed. As is explained on page 21, competitive practices can impel a firm to undertake activities that are aimed at increasing the volume of its own business without necessarily promoting services that consumers want.

Food's Share of Consumer Income. Probably the most quoted, and least valid, statistic relating to food marketing costs is the percent of the consumer's income dollar spent for food. Derived from data compiled and published by the U.S. Department of Commerce, it shows that the percent so spent dropped from about 25 percent in the early 1950s to 20 percent in 1960 and to 16 percent in the early 1970s. It has since climbed to 17 percent (see Fig. 5.4). The statistic is unreliable as a measure of performance in food marketing because the long downtrend mainly reflects the low income elasticity of demand for food, so clearly manifest during the rising national income of the 1950s and 1960s. As personal incomes increased, consumers spent only a small part of the incremental portion for food. The percent of their total income going to food consequently declined.

On the other hand, a relatively less ample supply of food in the inflationary 1970s caused the percent of income spent for food to turn upward.

The published data on percentage of consumers' income going to food purchases have been attacked as unrealistically low. Blakley has written of the "credibility gap" in such statistics. "In no way can the majority of consumers identify with an expenditure pattern" as low as the reported 16–17 percent. Blakley calculated that in

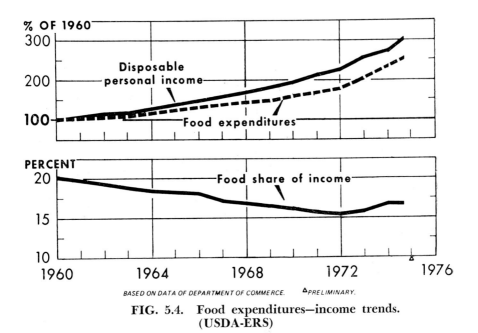

FIG. 5.4.   Food expenditures–income trends.
(USDA-ERS)

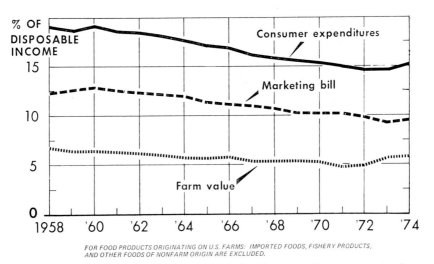

FIG. 5.5.   Consumer food expenditures, marketing
bill, and farm value as a proportion of
disposable income. (USDA-ERS)

1973 a four-person family of middle income would have had to spend 16 percent of its income to buy the U.S. Department of Agriculture's "low-cost diet" and 20½ percent for the "moderate-cost diet." A similar family of the lowest third of income would have had to pay out 35 percent of its income just for the low-cost diet.[9]

A similar series for only U.S.–produced food shows the shares of consumers' income going to farmers and to market agencies (Fig. 5.5). Downtrends for both ended in the 1970s, but the upturn was sharpest in the percent of income going to farmers.

Costs, Margins, and Farmer's Share Data. Statistics on costs, margins, and farmer's share commodity by commodity are companions to the marketing bill information just presented but differ primarily in that they relate to fixed quantities of foods—the familiar "market basket." The marketing bill, by contrast, pertains to the mix of food actually bought in each time period. In the language of statistics, costs and margins data are computed from fixed weights.

As another major difference, costs and margins data are based on prices at retail, whereas consumers' expenditures for food, the starting point for marketing bill estimates, are the sum of the monies spent in all places where food is consumed, including restaurants.

The two series are similar, however, in that estimates are made for both gross totals and cost components. However, cost-item breakdowns for individual foods are published only periodically.

Further information on the nature and source of costs and margins data is available from reports of the Economic Research Service and the National Commission on Food Marketing.[10]

Gross margins data are published in the *Agricultural Outlook* report of the Economic Research Service, issued 11 times a year.

Summary data for the combined market basket of all foods are reproduced in Table 5.4.

Regularly published price margin data show for most commodities only the retail price, farm value, and farm to retail spread. More complete data are provided for beef, pork, and bread. From time to time studies for individual commodities give more detailed information, such as farm-wholesale and wholesale-retail margins.

Margin data by commodities throw into sharp relief the differences among commodities in relative size of the farm value and of the value added in marketing. In 1975 the farm value was 66 percent of the retail price of eggs. It was only 7 percent of the retail price of canned beets. Farm value percentages for the other 46 commodities for which data are computed lie between these two extremes.

TABLE 5.4. Price and Margin for Market Basket of Farm Food.[a]

Year	Retail Cost	Farm Value	Farm-retail Margin	Farmer's Share
	($)	($)	($)	(%)
Average:				
1947–59	895	448	447	50
1957–59	989	397	592	40
1961	999	386	631	39
1962	1,009	395	614	39
1963	1,007	378	629	38
1964	1,009	377	632	37
1965	1,037	416	621	40
1966	1,092	445	647	41
1967	1,081	419	662	39
1968	1,119	441	678	39
1969	1,176	480	696	41
1970	1,223	476	747	39
1971	1,250	479	771	38
1972	1,311	524	787	40
1973	1,537	701	836	46
1974[b]	1,750	746	1,004	43
1975[b]				42

Source: U.S. Dept. of Agr., Econ. Res. Service, *Marketing and Transportation Situation*, Aug. 1972, p. 6; and subsequent issues. Also, *Agricultural Outlook*.

[a] The market basket contains the average quantities of domestic, farm originated food products purchased annually per household in 1960 and 1961 by wage earners and clerical worker families and workers living alone. Its retail cost is calculated from retail prices published by the Bureau of Labor Statistics. The farm value is the gross return to farmers for the farm products equivalent to foods in the market basket. The farm-retail margin is an estimate of the total gross margin received by marketing firms.

[b] Preliminary.

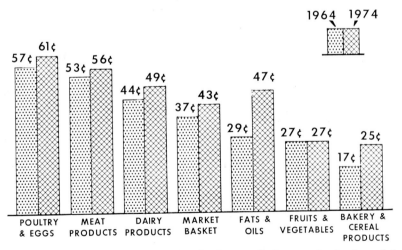

FIG. 5.6. Farmer's share of the marketbasket dollar, by food group. (USDA-ERS)

Figure 5.6 shows the percentage data for seven food groups. In general, the percentages are higher for foods of animal origin, lower for cereals, fruits, and vegetables.

What are the reasons for these wide differences? Gross margin figures carry no explanatory Baedeker. Involved are both physical factors and variations in competitive structure of the market. Margins for meat, for example, are affected by the limited processing given that high value product. Those for various processed foods carry a high charge for the processing. Vegetables produced on the West Coast bear a sizable transport cost.

Whether the competitive situation surrounding each food contributes to low or high marketing margins is a more difficult question to answer. The question invites searching inquiries into competitive structure and practice.

Yet one more series of descriptive data helps a little toward answering that question. These are data breaking the gross margins into functional components. Table 5.5 presents for a few commodities certain data published by the Economic Research Service. The National Commission on Food Marketing went even further into dissecting margins into the several services or functions. In Fig. 5.7 the commission's statistics for two contrasting foods, broilers and breakfast cereals, are graphed. They show the vast differences in the make-up of marketing costs in the two foods. Note, for example, the differences in the percent of retail price going to advertising and promotion, to containers and supplies, and to profits.

STRUCTURE AT PROCESSING AND RETAILING. It serves best to divide a review of the empirical structure of the food marketing system into two halves, each comprehensive. These are processing-wholesaling-retailing on the one hand and farm product marketing (primarily assembly and pricing) on the other. The two portions of the system are so different that they must be treated separately.

The processing and retailing system for food has been the subject of a number of investigations. The marketing of fibers and tobacco has been studied less. The U.S. Department of Agriculture and the Federal Trade Commission keep a stream of reports flowing on the food marketing system. Publications of the National Commission on Food Marketing, though dated in the later 1960s, are still a rich lode of information. The conflict within the commission as to an evaluation of the commission's findings does not detract from the validity of its reporting. On the contrary, if we believe that arguments arise easiest from significant rather than trivial issues, the commission's reporting covered significant features of the marketing system.

TABLE 5.5. Distribution of Retail Price of Selected Foods Into Farm Value and Value Received by Individual Marketing Functions, 1973.

Food	Farm value	Marketing Function					Retail price
		Assembly	Processing	Intercity transportation	Wholesaling	Retailing[a]	
				(¢)			
Beef, choice, lb.	89.9	1.5	5.8	1.1	8.9	28.3	135.5
Broilers, lb.	35.3	1.2	6.7	1.1	2.9	12.4	59.6
Milk, sold in stores, ½ gal.	33.2	2.5	11.6	[b]	13.0	5.1	65.4
Apples, 3 lb. bag	30.4	2.9	14.2	5.8	5.9	28.1	87.3
Tomatoes, Calif. whole, 303 can	2.4	.5	13.9	2.2	1.1	4.6	24.7
Bread, white, lb.	4.1[c]	.3	8.4[d]	.3	9.1	5.4	27.6

Source: U.S. Dept. of Agr., Econ. Res. Service, "Distribution of the Food Dollar by Marketing Function and Expense Item," *Marketing and Transportation Situation*, Nov. 1974, pp. 24-25.
[a] In-store costs only. Headquarters and warehousing expenses included in wholesaling.
[b] Included in wholesaling.
[c] Wheat only. Other ingredients included in processing.
[d] Flour milling and bread baking.

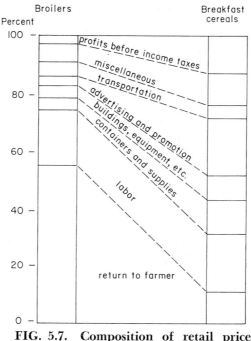

FIG. 5.7. Composition of retail price of broilers and breakfast cereals, 1964. Source: *Cost Components of Farm-Retail Price Spreads for Foods,* National Commission on Food Marketing, Technical Study No. 9, June 1966.

Food Retailing-Wholesaling. Marketing functions at the food retailing stage are in one sense almost the exact complement, or obverse, of those at local assembly. Retailing involves dispersion *to* many small household consumers, even as local assembly relates to collection *from* many comparatively small producers.

The dominant institution in food retailing obviously is the retail food chain. However, the chain extends through at least two stages in marketing, and not retailing alone. More accurate language would be to call it a retail-wholesale food chain.

Food chains are divided into the corporate and the affiliated. Affiliated chains in turn comprise the voluntary and cooperative. In voluntary associations, the wholesaler is the basic organizational unit and enters into affiliation with individual retail stores. In cooperative affiliates, retailers band together to procure supplies cooperatively.

Independent food stores, which require the services of independent wholesalers, remain sizable in number though small in aggregate volume of business.

In the mid-1960s, according to Food Commission data, about 47 percent of all food retailing was done by corporate chains, and 44 percent by voluntary and cooperative affiliates. The remaining 9 percent was credited to independents.[11]

Other classifications are possible. Among chains there are local, regional, and national firms. Individual retail food stores may be supermarkets, small self-service, or small old-fashioned personal service stores. Among the small self-service stores are chains that often use the term "mini-super." The personal service store is more likely to be found in rural areas or low income sectors of cities than elsewhere.

Food chain firms combine (integrate) vertically not only retailing and wholesaling, but a varying portion of the processing stage. Both corporate and affiliated chains almost invariably produce (directly or by contract) some of the processed foods they sell, such as milk, canned fruits and vegetables, and processed meats. They usually sell these foods under their private label.

The highly mixed network of vertical and horizontal relationships in food distribution is illustrated graphically in Chapter 4. The sketch is repeated here as Fig. 5.8.

The legend to the chart need not be described again, except to call attention to the four kinds of retailers that are shown: corporate chain, cooperative affiliate, voluntary affiliate, and independent.

Integration as far backward as the processor is shown to be fairly common. One instance is illustrated in which integration breaks only once, from local assembly to retailer. This is likely to be confined to unprocessed foods. Examples might be a retailer having livestock slaughter facilities that buys its cattle directly from a feedlot; or direct sale of eggs or fresh vegetables from a large producer to the procurement office of a retailer.

CONCENTRATION AT RETAIL. The standard questions about the structure of an industry are how concentrated it is, and how much differentiation of product is found.

United States total data on concentration in selling to household consumers have limited meaning. The question at issue is the degree of concentration in individual shopping districts. Do or do not consumers face a local oligopoly when they set out to do their food shopping?

As an average for 205 metropolitan areas, the top four retail food firms (which vary in identity from area to area) do 50 percent of the business. The top 20 account for 97 percent of the total food

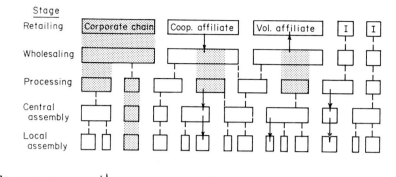

Ownership integration. ↕ Contractual integration. ┆ Buying and selling. I Independent retailer.

FIG. 5.8.   Illustrative sketch of food marketing structure as related to four kinds of retailers.

trade.[12] Around this average there are many variations, as may be seen in Table 5.6.

Paradoxically, the mobility of consumers rather than the number of local food stores can have the greater influence on whether or not consumers face a local oligopoly in food retailing. The mobility of middle-class families with their "second" automobiles has reduced tendencies toward local oligopoly. By the same token, low income families lacking transportation find themselves unable to comparative-shop and may be confined to one or two neighborhood stores.

TABLE 5.6.   Four-firm Concentration in Grocery Retailing in 205 Standard Metropolitan Statistical Areas, 1967.

Four-firm Concentration	Number of Cities
(%)	
20–30	3
30–40	26
40–50	63
50–60	73
60–70	35
70–80	4
80–90	1

Source: Willard F. Mueller, "Statement . . . before the Committee on the Judiciary, Subcommittee on Monopolies and Commerce, House of Representatives, concerning the Structure and Performance of the Food Industries, July 19, 1973," Univ. of Wisc., Madison, Dept. of Agr. Econ., p. 69.

The question of whether low income families are exploited by virtue of their immobility was a major topic at the White House Conference on Food, Nutrition and Health held in 1969. In general, the evidence relative to food chains is not that they exploit consumers in low income areas of cities but that they do not put stores there, leaving those consumers in the hands of small local stores.[13]

Concentration among food retailers is a more telling factor in their buying than in selling. This was the firm conclusion of the Food Commission, which pointed out that food chains not only enjoy some size and power in procurement, notably when buying from small suppliers, but add to that power by forming combined procurement organizations. In the commission's language, ". . . buyer concentration tends to be substantially higher than seller concentration; and . . . buyer concentration has increased continuously and markedly since 1948."[14]

The structural attribute of differentiation in food retailing has probably become less significant over time. The difference between supermarkets and quick service stores is genuine. But supermarkets tend to run to pattern (see below), and the quick service stores do also. Historically, geographic location has been a major differentiating factor in retailing. Shoppers' mobility has mitigated its importance (except for low income families); but if cost of transportation should continue to rise, the location of a store relative to consumers' homes might loom as a significant differentiating factor once again. That is, that would be the outcome unless neighborhood stores should proliferate once more. In that event, the whole historical cycle would be rerun.

Service differentiation gradually ebbed in food retailing as retail food stores converted from their original role epitomized in the arcade market, to the modern supermarket that serves as an emporium. In the arcade concept, still perpetuated in some cities, the retailer only provides stall space plus associated services, and the original producer or an intermediary sells the products of his farm or small processing establishment in that space. This makes possible a considerable distinctiveness in the products that various stall operators offer.

The opposite of this is the supermarket that handles branded packaged goods almost exclusively. It is truly difficult for one supermarket to provide a unique service when it, like all others, can only stock Campbell soups, three or four brands of breakfast foods, and McCormick spices on its shelves. Fresh fruits and vegetables have provided one arena for individualized services, but increasingly more fresh produce is now sold prepackaged. If and when meats are sold in frozen prepackaged form, the retail store will be little more than a local wholesale warehouse.

This characteristic of modern food retailing accounts for the ingenious and often costly efforts many retailers make to create an image of differentiation that may be genuine but often is only nominal or, at times, even fraudulent. These are touched on in Chapter 4 on market structure. They range from extended hours to giving food stamps to providing personal services such as check-cashing and carrying bags of groceries to buyers' automobiles. Of the same genre is the addition of more kinds of products. The latter requires a big store with a very large weekly volume of business. Differentiation by addition of more products runs directly counter to differentiation by location, because the larger the stores the fewer that can exist in each community. On the other hand, to the extent supermarket retailers become few and large, a greater opportunity opens up for small neighborhood retailers to operate under the shelter of supermarket giants.

Differentiation by adding new products or product lines has the disadvantage that the casualty rate for new items is high. Granted, the cost of introducing an unsuccessful item falls more heavily on the processor than the retailer, but the new-product "game" as a means of subtle differentiation is a part of modern retailing.

Private label products can serve as a differentiating technique for a retailer. However, most such foods are not highly distinctive. Private labeling comes about more as a way to wrestle with the power of large processors than for product differentiation.

Food retailers-wholesalers normally establish their pricing policy as a combination of full cost pricing and variable price merchandising. The former relates to standard markups product by product that reflect the competitive situation. The latter is attuned more to the customer-drawing power of each item. Private label products of larger retailers enter into the pricing strategy. They widen the retailer's latitude in pricing, because any restraint large processors may impose is avoided. Equally important, they give more flexibility in competition with retailers who try to assert price leadership. In addition, private labels can be used as a device of subtle stratification of the market. That is, there possibly is a demarcation among shoppers, between those who are loyal to nationally advertised brands and those who respond to private labels. It can be profitable to take advantage of this difference.

STRATEGY IN PROCUREMENT. Performance in food retailing and wholesaling is to be viewed not only on the selling but also on the procurement or buying side. As noted above, concentration in procurement exceeds that in selling.

However, concentration must be viewed not only in absolute terms but relatively. As food retailers-wholesalers get most of their supplies not from farmers but from processors, and many processors are themselves large, an oligopsony-oligopoly confrontation often emerges.

The Food Commission took note of retailers' procurement

TABLE 5.7. **Percentage of Value of Shipments in Food Manufacturing Industries Accounted for by the Four and Twenty Largest Companies, 1963, 1967, and 1972.**

| | Value of Shipments Accounted For by | | | | | |
| | 4 largest companies | | | 20 largest companies | | |
Industry	1963	1967	1972	1963	1967	1972
Meatpacking[a]	31	26	22	54	50	51
Sausages and other prepared meats[a]	16	15	19	35	34	38
Poultry dressing	...	...	17	...	...	42
Poultry and egg processing	...	...	23	...	...	65
Creamery butter	11	15	45	31	36	78
Cheese	44	44	42	59	61	65
Concentrated milk	40	41	39	71	74	76
Ice cream and frozen desserts	37	33	29	64	60	58
Fluid milk	23	22	18	40	42	42
Canned specialties[b]	67	69	67	94	94	94
Canned fruits and vegetables[b]	24	22	20	50	52	53
Dehydrated foods	37	32	33	80	75	76
Pickles, sauces, and salad dressing[b]	36	33	33	64	62	62
Frozen fruits and vegetables[b]	24	24	29	54	55	69
Frozen specialties[b]	...	...	42	...	...	70
Flour and other grain mill products	35	30	33	71	70	75
Cereal breakfast foods	86	88	90	99	99	99
Rice milling	44	46	43	86	89	92
Blended and prepared flour	70	68	68	92	93	92
Wet-corn milling	71	68	63	99	99	99
Bread, cake, and related products	23	26	29	45	47	50
Cookies and crackers	59	59	59	80	82	83
Raw cane sugar	47	43	44	82	82	84
Cane sugar refining	63	59	59	100	99	99
Beet sugar	66	66	66	100	100	100
Confectionery products	15	25	32	45	52	59
Cottonseed oil	41	42	43	72	80	80
Soybean oil	50	55	54	88	94	92
Vegetable oil	58	56	70	99	99	99
Shortening and cooking oils	42	43	44	92	93	93
Macaroni and spaghetti	31	31	38	71	73	76
Other food preparations	24	24	26	48	51	51

Source: U.S. Department of Commerce, Bureau of the Census, "Concentration Ratios in Manufacturing," *1972 Census of Manufacturers,* MC72(SR)-2, pp. 6–10.

[a] Percentages based on value added by manufacture.

[b] Percentages computed on value of production.

methods, and one of its staff members, Daniel Padberg, individually and jointly with Handy, has since written extensively on the subject.[15] Insofar as the large retailers cannot escape the hegemony of strong suppliers, such as processors with established brands (Del Monte, Campbell), a pricing contest ensues of the type Knutson has described for milk (see Chapter 4).[16] Because strongly entrenched suppliers neither want, nor are legally permitted, to offer price concessions, any merchandising strategy revolves around associated services. However, a service that amounts to a hidden price concession can be declared illegal.

When larger retailers seek to avoid fealty to processors by means of their own private labels, a characteristic pattern emerges. Insofar as the retailers get private label product by contracting for it instead of producing it in their own plants, they prefer to deal with small rather than large firms. The entire retailer-processor relationship takes on a crisscross pattern wherein small processors sell to large retailers, while small retailers depend heavily on the national brands produced by large processing firms.

Food Processing. Some features of the food processing stage can be inferred from the above account of food retailing-wholesaling. Food processing is essentially oligopolistic (and oligopsonistic). A few industries are nearly homogeneous. It is hard to declare any significant differentiation among sugar refiners, for example. However, most food processing firms are differentiated.

Data on concentration in various food processing industries are published regularly and always show a high figure for sugar refining, breakfast cereals, and a few other products. For certain others, as poultry dressing and manufacture of creamery butter, the concentration ratio is much lower. In Table 5.7 are data for 30 food industries for 1963, 1967, and 1972.

The table shows a 90 percent figure for four-firm concentration in cereal preparations in 1972, 67 percent in canned specialties, and 66 percent in beet sugar. The lowest figure for concentration is 17 percent.

In 1970, according to Willard Mueller, four food industries had a four-firm concentration ratio of 75 percent or more. These industries accounted for 21 percent of the value added by manufacturers for 41 food and related industries (see Table 5.8).

Since World War II, concentration in food processing has been reduced in industries that principally produce products that go to other manufacturers (intermediate goods). It has increased in industries that turn out products ready for delivery to household consumers. Moreover, the increase has been confined to industries marked by a high degree of product differentiation. Table 5.9 presents data.

CONGLOMERATION. Data by industries do not tell the full food industry concentration story. Many food processors are parts of conglomerate entities. Among meat packing firms, Armour is a part of the

TABLE 5.8. **Four-firm Concentration in 41 Food and Related Manufacturing Industries, by Quartiles, 1970.**

Four-Firm Concentration Ratio (%)	Number of Industries	Value Added by Manufacturers	
		Value	Percent of total
		(bil)	
75–100	4	$ 3.1	21.1
50–74	15	5.6	38.0
25–49	18	8.1	26.3
less than 25	4	4.5	14.6
Total	41	21.3	100.0

Source: Compiled by Willard F. Mueller from *Annual Survey of Manufactures, 1970,* and presented in "Statement of Willard Mueller . . . before the Committee on the Judiciary, Subcommittee on Monopolies and Commerce, House of Representatives, concerning the Structure and Performance of the Food Industries, July 19, 1973," Univ. of Wisc., Madison, Dept. of Agr. Econ., p. 5a.

Greyhound conglomerate, Wilson of L-T-V, Morrell of United Brands. Mighty Swift belongs to Esmark.

Probably the most diversified U.S. company is International Telephone and Telegraph Corporation. Its food processing activity, centered in its Continental Baking division, is big enough to have come under antitrust scrutiny, yet in 1973 it accounted for only 11 percent of the company's gross income, according to the corporation's annual report.

Conglomeration, a relative newcomer to the structural kingdom,

TABLE 5.9. **Trend in Four-firm Concentration in 31 Food and Related Industries, 1947–70.**

Year	All 31 industries	Producer or intermediate goods	By Industry Category			
			Consumer goods			
			All industries	By degree of differentiation		
				low	moderate	high
1947	45.0	50.9	42.2	28.5	33.3	53.0
1954	45.9	51.1	43.4	25.0	34.3	56.2
1958	45.1	50.2	42.7	23.0	34.1	56.5
1963	45.6	48.7	44.1	22.5	33.9	60.0
1967	45.6	47.7	44.7	21.8	33.9	61.3
1970	46.0	47.4	45.4	22.5	34.0	61.4

Source: Compiled by Willard F. Mueller from *Annual Survey of Manufactures, 1970,* and presented in "Statement of Willard Mueller . . . before the Committee on the Judiciary, Subcommittee on Monopolies and Commerce, House of Representatives, concerning the Structure and Performance of the Food Industries, July 19, 1973," Univ. of Wisc., Madison, Dept. of Agr. Econ., p. 1a.

has not received the statistical coverage that has mapped intraindustry concentration. It is not possible to cite summary statistics on the extent of conglomerate combination in food processing. Just a log of the instances, however, offers convincing evidence that conglomerate structure is extensive. It has gone much farther in food processing than in retailing.

MERCHANDISING PRACTICES AND COSTS. Food processing industries divide, as Mueller points out, into those of high and low reliance on differentiation of product. For those relying heavily on differentiation the evidence is that advertising, product development, and associated expenses become a large fraction of total sales. Table 5.10 summarizes data for eight food industries.

Conforming to principles set forth in Chapter 4, advertising and promotion in food industries is most aggressive for products that basically are fairly similar. The Food Commission reported that where products have intrinsic distinguishing characteristics, "either physically or in psychological appeal," it was found that "sales promotion plays a lesser role in the marketing mix."[17]

COMPETITIVE METHODS AND PRICING PRACTICES. Aside from product differentiation and advertising, the intensity of which varies by product, competitive methods among food processors tend to subordinate price competition to nonprice techniques of many kinds. The Food Commission summed up the situation in this language:

> Price competition, in the traditional sense, is essentially non-existent in grocery manufacturing, especially for the newer, convenience-type foods . . . given a choice, grocery manufacturers prefer not to compete on price

TABLE 5.10. Sales and Administrative Expenses as Percent of Value of Shipments, Eight Food Industries, 1954 and 1963.

Product	1954	1963
Confectionery products	15.0	11.4
Pickles	8.3	16.7
Coffee and other products	6.6	20.4
Flour mixes	25.5	23.4
Biscuits and crackers	22.7	26.0
Soft drinks	24.7	26.0
Flavorings and syrup	31.5	27.2
Cereals	21.6	29.2

Source: National Commission on Food Marketing, *Studies of Organization and Competition in Grocery Manufacturing* (Washington: U.S. Govt. Printing Office, 1966), p. 42.

but rather on quality and/or other aspects of what is called "nonprice" competition.

. . . Although there may be a large fringe of small sellers, competition is primarily oligopolistic. . . . In such a situation, each large seller carefully watches the actions of close competitors and generally reacts to any significant change in price, quality or selling effort.

Oligopolists tend to avoid price competition because, in general, they believe that a price cut responded to by competitors may not expand the total market sufficiently to improve profits . . .

. . . Grocery manufacturers generally prefer to employ: (1) Media advertising; (2) consumer-directed promotions such as coupons, free samples, cents-off deals; and (3) dealer-directed promotions such as trade allowances, in that order . . .[18]

DIFFERENCES BY COMMODITY. Data given above indicate differences among major classes of foods in degree of concentration and of reliance on product differentiation. Other structure and conduct characteristics are less visible and harder to report with confidence. However, a number of studies have been made—too many, in fact, to permit recounting here. A compilation by Moore and Walsh may be the single best reference work. Practices by commodity area, as described there, range from "joint-profit maximization . . . [with] prevalence of both price fixing and price leadership" in fluid milk to cost-barometric price leadership in bread. Competitive practices in bread baking were said to result in retail prices much higher than costs, and chronic underutilization of plants.[19]

Other sources of a wealth of information on individual food industries as well as on marketing practices for farm products in general are two reports of the Economic Research Service, *Agricultural Markets in Change*,[20] and the more up-to-date *Market Structure of the Food Industries*.[21] These are somewhat more reserved in their interpretation than the Moore and Walsh book.

STRUCTURE IN MARKETING FARM PRODUCTS FROM THE FARM. The market structure for the initial stages in the marketing system for agricultural products differs markedly from that for later stages.

Just to divide the entire marketing sequence into two halves for purpose of description, however, is to miss a very important point. The point goes back to the characterization of the entire system not just as a delivery and distribution system, but also as a value determining and directional control mechanism. Conventionally, the price of a product as "discovered" at successive stages in the marketing sequence was regarded as the instrument that controlled both final consumption and the subsequent production of both the basic product and its affiliated marketing services. This was the characteristic of the Agricultural Organization period in the evolution of marketing (Chapter 1). Manifestly, price no longer plays so operational a role. At processing, as has just been pointed out, price competition is subordinated to nonprice competition, and at retailing, the diversity of products handled by each firm not only facilitates but virtually mandates a strategic rather than solely cost-based markup policy. Moreover, the high degree of concentration among firms at both processing and retailing contrasts sharply with the nearly atomistic competition that has long been a hallmark of farm product markets.

But the more extreme case of turning away from price as a coordinating instrument is vertical integration. About a fifth of all farm products are now delivered under contractual or direct ownership arrangements that circumscribe the role of price (see Table 5.11).

The percentages for marketing under production contracts shown

TABLE 5.11. Estimated Percentage of Total Farm Output Produced under Contractual and Ownership Integration, 1970.

	Production Contracts	Ownership Integration
All farm products	17.2	4.8
All livestock and products	31.4	4.8
Fed cattle	18.0	4.0
Hogs	1.0	1.0
Fluid-grade milk	95.0	3.0
Manufacturing-grade milk	25.0	1.0
Eggs	20.0	20.0
Broilers	90.0	7.0
Turkeys	42.0	12.0
All crops	9.5	4.8
Feed grains	0.1	0.5
Food grains	2.0	0.5
Vegetables for fresh market	21.0	30.0
Vegetables for processing	85.0	10.0
Potatoes	45.0	25.0
Citrus fruits	55.0	30.0
Sugar beets	98.0	2.0
Sugar cane	40.0	60.0
Cotton	11.0	1.0
Tobacco	2.0	2.0
Oil bearing crops	1.0	0.5
Seed crops	80.0	0.5

Source: Ronald L. Mighell and William S. Hoofnagle, *Contract Production and Vertical Integration in Farming, 1960 and 1970*, U.S. Dept. of Agr., Econ. Res. Service, ERS-479, 1972.

in Table 5.11 may be on the high side. The high figure for milk, for example, is subject to challenge because cooperatives' delivery contracts hardly qualify as production contracts. On the other hand, a recent report indicates that 7 percent of all farm products are now marketed by large agribusiness firms. The 5 percent figure in Table 5.11 thus appears too low.[22]

In principle, production-and-delivery contracts could be exposed to organized market competition similar to futures trading in wheat or soybeans, but in practice this has not been done.

So we face the double dilemma that the long vaunted commodity price system for organizing and guiding the marketing system for farm products has been seriously compromised for a fifth of all marketing, and for the remaining four-fifths has been intermixed with nonprice elements. Prices reflected back to farm product markets no longer serve as only an indicator of consumers' wishes (demand). They are also highly influenced by the merchandising tactics employed and by oligopsony power.

That is to say, even though commodity pricing has obviously been replaced in a part of the marketing system, its continued existence in the remaining part may actually overportray its instrumental role.

Value created in merchandising serves as an example of the puzzle. Merchandising does create value, else it would not be practiced. Does any of that value redound to the producer of the basic product? Presumably very little. Certainly the merchandisers intend to latch onto it. Some farm partisans claim the opposite, namely, that merchandising absorbs some of the basic consumer demand and subtracts from the net demand that filters through to the farm product market. Regrettably, our techniques of analysis are not sharp enough to resolve the dispute. But the illustration makes it clear that our present-day marketing system for farm products is a major, even a devastating, departure from a wholly price oriented system in which values are transmitted in essentially pure form up and down the marketing sequence.

As is pointed out later, this asymmetry between farm product markets and processing-retailing has proved a major incentive for farmers' group action in marketing. The latter is one of the foci of current developments in farmers' marketing methods.

Still another force at work is of clear identity but uncertain motive power. It is the pressure for more orderliness in marketing. This refers to production and delivery in accordance with fairly exact specification as to quality and time. In the sketch of historical epochs in the marketing system offered in Chapter 1, a feature of progressive development is the increasing degree of control exercised over the initial production of a product, which thereby becomes subordinated.

Farm products do not lend themselves to precise control but many advances have been made in reducing the fortuitous element in farm production. Processing firms that have integrated into farming often justify their doing so on grounds of controlling their supply more accurately. For that matter, various public services to marketing, as standardization and grading, are aimed at improving quality control and at facilitating "orderly marketing" generally.

Decline of Organized Commodity Markets. The outcome of the several forces at work has been a decline not only in the role of price as an instrument but in organized price-making institutions. Organized commodity trading markets for making or discovering price have been on a steady decline.

Price "discovery" is used here in the sense defined by Thomsen and Foote, who distinguish that term from price "determination."[23] Discovery relates to the actual arriving at a price. (Tomek and Robinson say, "discovering or establishing" prices.[24]) Determination refers to the resolution of broad forces of supply and demand. Presumably, if the discovery process worked to absolute perfection, discovered prices would be the same as those indicated by forces of price determination. This epigram loses practical meaning where the market is clearly imperfect.

Local and central assembly markets have gradually given way to contractual or ownership integration, to direct trading, to various kinds of formula pricing, and to collective bargaining. Moreover, just as in processing and retailing price alone no longer controls the distribution of product and production of services, at the farm level commodity prices have been supplemented by various governmental activities as means to guide production. In earlier years acreage controls were in force. Beginning about 1965 the policy turned more to using direct "deficiency" payments to augment market prices received by farmers. The issue remains moot as to how, and how much, those payments affect the quantity of products produced.

Price Discovery Systems. Although both marketers and marketing economists speak freely of various ways in which trading prices are arrived at, no standard nomenclature of price discovery systems has come into general use. Probably the best reviews yet available are found in Rogers,[25] Rogers and Voss,[26] Tomek and Robinson,[27] and Rhodes.[28] An aspect of pricing that converts a beguilingly simple appearing idea into a complicated one is that pricing is ordinarily not done independently of other contractual commitments. Also not absent is strategic effort to bring price determination forces to bear on the price discovery process. That is, unless the conditions of perfect competition are fully met, each participant in the pricing process will try to influence the price in his own favor.

As an example of complications, it is a traditional view that pricing is done simultaneously with exchange of title to product. The fact that actual delivery may be scheduled for the future, as in futures market trading, does not violate this principle. But administered prices are announced independently of particular transactions, for they are just a price "tag." Bargained and committee pricing likewise may be carried on without regard to specific transactions.

To restate for clarity and emphasis: our common notion of price discovery is that a buyer and a seller, following little or much haggling, agree to transfer title to product at a price they negotiate. If there is communication among other persons who are potential buyers/sellers, the price the first traders arrive at becomes a datum that enters into subsequent haggling. If communication is swift and accurate, pricing tends to center toward a single value (for standard quality of product). Thereupon is exemplified the "law of one price."

The clearest of all examples of such a system is a central assembly market that operates on what Rhodes calls a market-clearing principle.[29]

Administered prices—the nonnegotiable price labels that processors, wholesalers, and retailers attach to their products—are set without regard for a particular transaction. But the sharpest departure is any commodity exchange trading in which the traders do not themselves enter into price making. They accept a price that has been made or discovered separately from their own transaction. They may use the published report of prices in other trading, or a price arrived at in some form of group negotiation (bargaining or committee pricing), or a private estimate (see below).

LINKAGE TO PRICE DETERMINING FACTORS. One of the murkiest aspects of the price discovery, price determination issue is to separate out the factors of efficient discovery from those of the economic forces that are expressed in the discovery operation.

The criteria for efficient price discovery are said to be many buyers, many sellers, good communication, accurate description of product, and well-chosen trading rules that are enforced strictly. These probably are met best in an assembly market or its equivalent of a trading mart such as a commodity exchange. They are met best of all if Rhodes's further criterion of market clearing be applied. What this means is that if there be only few sellers but many buyers, the pricing itself can be perfectly competitive if the sellers must commit their product for whatever it will bring. They cannot apply any reservation price, or themselves bid back their own products.

The same principle works in the other direction: a few buyers can invite bids from many suppliers, and competitiveness is not violated provided the buyers fill their total order irrespective of the prices submitted. The price discovery process cannot correct for the structure of the industry which leads to the supply or demand that is expressed, but the process can be so organized and conducted that it of itself is not an anticompetitive mechanism. Thus the rules about no withholding of committed product, etc., make good economic sense. The subject is as fascinating as it is elusive.

Administered pricing is used only in imperfect competition. Scitovsky declares that administered pricing applies only when the "price makers" are fewer in number and better informed than the "price takers."[30] Group bargained pricing obviously involves strategic contests between large organizations.

The nomenclature of Table 5.12 is offered as a reference list. It builds upon the work of other authors who have been cited. The object has been to show several kinds of distinctions among various systems of price discovery.

Systems 1 and 2(a) are the most traditional assembly-market method of discovering prices. The discovery technique has been re-

TABLE 5.12. **Systems for Price Discovery in the Marketing of Farm Products.**

System	Relationship of Transfer of Title to Price Discovery
Auction	
American	direct
Dutch	direct
Private treaty	
Central trading	direct[a]
Dispersed "direct" trading	direct[a]
Bid and acceptance	direct
Administered	none
Group-bargained	variable[b]
Marketwide supply-demand estimation	
Private	none
Group- or government-sponsored ("committee")	none
Formula	
Based on reported transactions	none
Based on supply-demand estimated prices	none
Governmental regulation	none

[a] Can be for immediate or future delivery.

[b] Bargained pricing may or may not be associated with specific ownership-transfer negotiations.

tained under arrangements in which the physical product is not brought to a central point, but trading is done by description. The latter offers a saving in cost of the physical assembly process. Rhodes's emphasis on market clearing in market pricing nevertheless applies incisively here. It is much easier to attach the market-clearing rule, with its benefits in protecting competitiveness, when physical product is assembled.

Dispersed direct trading has grown rapidly. It takes many forms. Livestock farmers sell their stock directly to slaughterers. An egg producer deals directly with a processor, wholesaler, or retailer. A fruit producer negotiates with a distant buyer.

Bid and acceptance and similar practices are harder to classify. They resemble an auction. A large seller invites potential buyers to bid what they will pay, or a large buyer solicits offers from potential sellers. The initiating firm accepts or rejects the responses as it sees fit.

These first two classes of price discovery systems relate pricing to transfer of title to product. For the most part, the other five classes dissociate ownership transfer from price discovery. The price is made separately from individual title transfer transactions. The cloudy exception is pricing by group bargaining. In general, though, even in bargaining a particular delivery is not made contingent upon a specifically negotiated (bargained) price.

Administered pricing, as previously noted, is the technical term used to describe all pricing where the seller announces a nonnegotiable selling price, or a buyer announces a firm paying price. Most processed or manufactured products of agriculture are sold by administered pricing. Administered paying prices are rarer, but some livestock slaughterers announce at the beginning of a day the price they will pay during that day. This is an administered paying price.

In administered pricing, the firm announcing the price must accept whatever volume of sales or purchases results.

Collective bargaining is still infrequent in the marketing of farm products. It is more common in pricing fruits and vegetables for processing than other commodities. Premium prices (above the marketing order price) for fluid milk are frequently bargained—although sometimes a farmers' cooperative only announces a premium, which is not bargaining.

In bargaining the representatives of producer organizations negotiate ("bargain") with processors to set a price that usually will apply to an entire season's marketings.

Supply-demand estimation pricing is of different character. In it, some organization makes its estimate of what price best fits the current market situation. The responsibility involved in such price making is awesome. It is still not common, but instances are found. Best known is the Urner-Barry pricing for eggs, and the National Provisioner Yellow Sheet pricing of beef carcasses and some other meat products. The original plan in the Urner-Barry egg pricing service was to disseminate information on prices arrived at in actual title transfer selling. As organized markets disappeared and an increasing volume of deliveries was made on the Urner-Barry quotation, that quotation took on more of the characteristics of supply-demand estimation. Critics of the Yellow Sheet operation claim that it has become a supply-demand, and not transaction-reporting, activity.

In cotton, the price reporting for major markets amounts to committee pricing. A formally organized committee pricing system had long been proposed for eggs, and in 1972 a Market Evaluation Committee system was set up that amounted to a modest version of committee pricing. The minimum pricing for fluid milk established by Milk Marketing Order administrators is also a kind of supply-demand estimation.

Formula pricing is a hybrid. Product is delivered following negotiation, itself often routine, of plus or minus margins from a later published price quotation. The base quotation can come from an organized market, or from supply-demand estimated prices. Many livestock are delivered directly to a packer and priced according to a central market price that is published. But the biggest volume of formula pricing is probably in eggs, where the Urner-Barry quotation becomes the base from which discounts are subtracted or premiums added—by "formula."

In Table 5.12, governmentally regulated prices are listed for completeness. With the possible exception of some state milk marketing orders, direct regulation of prices in the manner of a public utility is rare. The prices for milk named by a milk market administrator under a federal order are not regulated prices, for they are only minimums and the system itself can be voted out by the local producers. During periods of inflation the federal government can impose ceilings on certain prices. Commodity price supports can be a major price-making factor for eligible commodities in years of flush production or weak demand. However, they do not decree trading prices and at such times many sales are made at less than the support price.

Table 5.12 makes no special mention of markets for trading in commodity futures. Various kinds of price making can serve for transactions for future delivery as well as for spot delivery. Organized futures trading does take on a character of its own. Much descriptive material and many analytical studies are available. A survey article written by Gray and Rutledge is the most comprehensive source of information including bibliography.[31] Also see Chapters 12 and 13 in Tomek and Robinson's *Agricultural Product Prices*.[32]

TABLE 5.13. Résumé of Systems for "Discovering" Prices of Farm Products.

Eggs	Formula pricing based on Urner-Barry supply-demand quotations still dominates. The Egg Clearinghouse and the Market Evaluation Committee have gained some status. Eggs produced under contract are priced according to the contract but often the payment is a "piece wage" (payment per unit of production, with or without a correction factor for efficiency).
Broilers	Private treaty pricing in direct sales of chilled dressed broilers to large retailers. Some buyers occasionally use the bid and acceptance technique. Producers under contract are paid a "piece wage."
Fluid milk	Minimum classified prices (supply-demand estimation) are announced by the milk market administrator in federal order markets. A producers' cooperative may negotiate (group-bargain) a premium, or establish it unilaterally. In some states a state milk commission controls the price at one or more levels of distribution.
Manufactured dairy products	There is still some central market trading but direct trading outside markets is more common. For some products at some times government supports indirectly set a floor.
Meat animals	Pricing is now based on price reports from central terminal markets and from direct trading in several areas. Direct trading reports are especially important in pricing of fed cattle. Some "block" marketing is done, usually at a group-bargained premium (formula) over a published price.
Dressed meat	Much dressed beef is priced by formula, based on the National Provisioner Yellow Sheet published data, which in turn are partly a supply-demand estimate. Otherwise, most sales are at individually negotiated direct trading prices. The bid and acceptance technique is used by some buyers.
Cotton	Pricing is a blend of negotiated direct trading prices and joint government-trade supply-demand pricing.
Tobacco	Auctions, but government price support sets a floor.
Fresh fruits and vegetables	Much price making in direct trading but there are many different arrangements including production contracts and, for some products in some areas, still a substantial amount of pricing in open wholesale markets.
Fruits and vegetables for processing	Contracts are negotiated, with group-bargaining entered into in a number of cases. Where possible, contracts for annual crops are entered into prior to planting.
Grain	Central trading still dominates pricing but futures trading tends to set the national day-to-day pattern. Regional and local variations from central market prices reflect local conditions. Government price supports can virtually set a floor.

PRICE DISCOVERY SYSTEMS IN OPERATION. The resumé of price discovery systems set forth in Table 5.13 builds upon the work of Rogers and Voss. It incorporates a principle that has not won general acceptance, namely, that one particular kind of transaction usually sets a base price for other associated trading.

It should be noted that the transactions which establish a base price may occur at different stages for various commodities and may be only a small part of the total movement of a commodity. Central markets for meat animals, for example, though down to 12 percent of all cattle marketed and 17 percent of hogs (1973 data) continue to provide a general price reference. However, they have been superseded increasingly by price reporting from direct trading in several areas. Local auctions contribute to price discovery but play a less vital role.

Current Developments in Farm Product Marketing and Pricing. To summarize, the principal developments in the part commodity pricing plays in the marketing system for farm products have been:

1. Relegation of commodity price to a lesser role as nonprice competition increases at processing and retailing.
2. Replacement of market trading by vertical integration.
3. Decline of commodity trading on organized markets for price discovery—what Paul calls "increasing dispersion of price structure,"[33] and Forker, decentralization.[34]

Perhaps a fourth development should be added. It would be the reaction to the first three. Proposals to counteract the three developments in markets have themselves been three in number:

1. To strengthen organized commodity trading.
2. To develop new kinds of market institutions.
3. To utilize group action in marketing.

The first of these begins with extending the time-honored public services to new marketing practices. A clear example relates to information services in direct selling of meat animals. Selling direct to a packer offers some operating efficiencies but has the weakness that market information is harder to obtain from direct than from central market trading. The Market News Service of USDA has attempted to resolve this problem by providing, at considerable cost, market news reporting from areas of intensive direct selling of cattle and hogs.

It has been proposed that if it should be national policy to retain central markets for price discovery for any commodity or commodity group, processors should be required to buy a certain minimum percentage of their supplies from such markets.

Some innovation is to be seen in exploratory efforts to develop new kinds of price discovery institutions. These still fall in the category of traditional marketing; they are more adaptive than revolutionary. In the United States, the most originality has been shown in egg marketing. Impressive research studies have pointed to the advisability of committee pricing, which would provide for a formula pricing arrangement in which a formally organized committee representing both buying and selling interests would choose the base price. Egg industry committees and egg cooperatives have tried to set up a base price quotation system independent of the private firm of Urner-Barry. Also, a new egg trading market at Durham, New Hampshire, opened in July 1971.

In Canada, the province of Ontario and other provinces as well have shown more originality than the United States in devising new price discovery institutions. The Ontario hog marketing scheme (telegraphic auction) led to proposals such as that of Johnson for telegraphic selling and pricing of beef cattle in the United States,[35] and Schrader's for an electronic egg exchange.[36]

Group Action in Price Making. The ideas just narrated amount to trying to adjust the familiar types of marketing institutions to accommodate the changing times.

The policy direction of group action is more aggressively aimed at the kind of processing and retailing structure that now prevails. It departs furthest from traditional markets.

Group action takes the form of organizing large marketing cooperatives, or of bargaining collectively.

Farmers' marketing cooperatives were once advocated on grounds that they would countervail strong private firms and improve the quality of competition—make it more nearly perfect. A more recent advocacy is that they themselves be imperfectly competitive institutions, working on farmers' behalf.

Farmers' cooperatives can become price discovery mechanisms if they are large enough, or if they differentiate their product successfully enough, that they can impose administered prices. As long ago as the 1920s Aaron Sapiro advocated cooperatives big enough to be able to price products oligopolistically or, virtually, monopolistically. Success was limited. Even the cooperative federations of our day have seldom been able to do this. A few, however, have proved successful in integrating forward and merchandising their products under brand names. Sunkist lemons, Land O' Lakes butter, and Welch's grape juice are well-known examples.

Eric Thor and Ray Goldberg have been principal spokesmen for a proposal to form joint ventures between farmers' cooperatives and private merchandising firms. The private firm would make all the benefits of market development available to the cooperative that supplies the product, and both would share the benefits.[37] Critics have asked how the division of the benefits would be determined, and whether the merchandiser would get a disproportionate share.

COLLECTIVE BARGAINING FOR PRICE DISCOVERY. Collective bargaining associations, like cooperatives, seek to countervail on behalf of farmers some of the advantages allegedly arising from imperfect competition in the processing-retailing sector—both those of oligopsonistic structure and those originating in product differentiation and market development. Unlike many of the cooperatives, bargaining associations do not seek to contest with merchandisers on their terms, but try to protect their position by gaining control over a substantial part of the supply of the basic product. In addition, bargaining groups will often accept terms of quality control, and of orderly marketing in general, as one of the plus values they bring to the bargaining table.

Although some bargaining associations do not confine themselves to bargaining alone but perform some cooperative marketing services, in principle a bargaining association only negotiates price and other terms of trade for the production and delivery of a product. It does not itself take title to or handle a product.[38]

Moreover, in the strict sense of the term collective bargaining does not involve production control. From the farmers' standpoint, the object in bargaining is not to improve price by reducing the quantity produced ("price determination") but to get a higher price for a given volume of production ("price discovery").

In this sense bargaining is an appropriate price discovery device only under conditions of imperfect competition. In perfect competition it would have no place, no reason to exist. As Helmberger and Hoos put it, "As the degree of competition in buying approaches the limit of perfect competition, the potential for farmer gains erodes away and disappears in the long run."[39]

Inasmuch as price (and quantity) solutions in imperfect competition are indeterminate, collective bargaining may be viewed as one of the devices that may be used to resolve the indeterminacy.

This interpretation bears on the question often asked as to whether farmers' bargaining is intended to produce superequilibrium prices for farmers, or only to offset weaknesses in the pricing system. If imperfect competition does not yield objective equilibrium solutions, the question itself is inapplicable. For in that case there is no basis for making a comparison.

More accurate is an admission that both parties to a bargaining conference seek to maximize their advantage. A shelf of articles has been published on the strategy of bargaining. Most of them rely on some form of game theory.[40]

This is not to suggest that parties engaging in bargaining have no resources to employ in the negotiation strategy. Some of these are negative in nature and foreign to all the economic principles for price making in commodity market exchange. These are best summarized in the word "threat." A threat to withhold product, or divert to another outlet, or not to plant a contract crop, is an essential tool in farmers' bargaining. It should be noted that only rarely is the threat invoked. Usually the product is delivered, the crop planted.

On the positive side, each party to bargaining usually offers some promise of performance the other party finds attractive. This is the setting in which tomato farmers in Indiana a few years ago promised orderly delivery of tomatoes as a sweetener to the higher prices contained in the bargained contract.[41]

Ladd has formalized the positive and negative aspects of collective bargaining by his coinage of "opponent-gain power" and "opponent-pain power."[42]

EXTENT OF COLLECTIVE BARGAINING IN AGRICULTURE. As noted above, collective bargaining in agriculture has acquired more credibility as the marketing system as a whole has become more imperfectly competitive and as organized commodity markets have been displaced. Moreover, it offers some advantages over cooperative marketing for products that do not lend themselves well to product differentiation and forward integration.

On the other hand, collective bargaining faces a major obstacle in the reluctance of producers to band together for bargaining purposes. For this reason bargaining in agriculture has advanced farthest where a localization of activity is possible, or, as in fluid milk, where marketing orders plus the oligopsony structure of buyers have provided a favorable setting. In particular, bargaining has advanced most in the following commodities and kinds of activity:

1. In milk: negotiation of or, at times, virtually declaring "superpool" premiums over the minimum prices set by the Milk Market Administrator. Large dairy cooperative organizations undertake this bargaining as one of their major activities.
2. In contractual production: negotiation of the terms of contracts for contractually produced commodities, notably fruits and vegetables for processing. Efforts to organize contractual producers of poultry (mainly broilers) have been less successful. The bargaining associations are organized on a commodity basis but a sizable number are affiliated with the American Agricultural Marketing

Association, which is a wing of the American Farm Bureau Federation.

Most contract crops are highly localized. Some tomato-producing areas of the Midwest, for instance, may contain only a single processor. This is local monopsony. The tomato producers, lacking alternative outlets, frequently find a bargaining association to be not only their best recourse, but the only one.

3. NFO activities: negotiation of the terms of block delivery of commodities. When the National Farmers Organization first undertook bargaining it sought to enlist 60 percent of the producers of each commodity, so as to confront processors of that commodity from a strong bargaining position. Failing that ambitious goal, the organization turned to the tactic of negotiating block delivery of a specified quantity and quality of product to one or more individual processors located in an area. It has also entered into long-term delivery contracts. By offering block delivery to alternate outlets the NFO believes it can negotiate premium prices. In all likelihood, the amount of the premium is generally modest. Also, the system will work to the farmers' advantage only if processors have excess capacity.

The assembly of product for specified delivery borders on cooperative marketing. Indeed, the question of whether the NFO is a marketing cooperative became the subject of court tests.

SUMMARY. In brief summary, the system for delivering and pricing farm products has become more diverse and more decentralized over the years. It has also departed further from the structure of processing and retailing, which has turned ever further toward industrial-style market development built around differentiation of product. These trends have seriously compromised the time-honored concept of a straightforward internally linked sequence from farm to consumer. The asymmetry and disharmony between the initial and later stages is manifest. It has led to proposals that at one extreme would integrate agricultural marketing into the processing-retailing system, either on the latter's terms or, in the case of forward integration by cooperatives, on the farmers' terms. Other advocacies are to defend open exchange markets by legal means, to devise new price discovery institutions, and to solidify separate farmer interests into tight-knit bargaining groups. The last-named would not obstruct trends in delivery and merchandising systems but would use common confrontation to determine the terms of trade.*

*This is not intended to be an inventory of all institutions in the marketing of farm products. Various other institutions are named in later chapters. Those discussed here have a direct role in the making of price "or other terms of trade."

CHAPTER SIX

PERFORMANCE OF THE MARKETING SYSTEM: THE ROLE OF MARKETING RESEARCH

PREVIOUS CHAPTERS touched at various places on the quality of performance of the marketing system. Although efforts to measure—and to improve—performance have perhaps met as much frustration as success, the total investment in market studies has been truly enormous.

Three kinds of organizations have been involved. The first is marketing firms themselves. Predictably, they have directed their studies to matters of their own interests. Very often they have not seen fit to divulge their findings, yet they have contributed materially to research technique, particularly with regard to consumer acceptance and feasibility (market potential) studies.

The second kind of organization is the Land Grant Experiment Stations—United States Department of Agriculture network. Ever since the first states established agricultural experiment stations, marketing has claimed a part of the research activity. Federal funding, as from the Hatch Act of 1887, gave an impetus.

The big forward thrust came, however, with the enactment of the Research and Marketing (Hope-Flannagan) Act of 1946. In that postwar setting the action of Congress reflected a virtually idealized faith in what more efficient marketing might do. The hope and expectation was that better marketing would make the bountiful productivity of U.S. agriculture directly beneficial to consumers.

A companion goal was to lessen the need to resume the costly and unpopular prewar programs of restricting farm production. The opening language of the bill expressed the sponsors' grand hopes. Efficient marketing of farm products was declared to be "essential to a prosperous agriculture" and "indispensable to the maintenance of full employment and to the welfare, prosperity, and health of the nation." It called for the introduction of science to marketing. "It is . . . declared to be the policy of Congress to promote . . . a scientific approach to the problems of marketing, transportation, and distribution of agricultural products similar to the scientific methods which have been used so successfully during the past 84 years in . . . production. . . ."[1]

Appreciation is due Ben C. French for access to the manuscript of his forthcoming review article, "The Analysis of Productive Efficiency in Agricultural Marketing—Models, Methods, and Progress."

Quotas were set for a minimum percentage of funds to be devoted to marketing research. Although this device led to a sudden widening of the definition of marketing, the overall effect was to generate an intellectual ferment in marketing research during the late 1940s and 1950s that has not since been equaled.

The third sponsor of marketing inquiry is the governmental commission. This may be state or federal but the most exhaustive investigations have been done at the federal level. The prewar Temporary National Economic (O'Mahoney) Committee was precursor of the National Commission on Food Marketing that was active in the mid-1960s. Such commissions are without parallel in their potential capacity because (1) they are usually well funded and can engage top caliber staff, (2) they automatically give prestigious exposure to their findings, and (3) they have the benefit of subpoena power in conducting their investigations. Possession of subpoena power is essential to such an activity even though it is rarely employed. The need for it itself reveals something about the nature of imperfect competition. Firms operating in a highly imperfect environment find it advantageous to avoid the cooperative exchange of information that is more readily attained in perfect competition. As the marketing system grows more imperfectly competitive at all stages, it will likely prove necessary to employ more legal authority in order to conduct research into the workings of that system.

THE LANGUAGE OF INVESTIGATION. Not only the marketing system changes form over time. The language relating to it is equally inconstant. It evolves.

For many years, studies of the quality of the marketing system employed the term "efficiency" as their term of central focus. Frederick Waugh, in his 1954 book that compiled and condensed the best marketing studies then extant, devoted an entire chapter to the subject of efficiency.[2] The 1963 law establishing the Food Marketing Commission called for the commission ". . . to study and appraise the marketing structure of the food industry, including . . . the kind of food industry that would assure efficiency . . ."[3]

The term itself is of engineering origin. It only describes a ratio between output and input. Drawing on the term is only one more instance where the social science of economics has appropriated terms of good repute that were coined in the physical sciences.

In marketing studies, the term has been applied separately to concepts of operational efficiency and of pricing efficiency. Operational efficiency pertains to how well the physical part of marketing is done—the quantity and quality of services performed relative to resources used. Pricing efficiency, in the context of the language of this text, might better be expressed as coordinational efficiency. It refers to how well the marketing system carries out its function of giving directional coordination to the entire production and marketing sequence.

The term "performance" has come into increasing use. Marion and Handy titled their 1973 report, *Market Performance: Concepts and Measures*.[4] The term is less precise than the concept of efficiency, but probably more generally applicable.

MACRO OR SECTOR PERFORMANCE. Interest never ebbs in assessing macro performance of the economy—the total economy, or, with regard to the topic of this textbook, the marketing system for farm products that is so important a sector. We have gross measures of national product. Kendrick and a host of others have assessed grandly comprehensive productivity ratios, as well as sectoral ratios.[5]

Interest in these measures is entirely appropriate. A brief review of aggregative studies in farm product marketing follows. Yet the grand irony is that study of efficiency or performance is better suited to disaggregative than aggregative analysis. Marion and Handy give a good rundown of the impediments to aggregative as well as more limited studies.[6] The problems are not only those of (1) finding acceptable units of measurement, (2) circularity, and (3) the recently publicized issue of externalities. They are also that (1) goals for an aggregated economic system or marketing system are not the sum of the goals for its individual units,[7] and (2) resources are expended in pursuit of certain goals of individual units that do not contribute to systemwide goals. The latter includes the cost of engaging in many kinds of competition or rivalry among firms, the dominating example being promotion and advertising. Scitovsky puts the matter bluntly: "It would be meaningless to apply the criterion of economic efficiency to a measure aimed deliberately at changing the consumer's preferences or influencing his market behavior."[8]

Productivity in Marketing. Because of the complicating problems in analysis, studies of productivity at an aggregate level such as an industry have usually materialized as restatements of the issues rather than production of solid data. Insofar as estimates have been attempted they have centered on productivity of labor, notwithstanding the weakness of such partial analysis. When factors are combined, price data are commonly used for the weights. Productivity has been easier to measure in processing than in services. This too presents a handicap in marketing analysis, for much of marketing is composed of services.

During the surge of interest, even excitement, in marketing studies during the 1950s several national workshops took up the matter of calculating productivity. A 1950 report is representative.[9] The best single reference work on the subject is French's review article, recognized in the opening footnote to this chapter.[10]

Macro measures of marketing efficiency may be less popular now because, as Marion and Handy put it, "other dimensions have become more significant." Among them are "progressiveness, responsiveness to consumer and societal needs and demands, influence on equity . . . and the nature and type of externalities."[11] Nevertheless, the suspicion will not die that frustration is the major reason for reduced attention. Most marketing economists still run for refuge either to the venerable marketing cost and margin statistics, or productivity studies at the level of the firm.

COST AND MARGINS DATA. For many years the U.S. Department of Agriculture has collected and published data on price spreads or margins at successive stages in the marketing of farm products, the value of the "marketing bill," and estimates of major categories of cost. These data were summarized in Chapter 5 as a description of the magnitude and composition of the marketing system. They fulfill that purpose well.

The data have often been interpreted as, in the Marion/Handy words, "direct indicators of market performance." The authors add, "Unfortunately, the terminology of the farmer's share and the marketing bill carry equity or welfare connotations which in some cases has led [sic] to their misuse and misinterpretation."[12]

However, food marketing bill data have been further employed to arrive at a gross division of that bill into price and quantity components. This was done by Waldorf, for instance, by a "double-deflating" method.[13] Presumably, trends in the price component when compared with price trends in the total economy give a clue to comparative productivity trends in food marketing. A few notes on use of cost and margins studies for estimating productivity are included in the opening pages of Chapter 5. The techniques of analysis, however, have their critics.[14]

It would be easy to be too negative. Just to isolate various categories of cost, although not directly a source of concluding judgment, takes us partway along the path. The example of the contrasting spectra of costs in broilers and breakfast cereals (Fig. 5.7 in Chapter 5) is highly informative. Costs and margins data are a necessary and valuable starting point in examining performance.

Least reliable of all elements in cost-stratum analysis is the size of profits, either before or after taxes. Rather obviously, profits fail to distinguish between operational and pricing efficiency—do high profits indicate high operating efficiency or monopoly? They also are themselves an accounting phenomenon. Although Internal Revenue Service rules restrict the most imaginative accounting legerdemain, the data as published in any given year are significantly affected by accounting techniques by which they are calculated.

Structure-Performance Correlations. A whole body of cross-industry analyses relates differences in structure (usually with emphasis on degree of concentration and of product differentiation) to various measures of performance. Results are highly mixed, for reasons that Stern, among others, has pointed out.[15] Bain is one of the most quoted defenders of the visible relationships between structure and various performance criteria such as technical efficiency. Technical efficiency in production is in fact one of the criteria for which a fairly reliable relationship can be demonstrated: high concentration is not necessary for high technical efficiency and may impede it. Another example of a significant correlation is between concentration and progressiveness, and entry barriers and progressiveness. For a more complete scanning of the literature, refer to Marion and Handy.[16,17]

Vertical Systems Analysis. Much of the conceptualization of marketing system performance holds to the traditional horizontal orientation. In that long standing viewpoint, horizontal competition is both mainspring and regulator of vertical product flow. The structure-performance correlations just referred to are essentially horizontal.

A contrasting school does a sharp right turn and faces directly the organization of vertical relationships. This reflects the fact that performance as viewed horizontally has vertical implications, and it gets a fillip from the increasing tendency for marketing firms to extend themselves, or align, vertically. Marion and Handy note that "exchange in a vertical system often depends in part on negotiation skills, market power, and factors in addition to traditional demand and cost functions . . . ," and they report favorably Stern's preference to view "market channels as *social* systems performing economic functions" (original italics).[18,19]

As firms become more massive, more vertically aligned, and more conglomerate as well, the social system approach proposed by Stern takes on ever more credence.

Index of Consumer Satisfaction. A topic so important yet so analytically elusive as marketing performance has attracted a whole cadre of analysts. Among the more imaginative techniques is the construction of an index of consumer satisfaction (ICS). Marion and Handy describe the technique as "nonmetric scaling . . . to formulate social indicators of market performance."[20] "In computing the ICS, consumers are assumed to select from market alternatives that product which conforms most closely to the mix of attributes (price, quality, and so on) they perceive as important. Their overall satisfaction with the product will be determined by their satisfaction with the attributes."[21]

STUDIES OF CONSUMERS AND THEIR DEMAND. Marketing research has found one of its most fruitful applications in the area of consumer demand. Although in principle and in fact research can be directed toward both household and industrial consumers, the former preponderates and only it will be reported here. This kind of research lends itself to various levels of aggregation.

Four major types of consumer studies may be delineated. They will be discussed in successive order:

1. Demographic Studies. Demographic studies are primarily enumerative but they can be extended into formal correlation analysis between demographic characteristics and consumer behavior.

Demographic characteristics can include number of persons, their age distribution, their income distribution, race and other ethnic characteristics, vocation, residence (urban versus rural), and others

One of the more engaging demographic characteristics is the collection of intangible qualities loosely labeled as mores, life styles, and such. Only the most skillful and intrepid researchers are able to identify them in a fashion meaningful to market development or similar purpose.

2. Statistical Demand Analysis. The assumption underlying statistical demand analysis is that historical relationships between observed price of a product and its supply on the one hand and demand determining variables on the other (consumer income, price of competing products, etc.) can be used to predict what will happen under specified conditions in the future.

If several kinds of marketing research inventoried thus far in this chapter seem to be long on theory and short on application, the good record of work on demand analysis will reweight the balance and even restore faith in formal analysis.

Going back at least to the work of Henry Schultz[22] and others in the 1920s, the economic factors affecting production and utilization of farm products have been estimated with considerable success.

They have not only been determined with low error terms for past data, but they have proved reasonably reliable in predicting the future. They have likewise been used effectively in drawing up private marketing programs or making governmental policy.

These studies originate primarily from three sources. One is time series analysis, usually aggregated to a national basis. This is the most common. The second is cross-sectional analysis. For it, comprehensive data on food consumption (or purchases) are collected for a given period in time. The nationwide consumer purchase surveys conducted by the U.S. Department of Agriculture are the best example. In the 1965–66 survey, data were reported by family income, family size, residence, and region.[23]

Statistical analysis taken from the cross-sectional food purchase data yield coefficients that may differ widely from those obtained from time series analysis. A small body of literature addresses itself to the reasons for differences.[24]

The third source is purchase data obtained from household diaries. For these, a number of families record continuously their purchases or other acquisition of all food. The diaries give a wealth of data for analysis. Unfortunately, obtaining the data is a costly undertaking. The Michigan State[25] and Georgia Experiment Station[26] panels are among the best of recent years.

The coefficients of most interest drawn from demand analyses are those of income elasticity and price elasticity. An example of income elasticity data is found in a study published by Harmston and Hino, the summary data for which are presented in Table 6.1. Elasticity coefficients are calculated for two different income levels in each of two years. Commodities are then grouped by patterns that are observed. Alcoholic beverages, for example, showed a higher elasticity at the $15,000 income level than the $2,000 level in both 1955 and 1965. So did 11 other items. Coffee had a higher coefficient at the $15,000 than $2,000 income in 1955, but the relationship reversed in 1965. The "mixtures" item revealed the opposite direction of change, and so on, for other items in the table.

3. Consumer Preference, Shopping Behavior, and Similar Studies. Consumers have been interviewed, questionnaired, test-marketed, and observed from a watching post in a store—to the point, it would seem, of diminishing returns to researchers' enterprise, or to their own exhaustion of patience. Though the techniques may be furtive, among the most reliable of these studies are the observations of consumers' actual behavior, provided the display case or area is not itself conspicuous.

TABLE 6.1. Income Elasticities for Farm Commodities by Type of Shift from 1955 to 1965.

Commodity	Income Elasticity at $2,000		Income Elasticity at $15,000	
	1955	1965	1955	1965
Preferred superior for both years				
Alcoholic beverages	.864	.388	1.022	.962
Beef	.374	.232	.520	.445
Butter	.098	.101	.716	.492
Cheese	.276	.152	.361	.242
Dried fruits	.083	.267	.222	.456
Fresh fruits	.149	.229	.377	.453
Fresh vegetables	.113	.148	.344	.377
Frozen foods	.756	.566	.950	.836
Frozen milk dessert	.367	.264	.409	.267
Peanut butter and others	.418	.010	.503	.196
Poultry	.162	.155	.320	.210
Veal and lamb	.560	.572	1.025	.848
Preferred superior to nonpreferred superior				
Coffee	.142	.081	.249	.080
Eggs	.089	.024	.210	.017
Fresh fluid milk	.049	.140	.217	.124
Pork	.141	.090	.148	.087
Nonpreferred superior to preferred superior				
Mixtures	.485	.156	.484	.165
Salad oil and dressing	.262	.223	.220	.235
Nonpreferred superior for both years				
Canned foods	.291	.101	.198	.058
Preferred flour mix	.299	.278	.065	.149
Changing nature to nonpreferred superior				
Cold breakfast cereal	.212	.250	—.035	.124
Changing nature for both years				
Fresh potatoes	.004	.013	—.135	—.190
Margarine	.065	.075	—.193	—.092
Changing nature to inferior				
Bread	.226	—.009	—.025	—.038
Tea	.089	—.009	—.260	—.155
Inferior for both years				
Cornmeal grits	—.944	—.612	—1.296	—1.458
Dried vegetables	—.569	—.221	—1.014	—.735
Flour	—.535	—.371	—.818	—.744
Hot breakfast cereal	—.275	—.093	—.639	—.402
Processed milk	—.177	—.161	—.669	—.376
Shortenings	—.347	—.333	—.471	—.799

Source: Floyd K. Harmston and Hiroyuki Hino, "An Intertemporal Analysis of the Nature of Demand for Food Products," *Amer. J. Agr. Econ.* 52(1970):385.

To the consternation of technicians and cost to companies, many opinion-sampling or even test-marketing studies have not proved very reliable. The exceptional nature of the interviewing experience seems to bias a consumer's response.[27]

4. Sociological Studies. Sociological studies can be of a dozen types. When conducted perceptively, they can contribute to understanding of consumer behavior. For an example of reporting based on sociological, or sociopsychological, observations, see the quotation from Yankelovitch in Chapter 2, page 34.

THE OPERATIONAL EFFICIENCY OF THE FIRM. In the banner days of marketing research, approximately from 1948 to 1960, enthusiasm ran highest of all in studying the efficiency of the firm. Some of the research work was devoted to effectiveness of merchandising. In part, this amounted only to reporting from the firm's-eye-view the pattern of consumer (customer) behavior commented on above under the heading of consumer preference and shopping behavior.

In a heroic amplification, the same principle was carried forward to tests of response to multifirm, even industrywide, merchandising efforts. These studies took the form of analyzing the response in selected metropolitan markets to advertising and/or promotion of, for example, lamb[28] and milk.[29]

Nonetheless, the great majority of firm-efficiency studies have been devoted to studies of the internal operating efficiency of the firm. The Research and Marketing Act of 1946 was interpreted as giving a particularly strong endorsement to this research. Early work by Bressler in Connecticut[30] became prototype for engineering-type analyses of how a firm might organize its activities for an improved O/I efficiency ratio.

Implicit in this enthusiastic endeavor was a confidence that (1) improvements in operating efficiency would reduce operating costs and therefore total marketing costs, and the savings would be passed on to (divided among) farm producers and consumers; and (2) neoclassical economic theory would provide an adequate conceptual and technical base for the analysis.

Applying the engineering concept literally, Rudd reminded that "process analysis" can be divided into component operations, work elements, and therbligs—"the fundamental building blocks of accomplishment."[31] The word, therblig, was coined as a reverse spelling of the name of Frank G. Gilbreth, an early student of time and motion.

Internal efficiency studies have taken various forms. Many relate to economy of scale. Brewster's now classic 239-page report on cottonseed oil mills set a pattern for simulated ideal organization of a facility or an operation that has been duplicated in other studies.[32] Store layout has been a popular topic, and William Crow and his associates designed new wholesale produce markets throughout the nation, and in other nations too.[33]

French's interpretation and catalog of studies of operational efficiency in agricultural marketing is incisive. In general he concedes that the economics of efficiency in marketing is grounded in neoclassical theory but adds that "several types of modifications and extensions, growing substantially out of the work of agricultural economists, . . . are particularly relevant."[34] He classifies those special applications under five headings: production systems in marketing firms; plant costs and length of operations; multiple service plants; spatial components of marketing cost; and total systems analysis.

Not surprisingly, French encounters the greatest analytical difficulty in applying conventional neoclassical theory to the multiple-product or multiple-service feature of modern marketing firms. He cites various authors who have wrestled with the problem.[35]

French, writing in 1973, offered 100 references to "descriptive studies of plant cost records," 341 to "economic-engineering analysis of plant efficiency in agricultural marketing," 121 to economy of scale studies, and 30 to central market design studies.[36] He cited feasibility studies also, without tallying them.[37]

Similar research now being conducted has taken on somewhat more sophistication. As one enthusiasm dampener, studies of the structure of the market have indicated conclusively that pass-through of cost savings to farmers and consumers cannot be taken for granted. Many of the earlier operating-efficiency studies took no account of imperfection of markets for output and input in the sense that unit price would not be affected by the volume of operations. The indifference displayed amounted to a disregard of Brewster's instruction that increasing scale of operations could put some inelasticity into factor costs. Only comparatively recently have U.S. Department of Agriculture studies of economy of scale recognized that larger scale in farm product processing inherently involves a greater factor cost in procurement of raw material, distribution of product, or both. The cost may, of course, be borne internally or externally depending on the competitive structure of the market. French notes how "the total acquisition or distribution costs vary with the level of plant output."[38] Rogers and Rinear have introduced pecuniary diseconomies in their poultry processing research.[39] DeHaven has done likewise in milk pricing.[40]

PRICING EFFICIENCY RESEARCH. Few persons would deny that pricing efficiency is cohort to operating efficiency and at least its equal. Yet, perhaps because a nice analogy to the physical sciences is lacking, research into pricing or coordinative efficiency has been much more limited.

Research into pricing efficiency almost invariably consists of comparing observed data with an idealized norm defined by perfect competition. Most common subjects for examination are pricing accuracy spatially and by quality. In the former, price-topography maps are laid out with central markets as centers. Equal-transport-cost delineates the "perfect" geographical pattern of prices. Against this map actual observed prices can be compared. If the system works properly, the ideal and the actual will be identical.

Price patterns by quality are similar. Either a predominant grade of a product is used as a base for examining premiums or discounts for other grades, or grade differences are simply compared as such. Geography and price may be interlinked, as in a Farris study that showed local elevator pricing of grain in Indiana to be nearly "perfect" geographically for the most-quoted grade, but less so for other grades.[41]

Grade quality comparisons have been common in marketing research applied to livestock and meat. Failure of hog pricing to reflect consumer dislike for fat pork sufficiently to discourage production of a leaner ("meat-type") hog was reported, and deplored, for many years.

Pricing efficiency has also been examined according to alternate market channels. Again livestock affords an example, as direct and central marketing selling are compared.[42]

MARKET STRUCTURE RESEARCH. Of similar fabric but much more ambitious and comprehensive is the area known as market structure research. This also bears a close relationship to the structure-and-performance analyses referred to above. It is distinguished for its inquiry not into narrowly specified features of the marketing system for a product but for more comprehensive appraisals. Among examples are studies of retailing conducted by Mueller and Garoian,[43] Holdren,[44] and Padberg[45] among others. The investigations done by Walsh and several others that are compiled in the Moore and Walsh book;[46] studies of milk marketing such as those presented in Williams and Vose;[47] and of course several of the reports of the National Commission on Food Marketing.[48]

RESEARCH INTO GOVERNMENTAL MARKETING PROGRAMS. Also deserving of mention in an annotation of marketing research is that directed toward the operation of governmental programs for marketing. At one time such research dealt principally with the effectiveness of traditional services such as providing marketing information, standardization, and grading.[49] As new programs were added, new research was undertaken. As surrogate for a substantial body of studies done recently, selected work in the operation of supplementary food programs may be mentioned. Examples are reports by Madden and Yoder,[50] Feaster and Perkins,[51] and Breimyer and Love.[52]

RESEARCH INTO GOVERNMENTALLY AUTHORIZED COLLECTIVE ACTION. Governmentally authorized collective action has intermittently been the subject of a substantial investment in economic research. Various aspects of farmer marketing cooperatives have been studied, sometimes in depth and at length. Collective bargaining has largely been bypassed, primarily because the bargaining organizations, operating in highly imperfect competition, resist inquiry into their activities. However, court cases such as contests between the National Farmers Organization and Associated Milk Producers, Incorporated, and the Department of Justice indictment of the latter body opened up some data for research scrutiny.

Marketing agreements and orders have received occasional research inquiry, though not as much as their importance would justify. Illustrative examples are studies by Jamison,[53] Shafer,[54] and, with respect to milk, Dobson.[55]

The review of research related to the performance of the marketing system as presented in this chapter is a far from complete inventory. It does serve to indicate the major directions research has taken and its basic nature and content.

CHAPTER SEVEN

GOVERNMENTAL POLICIES IN MARKETING

LITERALLY DOZENS or even hundreds of laws and programs of government directly or indirectly bear on the marketing of agricultural products, as defined in the broadest sense. They can be classified according to the several languages that have been used in this textbook. For example, they divide relative to the stage in marketing to which they apply and according to the function(s) carried out at any stage. The Bainsian terminology fits, for some policies regulate structure, others pertain to conduct, and still others affect performance.

These pedagogical classifications fail to accommodate a kind of policy that has risen to prominence recently, namely, that of compensating directly for acknowledged deficiencies in the marketing—or economic—system. The most explicit example is transfer payments, such as certain deficiency payments made to farmers, and income maintenance schemes for consumers. Boulding and others have coined the term, the grants economy, to apply to them. Pfaff writes, "A whole class of nonmarket phenomena—or unilateral transfers or 'grants' have [sic] risen which to some degree compensate the operation of the market mechanism. A specific example can be found in the unemployment compensation 'grants' . . . The areas of health, welfare and education also exemplify. . . ."[1]

This chapter will focus primarily on policy that relates to the earlier stages in the marketing of farm products, principally local and central assembly. Except for brief comments on antitrust law and regulation of trade practices, less attention will be given to policy in food processing, wholesaling, and retailing. Debates about nutrition labeling, unit pricing, and similar practices at retail will not be reported.

Some overlap with other chapters is unavoidable. In Chapter 5 the latest thrusts regarding price discovery mechanisms are reviewed. Chapter 8 touches on policy in transportation.

A statement by Paarlberg serves well as introduction. It succinctly sets forth the points at issue in marketing policy for agriculture, casting them in language current in the 1970s. Professor Paarlberg, at that time director of economics for the U.S. Department of Agriculture, gives his opinion about why government has an "active role" and what

Credit is due Randall E. Torgerson and Gerald Engelman for help in drafting this chapter.

that role is. Moreover, this statement has a structural orientation, as does this chapter:

> The fact that the basic structure and performance aspects of the marketing system continue to undergo change places tremendous pressure on our knowledge and understanding of the relative bargaining and equity position between agriculture and the marketing sector. Moves toward further vertical and horizontal integration within agriculture itself raise serious questions about pricing practices and operating procedures. In recent years there has emerged a trend for large marketing firms to establish their own processing plants, develop their own private labels, and employ various techniques including contracting directly for farm products. This had enabled them to establish more control over many functions and channels of marketing. The open market which once was the primary mechanism whereby prices were set has diminished in importance with the appearance of various forms of integration. Some pricing points, once visible, have become invisible. Farmers are having to adjust to this new set of pressures in bargaining and otherwise dealing with a changed marketing system. These developments make it increasingly important that Government maintain an active role in monitoring the activities of the agricultural marketing system in order to encourage workable competition and assure fair returns to the production sector. Government has responded positively to enhance the position of the farmer through vital activities such as support of marketing orders and cooperatives; the provision of marketing intelligence through market news, price reporting, and evaluation of marketing costs and price spreads; grading and inspection services; and the provision of statistics, research and extension support.[2]

POLICIES TO PRESERVE, RESTORE, OR REPLICATE PERFECT COMPETITION. The conceptual principle known as perfect competition has enjoyed more standing in agriculture than perhaps any other part of the U.S. economy. Large numbers of producers and consumers are the anchor points to marketing, and the preferred image of a good middleman system has been that many buyers and sellers should haggle almost shoulder to shoulder over prices for standard product.

As Paarlberg notes, and as is also observed in this book, that image takes on reality less often now than formerly. But the principle of keeping something close to perfect competition has been a guidepost for marketing policy for many years and is far from defunct in the 1970s.

Also evident in the Paarlberg statement is that the issue of competitive structure finds expression not only in the broad "price determining" forces but also in "price discovery"—how prices are arrived at (see Chapter 5).

Governmental policies for marketing date from the last years of the 19th century. By that time the marketing of farm products had become almost detached from farming and held status of its own. Not only producers but consumers complained from time to time that the marketing system was not working well enough. Farmers voiced their protests when prices were declining. When prices of farm products and food swung upward, consumers took over the chant. It is significant that the first bill to create a bureau of markets in the U.S. Department of Agriculture was sponsored by Congressman Wickliffe, a spokesman for consumers. A little later farm groups joined in support, leading to enactment of a law in 1913.[3]

Market Information. No governmental service to marketing has been so recognized as proper or even essential to good marketing as the providing of market information. Basically, market information fits the principle of perfect competition. A market cannot be perfect without good information. In the language of theory, perfect knowledge separates "perfect" from merely "pure" competition. However, in this text the distinction is not followed.

Informational services have been engaged in for many decades, or perhaps a century.

MARKET NEWS, PRODUCTION STATISTICS, OUTLOOK INFORMATION. Informational services begin with market news reporting, which disseminates huge volumes of data about supplies, movement, and prices of individual products. Once radio and television came on the scene it was possible to broadcast trading information directly from markets, almost simultaneously with transactions. The federal-state market news services are conducted by the Agricultural Marketing Service and by the Departments of Agriculture of the various states.

Statistics of production, disappearance, and average prices are collected and published by the Bureau of the Census in the U.S. Department of Commerce and, in the U.S. Department of Agriculture, by the Statistical Reporting Service and the Economic Research Service. The SRS works jointly with departments of agriculture in the states.

Also an output of the Economic Research Service are periodical outlook reports. These are forecasts of the prospective economic situation for individual commodities, and for farm product markets as a whole.

Grades and Standardization. Publishing of grade standards and actual classification of product are another long-established marketing service.

Drawing up and publishing standards is closely related to the providing of market information and is sometimes so classified. The standards serve as descriptive categories by which market information can be reported. In fact, grade standards originated largely as an aid to market reporting, because market reporters needed terms by which to distinguish quality categories if they were to report price and other data. A set of grade standards served that purpose.

When standards were confined to providing a verbal tool for the convenience of market news reporters, they did little more than draw upon language already in use. Before long other applications of standards came into prominence. They raised questions about how standards should be chosen. They then led to activity to provide a physical grade classification service.

Standardization and control of the quality of the products of agriculture are difficult to achieve. It is not that farmers are careless or uninformed, although some producers still are not sufficiently sensitive to the quality of their products. It is basically a case that agriculture as an organic or "natural" process does not lend itself to industrial-type control of quality of output. Owing to the difficulty of control, grade classification or sorting becomes necessary.

Much grading is done by sellers or buyers themselves, and acceptance (or rejection) of the integrity of the operation can become a point of negotiation and dispute. Grading by its nature has something of a judicial quality. For this reason it is often performed by a third party. Very frequently the third party is a governmental agency.

Grading (classification or sorting) can be done at any of several stages in marketing, or it may in fact be repeated at successive stages. It is done most often at some point between the farm and processor, or between the farm and exporter for product that is exported.

For most products, federal (or state) grading is optional, and the service is provided for a fee that the marketing firm pays. However, for a few products such as cotton and tobacco grade classification is mandatory and the cost of the service is paid by the government.

Only a fraction of foods as sold at retail carry a federal grade identification. Fresh beef, eggs, and a few other foods are notable exceptions.

A number of consumers' organizations have advocated greater use of grade identification in retailing of food. To move in that direction would require a redefinition of many standards. It would also require legal mandate, for the trend has been toward identifying foods by the processor's brand label, not by an objective federal-state grade. Food processors generally have opposed grade labeling of foods at retail.

THE PURPOSES GRADING SERVES. Perennial disputes as to the criteria for setting up grade standards, and the desirability of grading services,

can be resolved only against an understanding of what operating purposes grading serves.

The time-honored value in providing a language for market
information has been mentioned.

Accepted grade standards are essential to trading by description
instead of inspection. A California fruit shipper can negotiate to ship
a carload of fruit to Philadelphia, priced according to accepted grade
standards. A Nebraska meat packer can likewise ship beef carcasses to
Boston, specified as Choice, yield grade two. Trading in this way
without personal inspection is obviously efficient. In this regard, part
of the grading service of the U.S. Department of Agriculture is to
provide appeal inspection—examining product that has been received
to resolve disagreement as to quality.

The ultimate in this regard is futures trading in commodities on
the basis of federal grades. Futures markets could not exist without
grade standards.

GRADES AND THE COORDINATIONAL FUNCTION OF MARKETS. In a broader
sense, a good system of grade standards and grading helps to make the
entire market system work better. It particularly helps the system to
perform its coordinational role—the role of enmeshing consumption,
market services, and initial farm production. This mission particularly
fits the third epoch in the evolution of marketing (see Chapter 1).

If grades are to assist in translating and communicating price
signals up and down the line between consumers and producers, there
must be a set of matching grade standards, stage by stage. To date,
most standards have been designed for wholesale trade in the original
or a processed product. Few standards have been specifically designed
for retailing.

Court tests about beef grading in the mid-1970s offer a clear illustration. Beef grades have long been tailored to wholesale trading in
carcasses. Standards for live animals were harmonized well, but the
Good, Choice, and other grade labels for dressed beef had been chosen
to facilitate pricing at wholesale and were not designed as consumer
grades. The proposals that reached the Court were to separate eating
quality criteria (of interest to consumers) from other criteria that
established value only at wholesale.

The amount of fat on a carcass or cut has been the criterion most
in contention. If excessive fat is not desired, the grade standards for
reflecting price back to producers must be chosen so as to discriminate
between acceptable and unacceptable degrees of fattiness.

GRADES AND MARKET STRATIFICATION. Grade standards also facilitate
stratification of the market. Once more beef grades afford an example.

From the beginning of beef grading, some leaders of the cattle industry saw grades as a way to separate out that portion of the market for beef that wanted a superior quality (according to consumers' tastes) and would pay a premium price for it. Beef grades still serve to stratify. The Prime grade is chosen by expensive restaurants. Middle income families that want a good steak for a backyard grill will often insist on Choice. For pot roasting, a less expensive grade can be selected.

Marketing Research. A nation dedicated to technical knowledge and scientific investigation would not fail to apply research techniques to the important economic sector of the marketing of agricultural products.

Although private firms have long engaged in research for their internal purposes, the image of a perfectly competitive marketing system virtually requires that the bulk of research be publicly funded. So it has been. Marketing research became general during the 1920s, expanded in the 1930s, and then blossomed following enactment of the Research and Marketing Act of 1946. It has since subsided.

It is not surprising that for much of the early research work the perfectly competitive model served as the template. However, farmers' cooperatives were a subject of research dating at least from the beginning of the 1920s, and in more recent years a considerable research effort has been directed toward various marketing activities that do not fit the perfectly competitive model.

Because marketing research is a subject of its own and has traditionally been appraised in terms of concepts of marketing efficiency, a separate review is presented in Chapter 6.

Antitrust and Trade Practice Regulation. The governmental activities of information, standardization, and research are sometimes regarded as facilitative. They assist a perfectly competitive marketing system but do not usually control its form of operation in any direct or obligatory sense. Furthermore, and significantly, in a perfectly competitive market such services are normally not resisted but welcomed. For in such a market, a participant is not able to influence the outcome of trading and therefore sees market services not as a threat but as an aid.

Contrariwise, as marketing becomes more imperfectly competitive individual marketers find it attractive to appropriate or influence market services to their private advantage. They also resist participating in voluntary activities such as providing market information or opening up their books to persons undertaking marketing research. The Food Commission some years ago, and other persons and agencies more recently, have advocated mandatory reporting of some kinds of market information.[4]

Of a different texture is the battery of government activities in antitrust and trade practice regulation. They come into being when markets depart from perfect competition. Antitrust and trade practice policy may be classified under the rubric of policies to restore or replicate perfect competition. The object has generally not been to regulate directly in the manner of a public utility but to lure, nudge, or force changes in structure and conduct so that the resulting performance would be a reasonable facsimile of that in perfect competition.

To change the metaphor, for antitrust and trade practice regulation in the United States the perfectly competitive model has been the conceptual lodestar.

A distinction might be made between laws and regulations aimed at market structure and those working through conduct. This is the Bainsian terminology explained in Chapter 4. Some laws are oriented more toward one than the other. But on the whole, the whole structure-conduct area is a cloudy sea, partly because there is no clearly definable relation between structure and conduct.

ANTITRUST REGULATION. Antimerger and antimonopoly law is rather clearly structural in nature. Much of the Sherman Act and Section 7 in particular of the Clayton Act can be so regarded. But it probably is necessary to look at all the many laws, and the agencies enforcing them, as a single big group. We would add to Sherman and Clayton the Federal Trade Commission Act and Robinson-Patman and Celler-Kefauver and similar laws. Also included would be laws setting up the Packers and Stockyards Administration and Commodity Futures Trading Commission, the Perishable Agricultural Commodities Act, the laws calling for sanitary inspection of meat and poultry, and a host of consumer laws relating to food identification, safety, and "truth in packaging."

Most antimerger and antimonopoly law, and the tradition surrounding it, is aimed at horizontal concentration. The object is to avoid a degree of concentration in an industry that would be clearly anticompetitive. Even the Packers and Stockyards Act has some antimonopoly powers.

A later uncertainty, not yet resolved, is how antitrust law can be applied to vertical and conglomerate structure. In the now-classic Brown Shoe decision of the U.S. Supreme Court, antitrust law was upheld as applicable to vertical integration. More specifically, the Court did not act against vertical integration as such but ruled that when vertical combination is associated with horizontal concentration the effect is anticompetitive. Therefore the Brown Shoe manufacturing firm, itself large, was not permitted to merge with the extensive Thom McAn shoe retail chain.[5]

To date, conglomerate integration has been even more of an antitrust puzzle. The Department of Justice has taken action against a number of conglomerate mergers. Some authorities declare that legal authority exists for a more aggressive anticonglomerate policy. Nevertheless, the situation is unclear and the approach taken still has a horizontal cast to it. That is, debates often are couched in terms of how a conglomerate merger affects the structure of an industry that has been "invaded" and do not consider its broader effects on the fabric of competition.

Various other proposals relating to conglomerates also appertain principally to the industries involved. This is true of the often-heard call for separate financial reporting for each industrial division of a conglomerate firm. It is true also of legislation proposed in the 1970s that would impose strict limits on how large a part of any industry could be in the hands of a single firm.

The phenomenon of giant conglomerate structure still appears alien, incomprehensible, and frustrating to legal action.

TRADE PRACTICE REGULATION. Without disavowing the thesis that for antitrust and trade practice policies the reference point is still perfect competition, we can also regard much trade practice regulation as fitting the idea of workable or effective competition. According to more recent philosophies, the notion of workable or effective competition may describe the norms for acceptable trade practices.

Implicit in much trade practice regulatory philosophy is an acceptance of an imperfectly competitive structure as a fact of economic life. This is an admission too that conduct options are open to managers. In a real sense, trade practice regulation amounts to a new consideration in the range of conduct options. Often the regulation acts as a limit, and in that way bears on managerial decisions.

Trade practice regulation has its own technique and even its own style. Even though all regulations are subject to court test, there are a range of advisory opinions and various formal and informal communications that often are accepted without challenge.

Do trade practice rules protect primarily businesses and traders, or consumers? In one sense the question is academic, for enforced standards of conduct that defend ethical against less ethical competitors ought to improve quality of service ("performance"). In a rough judgment, earlier attitudes may have stressed fairness and equity among business firms, but the more recent consumer movement probably tipped the scales in a consumer service direction.*

The question applies to laws relating specifically to agricultural products and food. All trading in those products is subject to general laws, except where the legislation specifies a division of jurisdiction. But a number of laws are essentially confined to the products of agriculture. Certain ones such as the Packers and Stockyards Act and Perishable Agricultural Commodities Act protect traders almost exclusively. The great body of law protecting consumers has to do with sanitation and safety of foods and their identification. Meat and poultry products, for example, are inspected with diligence. The trend has been for foods to receive more processing (manufacture) and in parallel fashion they have become more subject to scrutiny to protect against impurities and especially carcinogenous chemical residues.

Still another area of trade practice regulation deserves mention. Of recent origin, it makes no pretense of invoking perfectly competitive norms. Instead, it sets up a monitoring system over group action in marketing. The best example is the Agricultural Fair Practices Act.[6] It prescribes rules of conduct in collective bargaining. In the first court case brought under the law, illustrative of its powers, an Ohio milk company was enjoined from refusing to deal with an Ohio milk producer because of his membership in a producers' association.[7]

POLICIES TO COUNTERACT DEFICIENCIES. The various regulatory authorities of federal and state governments described to this point have in common the fact that they act not to predetermine the outcome (performance) of the marketing system, but instead to set the metes and bounds for the organizational structure and entrepreneurial conduct of business.

Not so with the second broad class of governmental policies. These of themselves do not recast the existing state of affairs. Instead, they are more supplementary and compensatory in nature. As such they have a performance component and may actually compensate directly for inadequacies in performance.

Demand Expansion: Commodity Purchases. Over several decades the federal government exerted a major influence over prices of several important commodities, through its price support activities. The program of nonrecourse loans resulted in sizable deliveries by farmers to

*The engaging issue of how diligently consumers should be protected against themselves (their own ignorance or foolishness) is taken up in Ivan L. Preston, "Reasonable Consumer or Ignorant Consumer? How the FTC Decides," *J. Consumer Affairs* 8 (1974): 131–43.

the Commodity Credit Corporation. The net effect was to increase prices to farmers and, to some extent, to consumers.

The U.S. Department of Agriculture has bought other products directly, under authorities such as section 32 of the Act of August 24, 1935, and the School Lunch Act. Section 32 makes 30 percent of all import duty revenues available for commodity purchases and for taking other measures to support the market for farm products. Commodities purchased have been distributed to low income families, to schools for their lunch programs, and to eligible institutions.

During the inflation in prices of food during the early 1970s all commodity procurement programs receded, but most remained in existence. Large scale action under them could resume.

Demand Expansion: Stratification of the Market. In Chapter 4 it is pointed out that under suitable conditions stratification of the market could enlarge total demand for a product. Several government programs for stratification have been undertaken. These will be described briefly.

EXPORT PROGRAMS. The oldest program is separation of domestic and foreign (export) markets, with subsidy often paid on exports. Most governments of the world have practiced this kind of stratification. Programs of the United States have taken three forms. One is to pay an outright subsidy on commercial exports. Usually these payments are on commodities for which domestic price supports hold prices above the so-called world levels. A second program comes under Public Law 480 and related laws. Commodities are exported on "concessionary" terms, which can range from direct grant to sale on long-term dollar credit. A third program is less visible. It is the policy gradually adopted beginning about the mid-1960s, whereby market prices are kept on the low side and any resulting deficiency in income to farmers is compensated by direct Treasury payments. This is an indirect export subsidy.

DOMESTIC FOOD PROGRAMS. Domestically, the several supplementary food programs are a major activity of stratification. In these too, delivery without cost to the recipient of food purchased in commodity operations of the U.S. Department of Agriculture may be regarded as an extreme or limiting case of stratification. But in the larger sense, the food stamp and child feeding programs are an unambiguous instance. In both programs the recipient pays a price that not only is less than the commercial market price but is graduated for persons

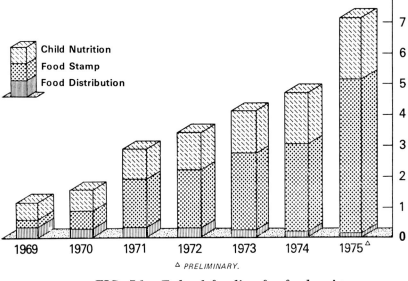

FIG. 7.1.   Federal funding for food assistance.
(USDA-ERS)

or families according to their capacity to pay. (The price paid gradu-
ates downward to zero.)

Supplementary food programs expanded rapidly beginning in
the later 1960s. (See Figs. 7.1 and 7.2.) At the end of the 1974–75
school year about 25 million school children were taking part in the
national school lunch program and 18 million persons were participating in the food stamp program. The family food distribution program was being phased out.[8]

Observers of these food programs have had a hang-up over
whether they are consumer-benefit or producer-benefit programs. The
argument is pointless. A parallel may be struck with any consumer
subsidy that is in the interest of both the consumer-recipient and the
supplier of products—*provided* the supplying industry has excess capacity. Supplementary food programs constitute at one and the same
time a transfer payment to consumers (partly commodity-specific) and
a market stratification and therefore market expansion device in the
marketing of agricultural products. From time to time the degree of
emphasis changes, however. Each change affects the design of the
program.

Child feeding programs build around the basic school lunch program. Federal, state, and local governments combine to make food

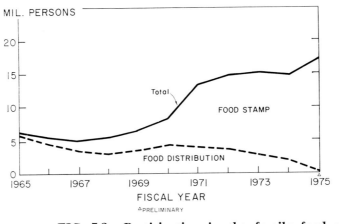

FIG. 7.2. Participation in the family food assistance programs (fiscal year average).
(USDA-ERS)

service available at a relatively low price. In addition, the federal
government subsidizes a further reduction in price to youth of families
of limited income. In 1975 about 10 million school children were
receiving school lunches free or at a reduced price.

The food stamp plan has become a major factor in the demand
for food. The Agriculture and Consumer Protection Act of 1973
called for it to replace the family food distribution program under
which packaged foods had been delivered to eligible low income families.

Perhaps more than any comparable program, the food stamp
plan was the product of abstract conceptual analysis. Frederick Waugh
especially perceived the potential advantage of stratification of the
market for food under the conditions of the 1930s when food was surplus and many consumers undernourished.[9] A prewar program became a wartime casualty, but in the early 1960s a revised program
was adopted first on a pilot basis and then permanently.

The essential features of the program are that lower income
families shall be enabled to buy at retail stores a quantity of food sufficient for a diet of balanced nutrition, and any shortfall in their capacity to pay the full cost will be subsidized. The mechanics are that
the stamps received by the participating family have a face value
scaled to the size of that family, but the cost to the family is propor-
tionate to its paying capacity as judged by its size and income. Adjustments for certain other expenses borne by the family, such as rent,
enter into the calculation. The stamps are virtual specie, accepted at
face value by participating grocers.

As adopted in the early 1960s the plan was puritan in nature. The cost to the family was fairly high and the family was required to buy the full quota of stamps or none at all. Also, a family was not allowed to participate one month and drop out the next. Since then the terms have been loosened—so much so that the author and promoter of the (postwar) law, Congresswoman Sullivan, disavowed the new version and voted against it. Among the changes, the cost to participants was reduced and the option was added of buying a certain fraction of the total monthly value of stamps.

The changes brought increased participation, although the rate of participation continued to fall short of expectations. They also reduced the food-specific nature of the program. Insofar as participants buy food at a bargain and use the money saved to buy other things, the federal subsidy amounts to a disguised general transfer payment rather than a supplemental food program.

The original intent in the food stamp plan was to charge a price for stamps equal to what the participating family would normally spend for food. And as the stamps would provide more food than the family would otherwise get for its normal expenditures, under the program families would eat better but save no money. Now that the terms are more liberal, participating families usually eat better but they also save money that they can use for other purposes.

The more reliable estimates are that as of 1975 around 50 or 60 percent of the governmental contribution (value of bonus stamps) became a net increase in food buying. The other 40 or 50 percent is a saving the families could spend discretionally.

Demand Expansion: Other Government Programs. Among other government programs to expand demand are domestic and foreign promotion, and research for new uses. Much of the governmental commodity market promotion is carried on in cooperation with private commodity organizations, including those set up under special law (see below). The more aggressive governmental activity has been directed to foreign markets.

Research to find new uses for farm products has centered at the several regional research laboratories of the U.S. Department of Agriculture.

Other Policies to Counteract Deficiencies. The policies listed thus far under the caption of counteracting deficiencies in marketing have all been demand-expansion programs. The domestic programs may be viewed and judged also according to how they help the consumer-beneficiaries, but this subject is not examined here.

In the U.S. tradition governmental action is seldom used directly to compensate for, or correct, a flaw in markets. A major exception may be appearing as major railroad lines virtually are taken over and controlled by governmental agencies. As a rule, though, we have few instances in the United States of governmental activity paralleling a private one, a pattern common in some South American countries (see Chapter 10).

PRICE CONTROL. In a sense, price control represents the ultimate in direct governmental action to supplant a faulty market function. In the United States, price control was instituted in World War II and the Korean conflict and during the inflation of 1971–74. The feasibility of price control is related directly to the prevailing method of price discovery. In general, administered prices are most readily controlled. Where commodity prices are arrived at in spot trading on open markets, price controls are harder to apply. Frequently, therefore, either the controls are confined to processed products as sold at processing and retail, or only markup practices are regulated. The latter is the pass-through device that was used under the Cost of Living Council controls of the early 1970s. In World War II and the Korean conflict, however, some farm products were subjected to firm ceilings.

GOVERNMENT AUTHORIZED GROUP ACTION IN MARKETING. There remains to be reviewed the various kinds of group action in marketing. All come under some form of legal authority and therefore are a part of governmental policy in marketing.

It is not difficult to classify the organizational forms. They are essentially cooperative marketing, collective bargaining, commodity promotion groups, and marketing agreements and orders. A fifth possibility is marketing boards, but they have not been adopted to date in the United States.

It is much harder to describe the functions performed, expressed in the language of this book.

The price discovery function that various kinds of farmers' organizations may undertake is examined in Chapter 5. In line with the message of that chapter, those groups' price discovery activities may substitute for market pricing that has become unacceptable or has disappeared.

In some other respects as well, group action may only fill a gap. It may mainly remedy deficiencies. Nevertheless it would be a benighted judgment to look at group action in marketing in so innocent a way. By and large, group action is sought in order to establish some sort, and some degree, of countervailing power.

Organizational Types. A thumbnail sketch of the major kinds of organizations will be followed by an examination of the functions performed.

AGRICULTURAL MARKETING COOPERATIVES. Farmers' marketing cooperatives are formed under state laws but have the protection of the federal Capper-Volstead Act. Essentially, Capper-Volstead waives certain antitrust statutes. It does not validate actions a cooperative might take that would otherwise be illegal. A number of publications examine the legal aspects of farmers' marketing cooperatives.[10]

Collective bargaining associations differ from marketing cooperatives in that they do not ordinarily take title to commodities or handle them but act as negotiating intermediary between producers and their buyers. A spokesman for the association represents his producer members in the negotiation. There is no one law that authorizes collective bargaining by farmers. Capper-Volstead applies obliquely; the extent of Capper-Volstead authority for bargaining is a moot issue. The Agricultural Fair Practices Act of 1967 sets some of the boundaries for the kind of action a bargaining association might enter into, and it protects it from certain kinds of harassment a marketing firm might use against it.[11]

COMMODITY PROMOTION GROUPS. Before the 1970s, organizations for the advertising and promotion of individual farm commodities were of two types. One category was those funded by voluntary contributions. Some were state and some national. Only a few national groups, as those for meat and wool, operated from a solid financial base. The second category was state commodity groups that obtained authority for "checkoff" funding—deductions made from all sales within the state. Almost always, a proposed activity required a two-thirds vote of producers. Any producer not wishing to contribute usually had the option of requesting a refund.

Later, more authority for funding of national promotion was granted by the Congress. Cotton producers won that permission. For commodities having a market order, or eligible for one, the common device was to add promotional authority to the order (see below).

MARKETING AGREEMENTS AND ORDERS. Marketing agreements and orders are legal instruments by which specified practices can be established and made enforceable for the marketing of a product. The agent for carrying out the terms of an agreement or order is a commercial handler or processor (which may be a cooperative). An agreement is a negotiated contract, binding only on the signatories. An order is more difficult to put in force and it applies to all the marketing sector covered in its terms. An order must be approved by a specified percentage of both producers and handlers, although the requirement for handler approval may be waived by the secretary of agriculture. The secretary himself has considerable authority of surveillance over orders and their administration.

Marketing orders, which are more significant than agreements, might be called enforced cooperation. Only certain powers are available, however, as explained later.

MARKETING BOARDS. Marketing boards have not been used in the United States but are common in Canada, England, Scandinavian countries, some African nations, and elsewhere. They can be powerful agents in marketing. The enabling law for a commodity board usually puts comprehensive powers into the hands of its directors. The powers may extend to not only total control of distribution of a product, but regulation of production. As though to ensure monopoly of action, some marketing board laws provide that all directors can be chosen from producers of the commodity. In other cases the directors must represent diverse interest groups, though producers are ordinarily a majority.

Powers Available and Functions Performed

MARKETING COOPERATIVES AND BARGAINING ASSOCIATIONS. The rationale for farmers' marketing cooperatives has been that they serve producers' interests; they return to the producer the profits in marketing, including those that can be derived from success in producing and merchandising a branded product; and they provide a yardstick of good competition that keeps other firms efficient and honest.

Although some cooperative leaders, notably Aaron Sapiro in the 1920s, dreamed of national cooperatives so big and powerful as to be major power wielders, most attempts to acquire that much size and influence have been unsuccessful.

That is, those attempts were unsuccessful when the cooperative had no allies. The companion structure to cooperatives that has magnified their power has been, above all else, the marketing order.

To some extent, bargaining associations also have fared less well independently than when linked to a marketing order. Certainly in milk marketing the big cooperatives have combined physical service in marketing with bargaining—bargaining for a superpool premium price, but also bargaining in representing members' interests before the administrator of the regional Milk Marketing Order.

On the other hand, a number of independent commodity bargaining associations, particularly in fruits and vegetables, have had

creditable success and some longevity. They find their greatest application when the market is oligopsonistic.

The National Farmers Organization has taken several tacks in
trying to be effective in bargaining. Failing to enlist as large a percentage of producers as had been hoped for, the NFO turned to block
marketing. By arranging for delivery of a specified quantity of a
product, to be assembled from NFO members, the organization has
been able to negotiate for the most advantageous sale. It can do this
successfully only if processors have unused capacity, so that they will
offer a premium price in order that they can utilize their capacity
while idling their competitors'.

The record of bargaining associations in price discovery is
touched on in Chapter 5. We observe there that association representatives have frequently found it necessary to promise, as a condition
for higher prices, conformity to quality standards and delivery terms
sought by the processor. In this respect, collective bargaining contributes to orderly marketing.

COMMODITY PROMOTION. The activities of commodity promotion
groups are almost self-defining. However, they extend far beyond
advertising. Emissaries are sent globe circling to represent clients'
interests with businesses and governments and to captivate consumers
in trade fairs. Technical information is disseminated.

Certain projects of research are funded in connection with promotion.

The drive toward group action in commodity promotion gets its
stimulus from the vigorous merchandising and promotional activities
of marketing firms, notably food processors. Commodity groups have
sought to emulate the practices in the hope of duplicating their apparent success. They do so in disregard of the warnings of most economists that advertising and promotion work best for branded products. Few farm products as sold from the farm carry a brand name.
Also, as various commodity groups get into the act they contend
against each other.

MARKETING ORDERS. Marketing orders are instruments of orderly marketing, of demand expansion through commodity promotion, of demand expansion through stratification of the market, and under some
circumstances of control of quantity of marketings. It is less certain
that they can control quantity of production. For milk alone, the
order provides a price discovery mechanism.

FIG. 7.3. Milk marketing areas under federal orders as of January 1, 1975. (USDA-AMS)

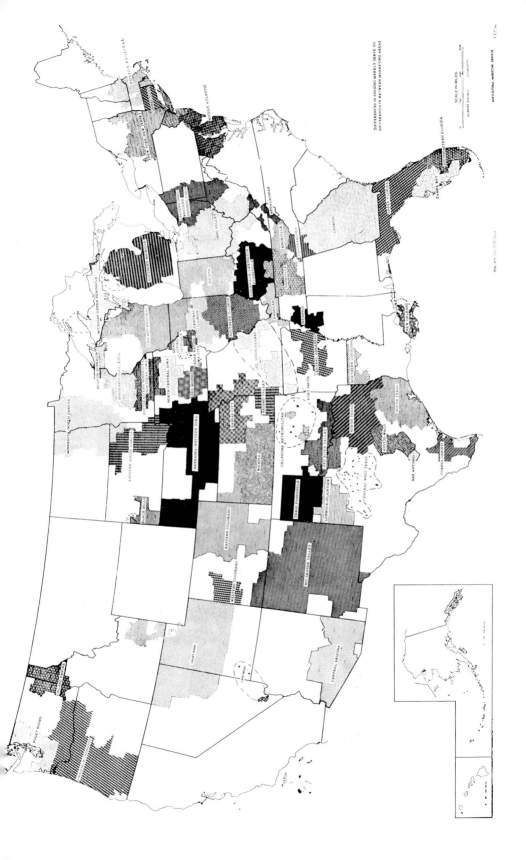

DIFFERENCES IN SHADING MERELY SERVE TO
DIFFERENTIATE BETWEEN MARKETING AREAS

SCALE IN MILES

AGRICULTURAL MARKETING SERVICE

Although it is hazardous to offer a generalized judgment about the consequences of marketing orders, their greatest power probably is attained when they are linked with large cooperatives, or, as in milk, with bargaining activity too. This liaison was referred to above.

More specifically, the authority contained in the enabling legislation for federal orders includes, in addition to the classified pricing for fluid milk, the following:

> Limiting marketings to a certain grade, size, or quality
> Allocating the quantity a handler may purchase or handle for producers
> Designating the quantity that may be marketed during a specified period
> Establishing a reserve pool
> Inspecting a commodity
> Fixing the size of containers used in handling the commodity
> Prohibiting unfair trade practices

To these must now be added, for a number of commodities, the funding of promotion.[12]

Several states have laws authorizing state marketing orders. They have usually concentrated on research and promotion. However, a number of states have set up state milk commissions. Powers vary widely, but in a few instances prices of milk are regulated at successive stages in distribution.

The federal milk marketing order is a mechanism for price discovery. It is also a means for expanding demand by stratification. In any market where a federal order is in force, the milk goes into fluid and processing uses at different prices. There may be only two pricing classes, or three. Usually the pool is marketwide, so that individual producers receive a price for their milk that reflects the market-total division into uses during the specified time period. (See Fig. 7.3.)

Classified pricing is market-expanding because demand for milk for fluid use is more inelastic than that for processing. At least, such a difference has been universally assumed. At any period when the federal government is acquiring manufactured dairy products as a means of price support, there can be no doubt that the manufactured stratum has elastic demand.

A number of fruit, vegetable, and tree nut orders contain a provision that permits certain kinds of market stratification. The process is usually called "diversion of surplus." The surplus may go into export or various alternate domestic uses. At times some nuts have been crushed for oil. Fresh lemons may go into the processing of frozen concentrated juice. Surplus diversion as a form of market stratification came about principally as a stabilizing device to be used in

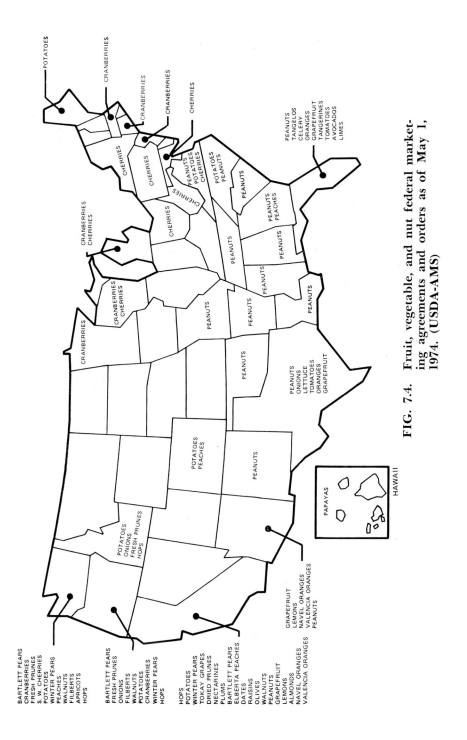

FIG. 7.4. Fruit, vegetable, and nut federal marketing agreements and orders as of May 1, 1974. (USDA-AMS)

years of exceptionally large crops. Annual yields of fruit and tree nut crops can vary sharply while demand is inelastic. Diversion of surplus in big harvest years serves to reduce fluctuations in prices. (See Fig. 7.4.)

Little objection is ever raised to provisions in marketing orders calling for standard grades or standard containers or spacing the shipment rate during a harvest season. The issue that exceeds all others in decibel count of concern is the extent to which the volume of marketings is restricted, thereby increasing prices. Volume can be limited by prohibiting shipment of inferior grades or by surplus diversion. If employed with enough vigor, diversion of surplus can serve not just to stabilize prices from year to year but to lift their average level. In addition, although the federal law does not authorize production control, the order for hops and one or two other crops has contained a provision for market delivery quotas that is at least borderline production control.

During periods of generally depressed prices of farm products, argument subsides about the price effects of marketing orders. During inflation, it resumes. Late in 1974 a special task force was commissioned to investigate the effects of orders on prices, after President Ford promised a review "to eliminate or modify those [orders] responsible for inflated prices." The group's report generally exonerates grade and size regulations from any charge of price enhancement, but it is less reasssuring about quantity control via "producer market allotments" as in hops and Florida celery.[13]

Group Action and the Public Interest. A marketing system or portion thereof is always subject to a goodness test. One such test is that of public interest.

The tone of the treatment of farmers' group action in this chapter has been somewhat sympathetic. Much of that action has an element of countervailing power, but the structure of marketing at processing and retailing contains enough power to justify being countervailed.

Nevertheless, the question arises as to where the balancing point is. A reading of public sentiment taken about 1974–75 would suggest that the largest milk marketing cooperatives had passed the balancing point.

To revert to language presented in Chapters 3 and 4, just as the structure of large business firms allows a wide conduct variable that can result in performance either for or against the public interest, even so do farmers' marketing organizations have options for favorable or unfavorable behavior.

In one respect the public has taken a precautionary measure regarding group action in agriculture that is less prevalent in private corporate business. It has lodged a surveillance obligation, and a virtual veto power, in the hands of government. Under both the Capper-Volstead Act and the Agricultural Marketing Agreement Act the secretary of agriculture is given weighty responsibility. Critics say the assignment is inappropriate, that the secretary is likely to be too friendly toward agricultural interests and too lax in protecting the public interest. They win some credence from the absence of any action taken against cooperatives during the half-century life of Capper-Volstead. But whether fully effective or not, a regulatory power exists and has been used often with respect to marketing orders. A summary judgment would be hard to come by, and none is offered here.

CHAPTER EIGHT

ECONOMICS OF TRANSPORTATION

COST OF TRANSPORT accounts for more than 7 percent of the cost of marketing farm products. Intercity truck and rail transport alone was estimated as 7 percent of the total marketing bill in 1974. Truck transport within cities and the cost of air and water shipping were additional.[1]

The economics of transportation, once an active subject of inquiry, was later almost neglected. Only in the mid-1970s did it begin to recapture economists' and policymakers' attention.

In much regional analysis for agricultural products the cost of transport is frequently assumed to be a linear function of distance. The assumption is invalid. Common carrier transport rates correlate only approximately with distance. The actual rate formula or pattern has much meaning to an economic region. A favorable rate structure can enhance regional development. Unfavorable rates retard it. It is almost as though the exceptions to linear correlation with distance have the most significance to regional analysis.

Bypassing of the economics of transportation is explained in part by the complexity of rate structure for common carriers. A more fundamental reason, however, is the complexity of the basic economics of providing transport services. This takes us back to the complicated economics of the modern large business firm. If in many large businesses a big overhead highly influences costing and pricing, in transportation the situation is magnified. Especially in rail transport does overhead cost dominate rate making.

The principle of large overhead and relatively small controllable variable cost even fits truck transport to some degree. Now that many common carriers guarantee minimum employment to essential employees, a sizable overhead charge is incurred. On the other hand, in an interesting anomaly, public financing of highway construction converts much of the essentially fixed investment in roadbed to a controllable variable cost. Trucks pay a fee for highway use via a fuel tax and a toll on toll roads and bridges. Annual license charges, however, are an overhead cost.

Thus, once again, institutional rules enter into the costing (and pricing) of a marketing service.

The counsel given by David E. Moser in the writing of this chapter is sincerely appreciated.

The high overhead feature of costs in transportation invites stratification of the market. It is easy to stratify transport rates, because transportation is a service. A service, unlike a physical good, cannot be resold. Moreover, the elasticity of demand differs for the various transport services, fulfilling the second requirement for stratification. The heart of the pricing issue in transportation is how much stratification should be engaged in and what form it should take.

Restraints on stratification have arisen more from ethical judgments than from inherent economics. The ethical or value judgment consideration in differential pricing policies raised in Chapter 2 comes into play repeatedly. It takes the form of a legal injunction against an "unduly discriminatory" transport rate structure.

This chapter reviews principles of cost structure and pricing as applied primarily to railroad transportation. The principles fit highway, water, and air transport also, but these other modes are not examined in detail. As in Chapter 3, the time dimensions are the short run and especially the intermediate run. Supposedly, current price and output decisions are made against an obligation to recover all of a firm's costs in the long run. The question could be asked at the mid-1970s whether railroads have set tariffs so low that the "quasi-rent" component of income will not reimburse all overhead costs. Whatever one's judgment, the picture presented in Chapter 3 holds true: in rail and other transport, as in all big business, managers constantly reconcile short- and long-term considerations in kind, quantity, and price of output. It is a never-ending game. It is usually played under conditions of less than full use of capacity.

THE ECONOMICS OF THE FRENCH FOOTBRIDGE. Although the economics of transportation is presented here as an application of the principles of high overhead and low controllable variable costs, historically it was the other way around. The manifest character of the economics of transport helped to direct attention to more generalized situations.

The instance of the French footbridge is so celebrated that it bears full quotation:

> A footbridge is built between two heavily-populated sections of a large city; it cost 150,000 francs; the income from a toll of 0^{fr} .05 a passage is only 5,000 francs; it is a losing proposition, and the entrepreneur who had borrowed most of the 150,000 francs could not pay the interest and was soon ruined. The bridge is bought by an intelligent man who studies the demand and seeks to increase his revenue. He is not allowed to raise his tariff, and neither an increase, nor a decrease, in the toll would raise his income sufficiently; he is obliged, then, to try new means. He notices that his bridge connects a factory district with

an area where the workers live; morning and evening these latter are obliged to make a long detour to get to their destinations. The bridge much reduces the distance, but a sacrifice of 10 centimes a day is much too big, in relation to their wages; if one demanded only 2 centimes, no one would hesitate to procure this satisfaction, and one would obtain thus one thousand new passages a day, which by reason of the tariff of 1 centime, would produce an income of 10 francs a day and 3,000 francs in the 300 workdays of the year. He tries now to get this extra income without reducing that of the 5,000 francs that he gets from the tariff of 0^{fr} .05. It is here that the imagination of the speculator should be exercised, and one will find without a doubt combinations that are better than those I shall propose and which are intended mainly to serve as models.

The proprietor of the bridge might insert into his tariff a clause such as: for the traveler dressed in work cap, blouse and vest, the toll is reduced to 0^{fr} .01. If he thus succeeds in defining satisfactorily the workers whom he wishes to benefit from the reduction, he will receive necessarily an income of 3,000 francs from the new business: but it is very possible that the former income of 5,000 francs may be diminished by some amount, because a certain number of travelers at 0^{fr} .05 will profit due to their costume, by the reduction which was not intended for them: this income might drop to 3,000 francs. The total receipts would be composed thus:

60,000 passages at 0^{fr} .05	3,000^{fr}
40,000 passages at 0^{fr} .01 from former users who escape the former tariff on account of their costume	400
300,000 passages at 0^{fr} .01 from new users	3,000
Total	6,400

One sees that this partial reduction of the tariff does not give the proprietor all that it could; he loses 1,600 francs from former users who profit in spite of him. Well, by new artifices, he can reduce this loss. Thus, he might stipulate that the reduction would apply only in the morning and evening at the hours when the factory opens and closes, or that it would apply only to workers who had identification cards. Whatever the combination adopted, it would raise the income to the extent that it distinguished best the travelers who received different utilities from using the bridge.

Thus the tariff of 0^{fr} .05 would produce	5,000 fr.
the same at 0^{fr} .01	4,000 fr.
And the combination of tolls at 0^{fr} .05 and at 0^{fr} .01 might produce about	8,000 fr.

Thus, depending upon whether you use this or that system of tolls, the bridge would be successful or unsuccessful, it will be profitable or unprofitable to the builder, it will be useful or useless to the public.[2]

COST CALCULATIONS FOR MINIMUM RAILROAD RATES.
The discussion that follows draws heavily on an analysis prepared by

10 of the nation's most distinguished economists,* relating to the nature of cost calculations for minimum railroad rates.[3] The group adopted cost terminology beginning with incremental cost as being the increase in total costs that results from an expansion in a firm's business. The authors note quickly that a very large part of costs in the operation of railroads cannot "be traced and attributed to specific blocks of output."[4] "Fixed costs, which are independent of volume and are not attributable to specific amount of traffic, are an important characteristic of railroad cost structures."[5] The 10 authors then declare their thesis that incremental costs of each particular service shall be a floor to rates charged; and that "it is essential that the burden of fixed costs be spread over as large a volume of traffic as can be developed with attractive rates in excess of the relevant incremental costs."[6] The latter calls for differential (stratified) pricing, which "is consistent with the public interest in the economical utilization of resources."[7]

This practice, in turn, requires taking demand for rail services into account in determining rates. Although the terms are not used in the article, the principle formerly called "charging what the traffic will bear" now converts to the more euphemistic "value of service."

The Baumol group's rationale parallels that of Chapter 3 of this book although the concepts and terms, taken from Interstate Commerce Commission usage, are not exactly the same. It restates the idea that multiple products of a firm must be priced so as to repay all overhead costs over time yet latitude is allowed in adjusting to competitive conditions. A body of transportation economists chooses to emphasize long run marginal cost concepts as a basis for pricing; manifestly, their point of view conflicts with that of the Baumol group and of this book.[8] The latitude allowed includes the opportunity for stratified pricing. The commonsense application has been that a higher rate should be charged for shipping diamonds than gravel.

The Flaw in "Fully Distributed Cost." The principle enunciated by Baumol and his associates will be recognized as a version of full cost pricing. As in all full cost pricing, no universal formula is to be used routinely in distributing costs and setting prices. "There is no single cost formula which will always and automatically be appropriate."[9]

Such a formula has in fact been proposed. It is called "fully distributed cost." It would allocate all overhead costs by a rigid statistical formula, without consideration of the competitive situation for individual products or services. It could be regarded as an example of full costing. It would be a bad example, because of its rigidity. Full costing is flexible. Baumol and his coauthors say directly, "the fully distributed cost doctrine does not reflect valid principles of pricing where fixed costs are significant."[10]

The summary of the group's analysis merits repetition:

*The distinguished composition of the group did not inhibit dissent. Cf., *J. Business* 36(1963): 336–47.

SUMMARY

1. In the determination of cost floors as a guide to the pricing of particular railroad services, or the services of any other transport mode, incremental costs of each particular service are the only relevant costs.

2. Rates for particular railroad services should be set at such amounts (subject to regulation of maximum rates and to legal rules against unjust discrimination) as will make the greatest total contribution to net income. Clearly, such maximizing rates would never fall below incremental costs.

3. Pricing which is not restricted by any minimum other than incremental cost can foster more efficient use of railroad resources and capacity and can therefore encourage lower costs and rates. This same principle applies to other modes of transportation.

4. The presence of large amounts of fixed costs and unused capacity in railroad facilities makes it especially important that railroad rates encourage a large volume of traffic.

5. Reduced rates which more than cover incremental costs and are designed by management to maximize contribution to net income do not constitute proof of predatory competition.

6. "Fully distributed" costs derived by apportioning unallocable costs have no economic significance in determining rate floors for particular railroad services. The application of such a criterion would arbitrarily force the railroads to maintain rates above the level which would yield maximum contribution to net income and would deprive them of much traffic for which they can compete economically. For similar reasons, restriction of railroad minimum rates according to the "full cost of the low-cost carrier" is economically unsound.[11]

The Unjust Discrimination Prohibition. In the second of their summary recommendations, Baumol and his associates acknowledge the rule against unfair discrimination. As judged by older connotations this is a contradiction of terms. Traditionally, discrimination has been regarded as undemocratic.

Yet the Interstate Commerce Act at one and the same time endorses discriminatory pricing and enjoins unjust discrimination. The value laden adjectives used so often to describe acceptable rates are "just and reasonable." The just and reasonable test must be applied not only to rates charged by railroads, but also to those of regulated motor carriers, barge lines, and freight forwarders.

In considering how to define just and reasonable, it helps to recall that the Interstate Commerce Act came into being primarily to correct the highly discriminatory, personalized concessions in railroad rates that had previously existed. It was enacted at a time of "robber barons" in the newly expanding U.S. industry. The Rockefellers and Hills and others played vicious games of reciprocal concessions. The consequences were favorable to the companies and the areas that benefited but devastating to all others.

Lauth and Heitz report that the Interstate Commerce Act "prohibits the railroads from the giving of undue or unreasonable preference or advantage, [or] subjecting others to undue or unreasonable prejudice or disadvantage. . . . Not only is preference and prejudice prohibited as to persons and corporations, but also as to associations, localities, ports or port districts, gateways, transit points, regions, territories or any particular description of traffic."[12]

The test of what is unjustly discriminatory also takes into account the nature and extent of competition with other modes of transport. However, this precept is complicated by the further principle that the rate structure shall "be administered so as to recognize and preserve the inherent advantages of each mode. . . ."[13] This means that rates charged by one mode (as railroads) shall not be designed so as to displace another mode (as barges) in a transport service for which the latter is regarded as the more suitable.

THE INTRICATE FABRIC OF RAILROAD FREIGHT RATE STRUCTURE. Although there is no reason to doubt that regulatory commissions try to act against unjust discrimination, the mechanics of the rate structure and rate making complicate their task exceedingly.

The complexity arises in part from the principle of discriminatory pricing itself. That principle allows a wide range of choice in setting "value of service" rates (or "what the traffic will bear"), without transgressing into the zone of unjust or unreasonable rates. The fact that the U.S. system consists of many private rail lines is another complicating factor.* Not only does the degree of competition among lines vary by product and by area, but rate schedules take into account "local" versus "joint," "proportional," and "combination" rates. Local rates apply over the lines of one carrier only. A joint rate involves two or more carriers, and proportional and combination rates may do so.

Further contributing to the prolix situation is the rate making procedure itself. The Interstate Commerce Commission does not itself set rates—though it may influence them considerably by the terms of what rates it denies. It does not even regularly examine and evaluate all rates. Although it is empowered to initiate investigations, for the most part it acts as an appeal board. Protests usually arise from either a shipper who is affected by a particular (higher) rate, or a competing carrier (or mode) that believes itself injured (by a lower rate). Some other third parties also are eligible to protest. For example, the secretary of agriculture has an obligation to review freight

*Developments during the 1970s are reducing the number.

rates on agricultural products, and a right to protest any rates or proposed rates that he believes to be inimical to the interests of agriculture.

For many products, railroad freight rates are quoted by classes (each class comprises a group of similar products). However, a number of important products, particularly raw materials, are granted special commodity rates. Most farm products move under commodity rates. These are usually lower than class rates.

The competitive consequences of the minutiae of railroad rates are far-reaching. Even small differences in rates can affect the economy of regions. For years, livestock and poultry farmers of the northeastern states have complained that freight rates on feed shipped to them do not match the concessions the Southern Railway among others has been able to provide the southeastern states. Comparative rates on raw versus processed products influence the location of processing. An example is relative rates on live animals versus meat shipped from the Midwest to the West Coast. These control the viability of much of the western meat packing industry. Closely akin is the issue of in-transit privileges. Historically, rates for shipment of a product such as grain permitted stopping the shipment at some intermediate point for processing (in the case of grain, for milling). In general, the trend has been to eliminate such privileges and to levy separate charges for individual services. Each such change helps some enterprise or area and hurts some other one. Moreover, it is often difficult to show conclusively which change improves or reduces the efficiency of the system as a whole.

TRUCK TRANSPORT. Transportation policy is no less complicated for truck than for other transportation. It may offer as much opportunity for selective determination of transport rates and therefore for just or unjust discrimination.

From the standpoint of regulatory laws, truck transport ranges from interstate common carriers which are regulated in a manner similar to the railroads, to farm trucks, which are scarcely regulated at all (except as to limits for retaining the classification).

One school of thought has declared that the cost structure for truck transportation, unlike rail, consists principally of controllable variable costs. Therefore, the argument goes, regulation is not necessary and may even be harmful.

No effort will be made here to resolve the issue. However, two counter arguments can be offered. One is that if unregulated motor trucks, in their competition with railroads, were to "skim the cream" of the freight traffic, leaving the railroads with all the less profitable hauls, the result could be to jeopardize the survivability of the rail-

roads without themselves providing an equivalent substitute service.*
The second and more intriguing argument opens up the issue of fixed
(overhead) costs. Truck, like railroad, transport involves the huge
overhead cost of a roadbed. The difference is that for trucks the public at large pays the basic cost. In the nature of the case the public
sets the terms of access to its highways. In this respect, any idea of
"free competition" in trucking is ill phrased.[14]

The proportion of controllable variable cost in truck transport
has declined as union labor contracts have increasingly called for
guaranteed employment. Although the "real" cost of a truck driver
may be confined to the time he is on the highway (plus servicing),
the financial cost is represented by his guaranteed wage, which is an
overhead cost.[15]

The economics of truck transport takes on another meaning
where a firm maintains a fleet of vehicles to transport its own products. Reportedly, flexibility of service can be an attraction. In this
respect, truck transport differs from rail, for although a few marketing
firms own rail freight cars none owns a railroad.

Truck transport as an internal division of a firm presents a problem no different from any other internal service. However, a number
of firms have learned how large a fixed (overhead) cost is in fact involved in truck transportation. The problem lies in synchronizing
the utilization of truck equipment with other physical operations of
the firm. Rather frequently, the synchronization proves so imperfect
that this kind of vertical integration is found financially impractical.
Some firms that set up their own trucking division later dispensed
with it. (Some others found that the burden of carrying a trucking
division was an incentive to merge with another firm, so as to enlarge
the shipping volume.)

SUMMARY AND EVALUATION. This brief review only opens up
the economic issues in the transportation of farm products. No de-
finitive interpretation is attempted. The principal message is to declare how much economic power lies in the hands of those who make
transport rates. The power arises from the high component of overhead costs in the transport cost structure (including much truck transport) which permits differential pricing in rates.

This awesome power is divided between transport companies
and the regulatory agencies of government. However, a larger share
than generally assumed rests with the former.

*A parallel is seen in the United Parcel Service, which skims the cream of the
package delivery business and leaves service to out-of-the-way places to the U.S.
Postal Service. A case can be made persuasively that where a natural-monopoly
public utility is involved, private appropriation of an attractive portion of the
service should not be permitted.

It hardly need be added that the potential consequences of rate making policy are heightened by virtue of the inelasticity of the demand for transport in the marketing of farm products.

If this chapter had been written from the standpoint of the regulatory agencies and public policy making, much more would have been said about regional discrimination (just or unjust) and how it can amount to determining whether a particular area or community receives, or is denied, access to common carrier freight service. Service can be denied by discontinuing spur line rail freight, for example, if no equivalent substitute is available. Denial of service is about the same thing as a limiting case of discriminatory pricing. In the melee of transport service and pricing foreordained for the later 1970s, public responsibility for assuring common carrier service may be as contentious as transport rate levels.[16] No area wants to be left without service.

Regional aspects of transport service and rates blend into the regional pattern of competition in marketing, which is the subject of the next chapter. Moreover, alleged preferences by region have been about the touchiest charge made of unjust discrimination.

It is timely to ask just what the regional competition record has been. It would be hard to sum up critical studies and probably would be inconclusive, too. Nevertheless, there is reason to doubt that freight transport rates have been carefully tooled to preserve something close to an idealized regional competitive structure in the marketing of agricultural products. The author's observation when he was directly involved in freight rate review was that most proposals to reduce preexisting rates received a favorable hearing irrespective of what competitive distortions would result. Only the most flagrantly violative cases were disallowed. An instance was entire-train rates for grain, which, though favorably publicized, were highly selective as to which shippers and which carriers could effectively use them. They probably were highly prejudicial against average sized shippers including the vast majority of farmer cooperatives. And because the shippers and carriers that could exploit entire-train rates served only certain regions, the rate decision (approval) selectively helped certain regions and selectively injured others.

Finally, this section on the economics of transportation gives dramatic emphasis to a theme that emerges at various points in this book. It is that the cost structure of nearly all modern industry including the processing and distribution of farm products offers opportunity for discriminatory pricing. Transportation is only an extreme example. Price discrimination, if applied with discretion, does not justify its cloudy connotations of the past, but if applied imprudently or with outright favoritism it fully merits the prohibition of "unjust discrimination" written so firmly into the Interstate Commerce Act.

CHAPTER NINE

LOCATION OF MARKETING ENTERPRISE AND COMPETITIVE STRUCTURE

S C A R C E L Y any part of the economics of the marketing of agricultural products is as fascinating as that of the location of enterprise. Scarcely any part has been as neglected.

Reduced to its simplest elements, marketing of the products of agriculture consists of progressive reduction of their bulk and perishability coincident with locational concentration, followed by progressive elaboration and attaching of services accompanied by locational dispersion. In simplest analogy it is a case of successive funneling, first in one direction and then in the other.

Both the original production and the final consumption are dispersed geographically. There are wide ranges of choices as to where the several physical operations of assembly, processing, and distribution are to take place. In many respects the economics of the marketing of the products of agriculture is the economics of geography.

But marketing economics is also the economics of competitive structure and performance, as is emphasized so often in other chapters. Competitive structure, in turn, is affected materially by the internal economics of the firm; and competitive performance reflects the managerial latitude in business conduct. It is important to examine the economics of location alongside the economics of competitive structure and associated performance. They are intimately interconnected. Such is the theme of this chapter.*

The original writing on the subject of enterprise location in agriculture was von Thünen's *Der isolierte Staat*.[1] Not only was it the foundation of location theory, but it has been credited with initiating the entire discipline of agricultural economics. Von Thünen's demonstration of zones or rings of enterprises surrounding a central city on a flat plain is noteworthy for its originality in its time. However, it is also noteworthy for omitting all consideration of competitive structure of enterprise.

Katzman notes this deficiency and strikes a contrast between the

*A much more developed treatment of some of the points made in this chapter may be found in Raymond G. Bressler, Jr., and Richard A. King, *Markets, Prices, and Interregional Trade* (New York: Wiley, 1970). See note 5 for other references on location theory.

"von Thünen paradigm" and the "urban-industrial hypothesis."[2] He embraces under the latter the count of enterprises in a market center, scale of enterprise, and cost of transportation. The same factors will be developed in this chapter. In effect, the industrial-urban hypothesis is applied to rural areas—or to all territory.

More specifically, the analysis that follows builds upon three basic principles. These are:

1. Locational advantage. No area is homogeneous, and within any area there are places that afford some degree of locational advantage to each kind of enterprise. The advantage may be
   a. Natural
   b. Institutional
   A natural advantage can take many forms—climate, waterway, access to fuel. Institutional advantages may be in transport tariffs, tax rates, or external economies that arise when businesses cluster.
2. Economy of scale. The greater the economy of scale relative to locational advantage, the greater is the probability of local monopoly or monopsony. The less the relative economy of scale, the greater will be the number of firms in a single location.
3. Cost of transport. Transport cost is obviously a function of distance, terrain, technology, cost of the resources used, and economy of scale in providing transportation. It is affected by various technological developments not only in transportation services but in product. Processing that reduces bulk cuts transport cost. So does improved packaging, and producing a more transportable product —as tomatoes with thick skins. On the other hand, requirements such as for refrigeration increase cost.

   Cost of transport is also affected by actions of public and private bodies to regulate costs. This last piece of the puzzle is ambiguous, but it probably classifies best as an institutional factor in the economics of location. We thus preserve the idea that the fundamental cost of transport is built in, native to the regional location problem.

To give this interpretation of location economics one further theoretical underpinning, the scheme of divisibility and mobility of factors of production may be recalled. It is presented near the end of Chapter 1. If all factors were perfectly divisible and mobile, all enterprises would be close to consumers and perfectly attuned to their individual wishes. Factors are not perfectly divisible—they show scale economy. They are not perfectly mobile—transport has a cost. The economics of the marketing of farm products is, from this analytical point of view, a matter of how indivisibility and immobility are counteracted and reconciled.

The process of reconciliation cannot be divorced from the devices dreamed up by men, individually and collectively. Hence the institutional element, put as 1.a in the above outline. The review of transportation economics in Chapter 8 shows how wide is the range of arbitrary choice in how transport is priced. Transport costs are by no means a linear function of distance. Not only are there long-haul, short-haul modulations, but the mosaic of rail and truck freight rates almost demolishes any simple principles of transport cost proportional to distance. It almost seems as though transportation rate makers have tried to convert industrial location into a function not of geography but of their expertise in juggling a "value of service"-determined rate structure.

Lest the exceptions be overemphasized, it must be admitted that in comparisons of long with short distances where a single mode is available (as railroads), cost of transport is approximately correlated with distance. But even so, small departures from linear relationships can be crucial to particular enterprises and particular communities—favorable or unfavorable as the case may be. The economic livelihood of a given place may trace to modest concessions received in transport rates.

It would be easy to load this review with a listing of other complications. The more complex any processing or servicing in marketing, the more difficult it is to determine what the basic locational factors are. The larger the role merchandising plays in the value of a product, the less controlling, we might suppose, are locational factors. Yet even this commonsense observation does not apply too well. Some firms that rely heavily on brand naming and promotion are circumspect in the location of their processing plants and distribution centers. The admitted complications nevertheless do not invalidate the basic analysis offered in pages that follow.

BASIC FACTORS IN LOCATIONAL ADVANTAGE. A common practice in studies of location of enterprise has been to classify enterprises into those for which location is raw-material oriented, market oriented, labor oriented, or otherwise largely predetermined by a single factor. Cheapness of transport and ingenuity in manipulating transport rates have reduced to some degree the applicability of this rather ingenuous approach. It nevertheless is instructive to begin by noting instances of a high degree of gravitational pull upon enterprise location. It can be exerted on the procurement side of a business, the distributional side, or both. In the processing of farm products perishability probably overrides all else. Fruits and vegetables for processing must often be processed close to where they are produced. This is true for tomatoes, for example. They must be canned within a few miles of where they are harvested.

A few foods require processing close to the location of consumers. At one time this was an invariable rule for fresh milk and for frozen products such as ice cream. Refrigerated truck transport has loosened the locational grip of consumer location, though it has not eliminated it entirely. Fresh baked goods probably qualify as the best example of a product that must be produced close to the homes of consumers.

Also, almost an axiom is that any processing of raw material that greatly reduces bulk is usually done at a location close to its original production.

Adding many services to a consumer product, however, orients toward the location of the labor supply or of the market. For most foods and other farm products the two are nearly the same. The ultimate in the service component is retail distribution, which has high, though not absolute, locational orientation toward the consuming population.

GEOGRAPHICAL DIFFERENTIATION OF HOMOGENEOUS PRODUCTS. It is almost always easiest, pedagogically, to begin with the geography of handling homogeneous products. This amounts to taking a single kind of differentiation into account at a time. Geography is a differentiating factor.

Two general conditions are to be assumed. One is that for every marketing operation there is some locational pull. This is a pull toward a particular location that can be weighed against the transport costs of assembly of raw materials and/or delivery (eventually, dispersion) of product. The balance between these two forces may be called the centralization factor. The second condition is that for every operation there is some degree of economy of scale. These conditions are a way of saying that there is less than perfect mobility and divisibility.

The General Rule for Homogeneous Products. *If the centralization factor exceeds economy of scale, two or more similar enterprises will be located at the favorable location.* If centralization exceeds scale economy substantially, the conditions are best for perfect competition.

If the centralization factor is less than economy of scale, there will be only one enterprise at each center. A notably weak tendency toward locational centralization combined with high economy of scale virtually makes anything close to perfect competition impossible.

Meat Packing as Illustration. The meat packing industry affords an illustration. At one time a strong centralizing pull drew the meat packing industry of the Midwest toward Chicago. The two most important factors favoring Chicago were an abundance of low-wage labor and a transportation system built to accommodate the city. It was the railroad era, when rail lines extended radially from large cities. As there is no great economy of scale in meat packing, the result was for a number of plants to coinhabit the Windy City.

Later, union wages reduced the labor advantage of the city while truck transport on improved highways recast transport. Meanwhile, new technology scarcely changed economy of scale in meat packing—though the shift from steam to electric power may have reduced it somewhat. The result is that meat packing plants are now scattered over the livestock producing areas. In some cities such as Omaha and Kansas City there is a small cluster of plants, but for the most part meat packing is now widely dispersed.

It is worth noting that the farmers who sell to meat packers are themselves more mobile than in the pre-Chicago era of a century ago. Nevertheless, the meat packing industry has in some respects gone through a complete cycle—from local butchers to big-city slaughterers and now back to local slaughterers.

The era of centralized meat packing may have been the time when the U.S. economy came closest to perfect competition. When improved transport first allowed a number of manufacturing firms to assemble in favored locations—and scale economies in very large plants were not yet stressed so much—a number of processing and distribution centers presented a competition that came reasonably close to fitting the perfect-competition model. Moreover, at that time differentiation of product was not pursued so avidly as it is today.

Imperfection in Early Markets. Prior to the time when new transport permitted clustering in cities, competition was far from perfect. Like the appealing doctrine of the Noble Savage, the notion that the early industrial economy of small businesses was competitively virtuous will not withstand scrutiny.

The best geometric analogy of the locational pattern in earlier times is a honeycomb structure (Fig. 9.1). Each cell was more or less independent. In each was a trade center. Although it might have had several grocery stores and other service businesses, the chances are it would have had only one or two butter or cheese plants, livestock slaughterers, or grain millers.

This is the competitive structure of local monopsony or oligopsony. Katzman makes the same point when he notes "market imper-

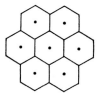

FIG. 9.1. Honeycomb of enterprise location under decentralization.

fections associated with monopoly and monopsony in rural areas dominated by small towns."[3]

Honeycombed Oligopsony and the Geography of Price. As a generalized pattern the honeycomb is less common now than previously, but it is far from absent. Local monopsonies or oligopsonies still exist in marketing or processing various farm products. They are to be found in grain elevators, local livestock slaughterers, poultry processors, and fruit and vegetable canning or freezing.

The geometry of a honeycomb controls the quality of competition and the geographic pattern of price. Competitive forces are of course present, but they show up strongest not at the center but at the fringe of each cell. Competition is keenest at the borders between trade territories.

That is to say, producers of agricultural products find that the degree of competitiveness among potential buyers of their products depends on their own location within the cells. A producer situated close to the center is disadvantaged. One living near the intersection of three trade territories is most likely to have the benefit of competitive bidding for his product.

Locational patterns of this kind induce various kinds of arrangements in freight absorption. The outlying supplier may in effect be excused from the consequence of his remoteness, because several firms compete to buy his product.

In a Missouri study of pricing of milk for manufacturing, De-Haven found haulage charges to be essentially uniform irrespective of the distance of a farmer from the milk plant.[4] Competitive concessions at the fringe took the form of hauling-cost absorption.

It is worth noting that if an outlying producer were up against a mountain range with no competitive buyers located beyond him, he would have no protection against paying all costs of transportation himself.

Scale Economy and Transport Costs. As noted above there has been almost a historical race between increase in economy of scale and improvement in transport. Transport first won. It particularly won in a fashion that increased centralization in location of industry. That was the time when railroads grew, and they, like the lines to and from Chicago, led to the new big cities. As industrial and commercial operations had not yet expanded so much, competition in urban centers was sharpened.

But if improved transport of the early industrial era brought more businesses into close competitive touch, the merger movement since has probably done the opposite. For various nearly homogeneous products, there are many instances not only of local oligopsony but of large regional cells with restricted competition within each one. Milk processing, for example, gives evidence of being organized as oligopolies/oligopsonies serving very large territories.

LOCALIZATION FOR DIFFERENTIATED PRODUCTS. To

summarize thus far, the economics of location of enterprise may be capsuled as a contest between forces of centralization as aided or hindered by cost of transport, and of economy of size or scale. However, for purposes of our study the greater meaning is not to the locational outcome as such but to the effect on the fabric of competition. An axiom of long standing is that marked economy of scale makes competition imperfect (oligopolistic). It has been pointed out in this chapter that forces of locational centralization work against economy of scale, in the direction of making competition more nearly perfect. But decentralization adds to imperfection.

These summary comments fit homogeneous product best. Product differentiation introduces a new element, as was pointed out before. It is a complicating element; but mainly product differentiation can work to offset locational advantages. Or, since location is itself a differentiating factor, we can say that differentiation of product can interfere with, reduce, and perhaps almost replace differentiation by geography.

Clearly, differentiation becomes an influential factor only at the stage at which, or past which, differentiation takes place. Kellogg's cereals, for example, are a differentiated product. The procurement of grain, a homogeneous product, conforms to appropriate locational principles. In selling its cereals, Kellogg strives for no locational differentiation, relying entirely on its product differentiation to win its market.

The example offered by Hotelling fits (see page 71). If a firm (such as Kellogg) belives its product can stand up in direct competition with competitors, the firm will not hesitate to locate at the spot that appears most advantageous for marketwide saturation. On the other hand, if the firm is timid and insecure it will seek a different location where it can get some geographical differentiation, albeit over a much smaller territory. In other words, the latter firm will add some geographic differentiation to its product differentiation.

LOCATION OF RETAILERS. The examples that have been cited have been selected mainly from food processing. Principles of the economics of location in retailing are no different from those that govern the location of processors. However, they take on a somewhat different application. Geographical location is always a differentiating factor of importance. In urban areas it applies almost solely to retailers' location in relation to consumers and scarcely at all to their procurement practices. In rural districts, however, location of a grocery may be affected significantly by the economics of procurement. Independent rural grocers who have depended on itinerant wholesalers have been hard pressed. They need badly to be stationed where they can have access to a good wholesale supply source.

The urban supermarket introduced scale economy into retailing, though the advantages of extraordinary size are nearly confined to the wide range of assortment it makes possible. Because of their large size, supermarkets tend to scatter except in densest urban areas. Each enjoys a small portion of oligopoly status.

Establishments that provide a sharply differentiated service, on the other hand, are most concerned for location relative to other stores of the same category. The small quick service shops that remain open long hours exist under the shadow of supermarkets, and they themselves scatter.

As retail food stores conform to the pattern of the honeycomb with local oligopoly, even though the accompanying power is usually gentle,* a question may arise as to competitiveness at the fringes of areas. The principle of sharper competition at the border applies. Some years ago, when grocers provided home delivery service, the grocer absorbed the extra cost of reaching his more distant customers. But when supermarkets came on the scene, housewives were induced to drive their station wagons to the brightly lighted food emporiums. In doing so they themselves absorb the cost of distributional transport. Obviously, those living most distant from the stores absorb the most cost. Those same outlying customers, however, are more likely to be equidistant from several stores. They therefore become the agents of arbitrage to keep locally oligopolistic retailers' prices approximately in line. The geometry of the honeycomb still fits.

*Their touch may not be so light in central cities or in rural areas.

RISING COST OF TRANSPORTATION. As this text was being written a sharp upsurge in transportation cost was being witnessed and felt. Prospects are for transport costs to be relatively higher in the future than in the past. If this proves to be the case, a considerable reshuffling of enterprise location can be expected. To the extent it occurs, the quality of competition will again be altered.

It seems unlikely that economy of scale in marketing enterprises will change very much. Therefore the net consequence will be to create pressure for some decentralization in enterprise location.

Much will depend, to be sure, on the relative degree of cost increase among various modes of transport and various classes of traffic. Nevertheless, the generalized outcome is likely to be a trend toward decentralization.

From 1950 to the early 1970s, the cost of transporting farm products and food, per ton mile, relative to value was probably the lowest in history. If it can be assumed that the transport rate system was in fact virtually free of unfair discriminiation, the advantage of location was maximized, or disadvantage minimized. Even though the assumption is too heroic, to the extent it is valid the situation favored operational efficiency and a higher degree of competition among marketing firms. By any test, higher transport costs in the future will be a retrogression.

A few inferences can be drawn. On balance, the prospect of a net effect toward decentralization can hardly be challenged. Industries that have depended on long-distance movement of bulky products, such as fresh fluid milk and manufactured feedstuffs, will be highly vulnerable. Some of the apparent advantage of economy of scale of large milk processing plants may vanish when higher costs of long distance procurement and distribution are taken into account.

Not all adjustments will be confined to relocation of enterprise. In milk, the principal effect might be to shift toward concentrated products instead of shipping immense tonnages of the water content of milk across large areas of the country. Public transit (as rail) may be used more, and new efficiencies in rail transport might be brought into use.

Because transport will be more costly, the system of rate making will attract more critical attention. Public bodies that escape public scrutiny when costs are low can find themselves under a giant lens when costs rise.

The net effect on competition will be to increase regional protection against sharp competition: regional differentiation will grow. This general statement applies best to homogeneous products. To the extent products are distributed regionally or nationally on the basis of product differentiation, moderate rises in transport costs will have somewhat less effect. Those products will continue to fight for a share of a big market on the basis of their own distinguishing features and are less likely to retreat to the shelter of geographic area boundaries.[5]

CHAPTER TEN

MARKETING IN ECONOMIC DEVELOPMENT

T H I S   C H A P T E R is added in respectful recognition of the
fact that "marketing in economic development" is commonly regarded
as a special subject. Much literature has been published under that
title. The writings draw largely on experiences in lower income
countries of the world.

Yet in a larger sense the economics of marketing always involves
the idea of development. Every nation seeks to correct past deficiencies and to make forward progress. Individual firms likewise have as-
pirations for improvement and for growth.

In comparisons of agricultural marketing systems among higher
and lower income countries of the world, differences are more of degree than of kind.

Because the conventional approach to development is accepted,
this chapter will shift approach and vocabulary from what has been
presented in preceding chapters. It will not be in conflict, however.

The text that follows is abstracted from another publication of
the author. It particularly focuses on the institutions for marketing
agricultural products in less developed countries.[1]

THE COMMON DENOMINATOR. Some elements in the role of
product markets in agricultural development can be generalized from
nation to nation. A great many cannot. But one generalized starting
point seems almost unchallengeable. It is that economic development
universally involves attaining more specialization in economic enterprise than prevails in primitive economies.

Specialization is often thought of in terms of Adam Smith's pin
making. It is more complicated than that. Belshaw calls it "differentiation of role."[2] It includes specialization in both technical process
and administrative direction (management).

It is both horizontal and vertical. It can apply to any of the
functions performed at each of the steps or stages in the marketing
system, as outlined in early chapters of this book.

As the degree of specialization increases the question of how to

The major assistance of William J. Staub in the writing of this chapter is grate-
fully acknowledged.

connect the individual parts comes to the fore. It is a question of the mechanism for interrelating or linking them. In the language of this text, it is a question of the structural organization of the market as it bears on the operational and coordinational missions of a marketing system.

As explained in Chapter 1, the historical trend was to move first toward more decomposition or disintegration, as specialization of process was accompanied by specialization of business enterprise. The trend is still underway in some less developed countries. As it proceeds a market exchange system usually grows in scope and importance.

But market exchange is not the only possible system. Nor do enterprises have to remain atomistic. Chapter 1 describes the reintegration taking place during the fourth epoch in developed nations, where a market exchange system is no longer relied on so much. In other countries also, organizational systems other than market exchange may be employed.

Use of the historical-epoch model in examining the economics of development has the weakness of implying that any nation moves progressively and uniformly from period to period. Seldom does development take place in this manner. In almost any country at any given time there exists a mixture of marketing systems. Some may be almost primitive. A few may be ultramodern. There usually are instances of coexistence of several levels of marketing development.[3]

Nevertheless, in many developing nations of the world today the marketing system for farm products tends to fall roughly in epochs two and three as defined in Chapter 1. It will be remembered that, in the language of the dual missions of marketing, those two epochs differ less in the delivery of product than in the coordinative or control mechanism.

It is therefore particularly instructive to examine the marketing system of developing nations with separate regard for the distributive or delivery methods and the coordinative mechanism. For the latter purpose a price oriented market exchange system will often be relied upon, but not always. Governmental control, for example, may enter into pricing or other marketing activities.

Authors who have studied market development tend to fall into two camps as to which aspect of the marketing mission they emphasize. Among those who stress the coordinative mission is Abbott, who writes about shortcomings in various developing nations in getting incentives back to farmers.[4] Schultz, likewise, has long been concerned with the form and adequacy of a system of incentives.[5]

ANOTHER DUALITY: PHYSICAL INFRASTRUCTURE AND INSTITUTIONS. Any system of marketing, including market exchange, invariably embraces both the necessary physical facilities, including a network of transport, and the supporting institutional structure.* On this pairing of requirements also, individual writers tend to show partiality. Some give much attention to the inadequacy of storage, of wholesale market facilities, of highways, of other infrastructure. Others stoutly defend the crucial role of institutions, reporting various instances of institutional shortcomings. They also proclaim a psychological handicap to their homiletics. Human beings, they say, have a psychic preference for dealing with material things rather than comparatively ephemeral institutions.

Collins and Holton, for example, declare that development plans typically "call for improved distribution facilities . . . [when] more often the really critical need is a change in the organization and operation of the distributive sector. . ." Further, "materials are notably more malleable than men. . . ."[6]

The contest is easily resolved by once again separating what can be generalized from what cannot. Both infrastructure and well-designed institutions are essential to a good system of marketing. In a given case, the greater deficiency and more pressing need may be for a certain infrastructure. But if institutions are deficient, their improvement may take priority. Not infrequently the two will be inseparable and equal: new public commercial warehouses, to be fully useful, will likely require (1) an inspection service to assure integrity and (2) lending practices by banks that accept warehouse receipts as collateral. All these become empirical questions, resolvable only in terms of specified place and time. To try to calibrate globally is pointless. The actual situation at any place and time is what counts.

THE SOCIOCULTURAL SETTING. As though to complicate the marketing question even further, no system exists *in vacuo*. It is embedded in the political and social system of any community or nation. For example, Polanyi argues, as expressed in Shaffer's paraphrase, that "the liberal state was a creation of the self-adjusting market and the key to the institutional system of the nineteenth century lay in the laws governing the market economy."[7]

Kriesberg reminded a 1970 seminar on the marketing challenge in developing nations that the marketing system has to serve the needs

---

*Market institutions are considered here to encompass all the practices and arrangements under which marketing is done, ranging from entrepreneurship to restrictive or supporting laws. Some writers on economic development would include custom, convention, even taboos and folklore.

of producers but it must also make certain that gains in production are widely shared, in the interest of social stability. Taking note of the "critical issue" of "equity in the distribution of the goods of a more productive economy," Kriesberg adds, "Food is so basic that a political (as well as moral) case can be made for . . . [improved] distribution. . . ."[8]

These enlightened or even idealized comments bring joltingly to mind the circumstances that prevail in many communities of developing nations. The all too common situation and its implications are described by Myrdal in powerful language:

> In a stagnant community, with low levels of living and education, which has inherited a rigid and inegalitarian social and economic structure, the difficulties of building up institutions for self-government, collective bargaining, and cooperation are immense. The fundamentally different problem facing the state in under-developed countries is that it will have to plan to build up such institutions.[9]

Breimyer calls attention to the crude economics of the most primitive circumstances, where "demand schedules are practically nonexistent," and it is "doubtful that any system approaching a free market would be permitted."[10]

When a system of production and marketing becomes more specialized, it becomes more dependent upon a stable and culturally advanced community. A market exchange economy probably can work well only if the population is relatively literate, distribution of wealth is not too uneven, traditions of the citizens are conducive to responsible individual performance within a large organization, and central government is capable and enterprising.

The counterpart conclusion is that unless the social and political structure is reasonably advanced the marketing system cannot develop greatly.

The contrasts between simple and more complex exchange systems can be set forth in terms of the complementary services that are necessary. When a *campesino* takes his produce to a village market aud himself sells it to a local buyer, the transaction needs only simple supporting services other than police protection against brigands. If he instead ships corn to a distant market, perhaps for storage pending sale later, he relies on a complicated institutional system. He depends not only on the integrity of each transaction, but on the efficiency of a price-making mechanism. The latter seldom can be assured unless central government provides basic services, including restraining syndicates or monopolies from obstructing competitive trading.

Usually, the ambience for market institutions is to be appraised not in absolute terms but as a matter of degree. If a system approximating market exchange is to be established, it must be sufficiently competitive and efficient that no grave injustice is likely to be done. The concept of workable or effective competition described in Chapter 4 can be applied to developing economies.

If satisfactory private market institutions cannot be established, the only recourses are to keep the market system simple, at the cost of retarded development, or to rely more on central government. The second is realistic if the institution of government is itself reasonably dependable.

THE ISSUE OF CHOOSING PRIORITIES. In any program for development one operational question invariably arises: As it is not possible to move forward on all fronts simultaneously, which are to be chosen for priority? In most situations it is necessary to move ahead first on certain carefully selected ones—the concept of leading thrusts. Moreover, a survey of the existing situation may reveal some glaring deficiencies that call for priority of attention. But finally, one returns to the principle that development must eventually involve many aspects of an economy.*

Further, this simple axiom needs emphasis if only because it happens so often that individuals and organizations that offer advice on how to inaugurate or speed development reveal a kind of professional favoritism. This is true of both native officials and technical aid specialists of outside countries, including those from the United States. The soil scientists want to add nitrogen to soils; the conservationists seek to build dams; the retail trade specialist offers to cover the place with supermarkets; and the conventional farm marketing man hurries to establish a market news service and build a grain storage elevator. Indulging one's own competency is one of the human hazards of counsel for development.

Moreover, the consequences of unbalanced measures may not be innocent. In marketing, a common mistake with regard to physical facilities is to advocate constructing new facilities that are costly of capital and laborsaving—in an economy where labor is surplus and capital scarce. "Wasteful" employment in marketing adds nothing to cost of marketing if labor receives only a residual income. Recommendations for institutional change may be in error if they call for

*The notion of internally balanced composites of institutions, put into Ruttan's nomenclature, denies growth stage theories and comes close to dynamic dualism. See Vernon W. Ruttan, *Growth Stage Theories, Dual Economy Models and Agricultural Development Policy,* Univ. of Guelph, Dept. of Agr. Econ., Publ. No. AE-1968/2.

cooperatives where either leadership or the discipline of group action is absent, or for private agencies that easily would become monopolistic. Instances are legion of "good advice for the wrong place," which is indistinguishable from outright bad advice.

THE SUBSISTENCE SECTOR. For illustration rather than any rigid cataloguing, the remainder of this discussion is divided into marketing in the subsistence sector, in the commercial sector, and in the export sector.

The subsistence sector may be best defined by the high percentage of its production that is consumed by the producing family, or in any event, outside of market exchange. Characteristically it is also a sector of small land holdings, of illiteracy, of rudimentary social structure.

Obviously, a handicap to efficient marketing is the rather small volume of marketable output. Moreover, the marketed product may be variable as to season and quality.

Two mistakes could easily be made. One would be to write off the sector entirely. The other is to assume that few if any market services are needed.

The former is a mistake for political reasons if not economic ones. Often, this is the sector that is properly the object of technical aid efforts. The latter assumption is in error because market services can be fairly numerous while kept simple.

By no means should improvement in production for self-sufficiency be discouraged. Benefits can frequently be obtained by increasing indigenous production for local consumption. This can amount to converting subsistence agriculture to small-scale commercial agriculture. Johnston and Mellor comment on this kind of development in some countries.[11]

Services to Local Markets. With regard to subsistence sector markets, a necessary distinction is between local markets (of the same village, or neighboring villages) and distant urban markets. Village markets exist by the thousands, yet these remain largely outside the expertise of economists. They often employ labor in a way that seems wasteful yet until alternative employment becomes available, there is no reason to think that the practice is socially undesirable or that it adds to cost of marketing. In the words of Holton, "the phenomenon of the unemployed taking refuge in trade may be a satisfactory substitute for a comprehensive unemployment insurance program."[12] Similarly, Lawson observed in Ghana that "the long chain of distribution which utilizes thousands of small-scale traders is in fact a rational use of existing economic resources."[13]

Can these markets benefit from conventional market services? For staple products, probably so. The simplest kind of price reporting, as by means of blackboards, may be helpful. However, classification schemes (grades and standards) other than the simplest one probably have little important application.

According to some authors, local markets are not invariably free of restrictive trade practices such as guild rules or exclusiveness of access to stall space.

Services to Central Markets. More difficult to prescribe for are markets for surplus that goes to distant urban centers, or possibly even to export. In this portion of marketing, plus that from smaller commercial farms, markets are likely to be the most deficient in various respects including freedom from exploitation. This is where the money lender may dominate local marketing, where the itinerant trucker may take advantage of uninformed sellers, where infrastructure is deficient. Yet the volume of trade may not make a sound market system profitable.

In circumstances such as these, neither improved marketing institutions nor better physical facilities (including roads) likely will spring up of their own accord. Moreover, action by government may not prove worth the cost in the short run. But the commercial sale of surplus products by the subsistence sector may be vital to the survival of the economy of that sector. Furthermore, there must rest hope that the sector itself will develop and become commercial. So government investment in contemporary improvements in marketing may have a longer run developmental aspect. Furthermore, it may be politically and sociologically unavoidable. In developing and developed nations alike, some subsidization from centers of wealth to backward or impoverished areas in inescapable.

The call is not for elaborate services but essential ones at minimal levels of sophistication. This may mean constructing crude access roads, providing simple kinds of market information, or encouraging the beginning of credit unions or production credit. Better sources of credit could free farmers from practices such as precommitting their cash crops to money lenders. For some storable commodities a price support and storage program may be desirable, and if it is begun precautions must be taken to ensure that it reaches the subsistence sector.

DOMESTIC COMMERCIAL SECTOR. For commercial agriculture the repertory of activities and services developed in the United States and similar nations can be drawn on as a shopping list. Never can any or all be prescribed without careful analysis. Further, easy analogy with familiar conditions in the United States can be a trap; the local problems may be surprisingly complex.

The sector is itself highly variable, and the label "domestic commercial" takes some liberties. Farm units may range from tiny to huge, and their organizational structure may take a variety of forms. Moreover, there may be considerable production for export. However, a contrast can be sketched with the large-scale export agriculture described below.

Even though circumstances are not uniform, as a rule simplified versions of traditional services such as market information, grading and standardization, and certain kinds of trade practice regulation are well suited. With regard to infrastructure, the decision to build or not to build a road is at least clear cut. Other infrastructure can be more clouded. Almost always, storage and processing facilities are needed. Regrettably, too often there is an economy of scale in those facilities that leads to monopoly. In smaller countries the quantity of product marketed may not be large enough to support a sufficient number of firms to assure active competition. The choices are to retain smaller, more numerous facilities at some loss of operating efficiency; to form farmer or consumer cooperatives; to apply government regulation over market practices; or to conduct a parallel government action to serve as a yardstick.

In an excellent study, Haag and Rioseco describe the market system that was brought about for the commercial agriculture of the Yaqui Valley of Mexico. Of the 9,000 farmers in the valley, 5,400 were *ejidatarios,* 1,200 were *colonos,* and more than 2,200 were private landowners. Virtually all the crops produced were marketed. Government support in the form of buying and production credit agencies was a pervasive influence on the agriculture of the valley. The government agencies set minimum prices. A government bank provided production credit to the farmer, and it had the right to designate either a government buying agency or a private wholesaler as the market to which the borrower must deliver his product.

Reportedly, the wheat and corn cultivators netted about 95 percent of the stated purchase prices for their products. In scarcely more than decade, the acreage planted to cash crops was doubled.[14] Rather frequently, the problem of adequate markets arises when a developing nation opens up new land areas. Too often, colonists have been helped to settle on new land when adequate provision has not been made for the physical or institutional requirements for good marketing.

LARGE-SCALE EXPORT SECTOR. A number of developing nations have an export sector that is almost a world apart. It features large holdings operated with hired labor and professional management. Owners may live in the capital city, or they may be investors from other nations. The marketing process is highly advanced. The producing firms may be nearly self-sufficient in providing marketing services, either independently or through commodity organizations. Even government service may be highly client oriented, confined to that sector.

The export sector of various nations often includes a marketing institution that is virtually unique to that sector, namely, the marketing board. The board will usually have a sizeable industry representation as part of its membership and leadership.

An even more singular export institution is the arrangement for participating in an international commodity agreement. Agreements are in force for several major products. Adjusting to the terms of an agreement may put a strain on the commodity organization, the marketing board, or the government agency that provides storage or credit services to the industry. Almost certainly, in some years part of the available supply cannot be exported. The surplus must be stored. Not only are facilities and finance required, but a question arises as to equity of treatment of individual producers. Further, steps to restrain production in the future may be necessary. Commodity agreements may simplify some aspects of foreign trade, but they make life more complicated domestically.

Governmental service to the export sector may include engaging in market promotion abroad and in political negotiation as well. Almost always, farm products sold in export are given tight inspection for quality. Some developing nations are more circumspect in protecting the worldwide reputation of their export products than are developed ones!

INCENTIVE PRICING: FOR PRODUCTION, FOR CONSUMPTION. This discussion has thus far omitted one subject that always is prominent in policy making for developing nations, namely, a price policy. Implicitly assumed herein has been the idea that if a market exchange system can be helped to function efficiently, there is a good chance that the price returned to producers will be high enough to have incentive effect.

It is sometimes argued that in order to get fastest acceleration in production, there must be a subsidy in addition—a bonus to make further output more attractive. This is clearly one more issue that cannot be resolved in general terms. Doubtless, a subsidy incentive will sometimes be necessary.

Nevertheless, most developing nations do not have the fiscal resources to enable them to offer large incentive payments to producers. Further, an expanded production that rests on *un*subsidized expansion in output is the goal that is sought.

Questions may properly be raised as to whether generous subsidy is in fact essential for expanded output. There appears to be a delicate balance between economic pressure and economic incentive that provides the most stimulative setting for development. This is particularly true if the means for expansion of output are provided by technology.

More and more evidence coming to light gives reason to distrust the dogma promulgated by developed nations as to the interplay of price incentive and resource adjustment in development. Boulding and Singh, with a slight suggestion of tongue-in-cheek, remark on "curiously perverse reaction to adversity" and within a "general theory of social dynamics" they "distinguish at least four reactions" to disappointment.[15]

A further conundrum poses itself. It concerns incentives to consumption. These could achieve the maximum welfare benefit from farm production and enhance demand and prices as well. Even in developed countries a fraction of the consuming population lacks enough purchasing power to be strong buyers of food, and to have adequate diets. Conditions in some developing countries are much worse. Wise policy may call for establishing multiple pricing of basic food products. Among other merits, such a policy best converts physical need for food into demand for farm products at the farm; it narrows the discrepancy between "physical demand" and "money demand."

THE ROLE OF GOVERNMENT. The government role in marketing in developing nations is usually about the same as in the United States and other advanced countries. It includes providing information and grading services, credit, certification of public storage warehouses, promotion, storage and price support, and regulation of trade practices—also multiple pricing of food to consumers. Mentioned less often in foregoing pages were measures to sponsor self-help actions by farmers, as in forming cooperatives, not because they lack potential value but because favorable conditions often are not present.

But in some instances a more aggressive role for government may be necessary. The most notable and perhaps most controversial is direct government intervention for so-called yardstick purposes. The agency so engaged might be wholly governmental or mixed. The rationale for it is that in some smaller national economies private firms cannot be kept competitive. The market just is not big enough to support the number of firms needed for competition. There is a choice, as noted above, of deliberately retaining a small-scale and decentralized marketing system or of relying on countervailing activity by government. A number of developing nations now conduct a modest government activity alongside the private ones. Presumably, the private firm and government agency keep each other honest.

Yet this picture of alternatives may be too simple. Blends and combinations of private and governmental institutions have been devised in some nations. Even though they appear strange to eyes in the United States, they may be a rational invention for the circumstances. These can be industry-government combinations, or they can be of other makeup.

ALTERNATIVES TO A MARKET SYSTEM. Although discussion at the outset of this chapter took note of various kinds of structural organization for marketing and posed the basic question of choice among them, most of the later detail has related to a market exchange system.

As a socialist system of total direction by central government is assumed to be unacceptable in most or all developing nations, the most relevant alternative is that of integration in private hands. In its most extreme form it would embrace all production from the farm to retail distribution. Integrated firms of considerable size and scope are now found in some developing nations. Often, they are financed by capital from outside the country.

The implications of vertical integration, and of conglomerate structure as well, are sketched in earlier chapters. Perhaps developing nations would be even more susceptible to the consequence than developed nations are. The more general outcome might be forms of cartelization. Checks and balances would be applied not so much through market buying and selling as through contest leading to bargained arrangements among various groups. Quite likely, the government would involve itself in providing surveillance over bargaining techniques and in representing the interests of consumers.

In a developing economy of limited size, the hard fact is that it is difficult to establish a viable market exchange system impelled by competitive forces alone. One can be sympathetic with Cook's injunction that developing nations may have to "learn to live with monopoly as one price of self-sufficiency."[16] On the other hand, in those instances where there is little hope of preserving even a minimum acceptable degree of competition, the best alternative might be, as Collins and Holton suggest, to treat the private firm as a public utility.[17,18]

DEVELOPMENT OF THE INSTRUMENT OF GOVERNMENT.
That the capacity of government to perform marketing services effectively varies widely by countries is generally acknowledged. It leads to Cook's further observation that "the quality of government must be taken into account in deciding the form of government intervention."[19] But this is not the only conclusion to be reached. Another is that as an evolving modern market system in a developing economy necessarily relies on central government in some manner, a part of economic development must be the development of capacity for responsible performance by government. In fact, among all institutions for marketing, that of an effective and stable government may be the most important.

Nor is good government an act of God. It too can be cultivated. Further, as Raup insists, there are choices as to forms of "administrative structure" in government.[20] Improvement of the capacity of government may well be one of the underappreciated and undersupported elements in the mix that is known as "planning for development" of a nation that wants to improve its economic and social station.

MAKING HASTE SLOWLY—AND INTEGRALLY.
Progress will usually come at measured pace rather than breakneck speed. However, there will be exceptions. Kriesberg is one among several authors who point out the arithmetic of how fast marketings can increase when a subsistence sector catches fire.[21] The result can be to force grain or other product on the market at a rate that exceeds the capacity of facilities and market institutions to handle it. Wharton calls this unsettling experience the "Pandora's box" of the Green Revolution.[22]

Although planning and prodding ought to speed progress, undertaking herculean action on a few selected fronts while neglecting all else would usually be a mistake. As noted above, to add physical facilities that soak up scarce capital funds while displacing workers from employment faster than industrial expansion can re-employ them reflects doubtful wisdom. As another illustration, coating a country with asphalt highways overnight may do some good but other aids to marketing would often yield a higher return to the marginal investment dollar.

In most developing nations the three sectors used for illustration in this chapter may each persist for many years, and with good reason. However, the power of government may have to intercede to prevent one sector from impinging on, and harming, another.

Boulding and Singh forthrightly defend not only retaining but consciously supporting two contrasting subeconomies, a combination they call "technological dualism." Developmental tactics would be "capital-intensive for the basic producer goods" and "labor-intensive for a variety of consumer goods and light engineering industries."[23]

When all is said and done, generalizations are suspect and particularizations hard to come by. Improvements in a system of product markets can contribute greatly to the development of a nation. More than that, they are crucial to it. Yet they are only one part of an overall scheme for development, one link in a chain. The game of fighting for priority of attention is a bad game.

And it may not be denigrating of economists' expertise to accept the words of Lee Martin: "Decisions to accomplish . . . goals [in marketing] will call more for ingenuity in organization and human relations than for elaborate economic analysis."[24]

CONCLUSION. The thread that runs through this chapter is a reluctance to form universal judgments as to desirable policies for product markets in developing countries. On the one hand, if a nation is to pursue a higher degree of specialization, including geographical division of enterprise, it must have a viable system of markets of some kind. On the other hand, a highly sophisticated marketing system requires a network of supporting activities that often is hard to bring about in a developing economy. Particularly does a self-regulating market exchange system rest on cultural and political maturity in the nation as a whole.

Frequently, the best policy calls for a system of mixed makeup, containing roles for both government and private organizations. Boards and commissions of joint composition may be needed as well.

Moreover, if a market structure capable of supporting a more advanced production system is not forthcoming, technological gains in production may have to be restrained. Although precisely coordinated advance in all sectors is not mandated, neither can a marked imbalance be lived with for an indefinite period of time.

On the whole, there is reason for pragmatism in preference to conforming to a single doctrine of development. But this does not depreciate critical analysis as a base for planning and stimulating the agricultural market development of a nation. On the contrary, more ingenious analysis is made essential, and if the techniques and tools are less stereotyped they are also less constrained.

NOTES

CHAPTER ONE MARKETING IN THE ECONOMIC SYSTEM

1. James M. Buchanan, "A Future for 'Agricultural Economics'?" *Am. J. Agr. Econ.* 51 (1969): 1027–36.
2. Kenneth Boulding, "Towards a Pure Theory of Threat Systems," *Am. Econ. Rev.* 53 (1963): 424–34.
3. A. Allan Schmid and James D. Shaffer, "Marketing in Social Perspective," in *Agricultural Market Analysis,* Vernon L. Sorenson, ed. (East Lansing: Bureau of Business and Economic Research, Michigan State University, 1964), p. 20.
4. Harold F. Breimyer, "Man, Physical Resources, and Economic Organization," *Am. J. Agr. Econ.* 55 (1973): 1–9.
5. James D. Shaffer, *A Working Paper Concerning Publicly Supported Economic Research in Agricultural Marketing,* U.S. Dept. Agr., Econ. Res. Serv., 1968, p. 16.
6. Andreas G. Papandreou, *Paternalistic Capitalism* (Minneapolis: Univ. of Minnesota Press, 1972), p. 5.
7. Richard L. Kohls and W. David Downey, *Marketing of Agricultural Products* (New York: Macmillan, 1972), pp. 8–9.
8. Harold F. Breimyer, "The Economics of Agricultural Marketing: A Survey," *Rev. Marketing and Agr. Econ.* (Australia) 41 (1973): 115–65.
9. John Phillips, "A Revised Approach to Marketing," *Rev. Marketing and Agr. Econ.* (Australia) 36 (1968): 28–36.
10. Henry H. Bakken, *Theory of Markets and Marketing* (Madison: Mimir Publishers, 1953), p. 34.
11. James D. Shaffer, "Changing Orientations of Marketing Research," *Am. J. Agr. Econ.* 50 (1968): 1437–49.
12. Shaffer, *A Working Paper,* p. 1.
13. Ibid., p. 5.
14. Kohls and Downey, pp. 20, 24.
15. Charles F. Phillips and Delbert J. Duncan, *Marketing Principles and Methods,* 6th ed. (Homewood, Ill.: Richard D. Irwin, 1968), p. 3.
16. Edward A. Duddy and David A. Revzan, *Marketing, An Institutional Approach,* 2d ed. (New York: McGraw-Hill, 1953), p. 16.
17. Richard M. Cyert and James G. March, *A Behavioral Theory of the Firm* (Englewood Cliffs: Prentice-Hall, 1963).
18. Kenneth E. Boulding, *The Organizational Revolution* (Chicago: Quadrangle, 1968).
19. John Kenneth Galbraith, *The New Industrial State* (Boston: Houghton Mifflin, 1967).
20. Robert Bartels, "The Theory of Marketing," *J. Marketing* 32 (1968): 29–33.
21. Robert Bartels, "The Identity Crisis in Marketing," *J. Marketing* 38 (1974): 73–76.
22. Ibid., p. 76.
23. Peter F. Drucker, "Marketing and Economic Development," *J. Marketing* 22 (1958): 252–59.
24. William Lazer, "Marketing's Changing Social Relationships" *J. Marketing* 33 (1969): 3–9.
25. Philip Kotler, *Marketing Management,* 2d ed. (Englewood Cliffs: Prentice-Hall, 1972).
26. W. T. Tucker, "Future Directions in Marketing Theory," *J. Marketing* 38 (1974): 30–35.

27. F. Kelly Shuptrine and Frank A. Osmanski, "Marketing's Changing Role: Expanding or Contracting?" *J. Marketing* 39 (1975): 58–66.

28. Richard P. Bagozzi, "Marketing as an Organized Behavioral System of Exchange," *J. Marketing* 38 (1974): 77–81.

29. Wroe Alderson, *Dynamic Marketing Behavior* (Homewood, Ill.: Richard D. Irwin, 1965), pp. 10–11.

30. Ibid., p. 21.

31. Bakken, p. 43.

32. George W. Robbins, "Notions about the Origins of Marketing," *J. Marketing* 11 (1947): 228–36.

33. John Hicks, *A Theory of Economic History* (Oxford: Clarendon Press, 1969); and review by Allen B. Paul in *Agr. Econ. Res.* 22 (1970): 83–84.

34. Miriam Beard, "Swordsmen and Salesmen in the Homeric Age," in *A History of Business from Babylon to the Monopolists* (Ann Arbor: Univ. of Michigan Press, 1962), quoted in Harvard Business School, *The World of Business*, Edward C. Burks, Donald T. Clark, and Ralph W. Hidy, eds., vol. 1 (New York: Simon and Schuster, 1962), p. 160.

35. Richard Thurnwald, *Economics in Primitive Communities* (London: Oxford Univ. Press, 1932). Quotation from *Trade and Market in the Early Empires: Economics in History and Theory*, Karl Polanyi, Conrad M. Arensberg, and Harry W. Pearson, eds. (Glencoe, N.Y.: Free Press, 1947), pp. 346–47.

36. Karl Polanyi, *The Great Transformation* (New York: Rinehart, 1944), p. 71.

37. George Burton Hotchkiss, *Milestones of Marketing* (New York: Macmillan, 1938), p. 19.

38. John R. Commons, *Institutional Economics* (New York: MacMillan, 1934), p. 393.

39. Karl Polanyi, *The Great Transformation* (New York: Rinehart, 1944), pp. 68–69, in Duddy and Revzan, pp. 4–5.

40. Joan Robinson, "The Basic Theory of Normal Price," *Quar. J. Econ.* 76 (1962): 1–19.

41. E. Jerome McCarthy, *Basic Marketing: A Managerial Approach*, 4th ed. (Homewood, Ill.: Richard D. Irwin, 1971), p. 19.

42. David McCord Wright, "What is the Economic System?" *Quar. J. Econ.* 72 (1958): 198–210.

43. E. Jerome McCarthy, "Are Effective Marketing Institutions Necessary and Sufficient Conditions for Economic Development?" *Toward Scientific Marketing*, proceedings of winter conference of Am. Marketing Assn., Dec. 1963.

44. Duddy and Revzan, p. 6.

CHAPTER TWO WELFARE GOALS IN MARKETING

1. Edgar Z. Friedenberg, "Thoughts on Liberty and Rancor," *Harper's* 250 (June 1975): 41–46.

2. John M. Brewster, "The Cultural Crisis of Our Time," in *A Philosopher Among Economists, Selected Works of John M. Brewster*, J. Patrick Madden and David E. Brewster, eds. (Philadelphia: J. T. Murphy, 1970), p. 9.

3. Thorstein Veblen, *The Theory of the Leisure Class* (New York: Modern Library, 1934), pp. 68–101.

4. E. J. Mishan, *Welfare Economics* (New York: Random House, 1964), pp. 4–5.

5. William J. Baumol, *Welfare Economics and the Theory of the State*, 2d ed. (Cambridge: Harvard Univ. Press, 1965).

6. Ibid.

7. Harold F. Breimyer, "Man, Physical Resources, and Economic Organization," *Am. J. Agr. Econ.* 55 (1973): 1–9.

8. Robert A. Brady, review of K. William Kapp, *The Social Costs of Private Enterprise*, in *Am. Econ. Rev.* 41 (1951): 435–37.

9. "Underlying Objectives of Marketing Efficiency Programs," Report of Work Group I, in *Marketing Efficiency in a Changing Economy*, Report of National

Workshop on Agricultural Marketing, University of Kentucky, June 17–24, 1955, U.S. Dept. of Agr., Agr. Marketing Service, 1955.

10. University of Kansas, March 1968. From press reports of the time.

11. Andreas G. Papandreau, *Paternalistic Capitalism* (Minneapolis: Univ. of Minnesota Press, 1972), p. 19.

12. Tibor Scitovsky, *Welfare and Competition* (Homewood, Ill.: Richard D. Irwin, 1971).

13. Ibid., p. 9.

14. Ibid., p. 10.

15. Ibid., p. 72.

16. Alexander Gray, *The Development of Economic Doctrine* (London: Longmans, Green, 1931), pp. 330–31.

17. Hendrik S. Houthakker, "The Present State of Consumption Theory," *Econometrica* (1961): 704–40.

18. William J. Baumol, *Economic Theory and Operations Analysis*, 2d ed. (Englewood Cliffs: Prentice-Hall, 1965), p. 183.

19. Houthakker, p. 718.

20. Gordon A. King, "An Appraisal of the Strengths and Weaknesses of the Econometric Approach," *J. Farm Econ.* 45 (1963): 1408–19.

21. Robert Ferber, "Consumer Economics, a Survey," *J. Econ. Literature* 51 (1973): 1303–42.

22. Wroe Alderson, *Marketing Behavior and Executive Action* (Homewood, Ill.: Richard D. Irwin, 1957), p. 165.

23. Ibid., pp. 163–93.

24. A. Allan Schmid and James D. Shaffer, "Marketing in Social Perspective," in *Agricultural Market Analysis*, Vernon L. Sorenson, ed. (East Lansing: Michigan State Univ. Bureau of Business and Economic Research, 1964), p. 12.

25. Ibid., p. 14.

26. "Yankelovich Describes Types of Trends," *Marketing News*, American Marketing Association, Mid-May 1971, p. 7.

27. Yankelovich, Skelly, and White, Inc., "Survey Pinpoints Fading American Dream," *Columbia Missourian*, April 30, 1975, p. 1.

28. John F. Due, *Intermediate Economic Analysis*, rev. ed. (Chicago: Richard D. Irwin, 1951), p. 388.

29. Ibid., pp. 389–90.

30. Randall E. Torgerson, *The Cooperative Systems Approach to Improving Farm Incomes* (Ph.D. thesis, University of Wisconsin, 1968). Herbert Simon reference is to "Theories of Decision-making in Economics and Behavioral Science," *Am. Econ. Rev.* 41 (1959): 254–83.

31. William J. Baumol, *Business Behavior, Value and Growth* (New York: Macmillan, 1959), ch. 6. (Quoted in Torgerson, p. 46.)

32. James Nielson and Vernon L. Sorenson, "The Firm as a Focal Point in Market Analysis," in *Agricultural Market Analysis*, p. 75. McDonald reference is to John McDonald, "How Businessmen Make Decisions," *Fortune* 52 (1955): 84.

33. Due, *Intermediate Economic Analysis*, p. 522.

34. Ibid., p. 517.

35. Kenneth E. Boulding, *Economic Analysis*, rev. ed. (New York: Harper, 1948), p. 661.

36. Quoted by Tibor Scitovsky, "The State of Welfare Economics," *Am. Econ. Rev.* 41 (1951): 303–15.

37. Mishan, *Welfare Economics*, is an excellent review source.

38. Arnold Brekke and Norman Zellner, "Conflicts Between Some Assumptions Underlying Production and Welfare Economics," *J. Farm Econ.* 34 (1952): 96–102.

39. Mishan, p. 175.

40. Nicholas Georgescu-Roegen, "Utility," *International Encyclopedia of the Social Sciences*, David L. Sills, ed. (New York: Macmillan and the Free Press, 1968), vol. 16, p. 264.

41. Francis M. Bator, "The Simple Analytics of Welfare Maximization," *Am. Econ. Rev.* 47 (1957): 22–59.

42. Quoted by Mishan, p. 47.

43. John Maurice Clark, *Competition as a Dynamic Process* (Washington: Brookings Institution, 1961), pp. 70–71.

CHAPTER THREE ECONOMICS OF THE MARKETING FIRM

1. Richard H. Leftwich, *The Price System and Resource Allocation,* rev. ed. (New York: Holt, Rinehart and Winston, 1965), p. 95.
2. Campbell R. McConnell, *Economics: Principles, Problems, and Policies,* 4th ed. (New York: McGraw-Hill, 1969), p. 120.
3. John F. Due, *Intermediate Economic Analysis* (Chicago: Richard D. Irwin, 1950), p. 31.
4. Richard G. Lipsey and Peter O. Steiner, *Economics,* 3d ed. (New York: Harper & Row, 1972), p. 53.
5. P. J. D. Wiles, *Price, Cost and Output* (Oxford: Basil Blackwell, 1961), p. x.
6. Paul E. Nelson, Jr., "Altering Marketing Concepts to Modern Conditions," *J. Farm Econ.* 40 (1958): 1511–22.
7. James Nielson and Vernon L. Sorenson, "The Firm as a Focal Point in Market Analysis," in *Agricultural Market Analysis,* Vernon L. Sorenson, ed. (East Lansing: Michigan State Univ., Bureau of Business and Economic Research, 1964), p. 72.
8. Richard M. Cyert and Charles L. Hedrick, "Theory of the Firm: Past, Present, and Future: An Interpretation," *J. Econ. Literature* 10 (1972): 398–412.
9. Cyert and Hedrick, pp. 398–403.
10. Wiles, p. 8.
11. John Maurice Clark, *Competition as a Dynamic Process* (Washington: Brookings Institution, 1961), p. 364.
12. Ibid., pp. 363–64.
13. William J. Baumol and David F. Bradford, "Optimal Departures from Marginal Cost Pricing," *Am. Econ. Rev.* 60 (1970): 265–83.
14. Wiles, p. 45.
15. Martin Shubik, "A Curmudgeon's Guide to Microeconomics," *J. Econ. Literature* 8 (1970): 405–34.
16. Peter F. Morris, "Finding a Fair Price for Widgets," *Management Review* 59 (1970): 21–26.
17. Alfred R. Oxenfeldt, "A Decision-making Structure for Price Decisions," *J. Marketing* 37 (1973): 48–53.
18. Robert A. Lynn, "Unit Volume as a Goal for Pricing," *J. Marketing* 32 (1968): 34–39.

CHAPTER FOUR COMPETITIVE STRUCTURE OF THE MARKET

1. Richard M. Cyert and Charles L. Hedrick, "Theory of the Firm: Past, Present, and Future: An Interpretation," *J. Econ. Literature* 10 (1972): 398–412.
2. Harold Hotelling, "Stability in Competition," in American Economic Association, *Readings in Price Theory* (Chicago and Homewood, Ill.: Richard D. Irwin, 1952): 471.
3. Ibid., p. 482.
4. Jacob Viner, "The Economist in History," *Am. Econ. Rev.* 53 (May 1963): 1–22.
5. E. J. Mishan, *Welfare Economics* (New York: Random House, 1964), p. 25.
6. John P. Doll, V. James Rhodes, and Jerry G. West, *Economics of Agricultural Production, Markets, and Policy* (Homewood, Ill.: Richard D. Irwin, 1968), p. 266.
7. Eugene R. Beem and A. R. Oxenfeldt, "A Diversity Theory for Market Processes in Food Retailing," *J. Farm Econ.* 48 (Aug. 1966, part II): 69–95.
8. Harold F. Breimyer, "Cost-Escalating Imitation in Market Services," *Am. J. Agr. Econ.* 50 (1968): 767–69.

9. Paul E. Nelson and Lee E. Preston, *Price Merchandising in Food Retailing: A Case Study* (Berkeley: Univ. of Calif. Grad. School of Bus. Admin. 1968).
10. George J. Stigler, "The Kinky Oligopoly Demand Curve and Rigid Prices," *J. Pol. Econ.* 55 (1947): 432–49.
11. Sidney Siegel and Lawrence E. Fouraker, *Bargaining and Group Decision Making: Experiments in Bilateral Monopoly* (New York: McGraw-Hill, 1960).
12. George J. Stigler, "A Theory of Oligopoly," *Five Lectures on Economic Problems* (London: Longmans, Green, 1949).
13. Joe S. Bain, *Industrial Organization,* 2d ed. (New York: Wiley, 1968).
14. Robert L. Clodius and Willard F. Mueller, "Market Structure Analysis as an Orientation for Research in Agricultural Economics," *J. Farm Econ.* 43 (1961): 515–53.
15. Stephen H. Sosnick, "A Critique of Concepts of Workable Competition," *Quar. J. Econ.* 72 (1958): 380–423.
16. Stephen H. Sosnick, "Operational Criteria for Evaluating Market Performance," *Market Structure Research,* Paul L. Farris, ed. (Ames: Iowa State Univ. Press, 1964), pp. 81–125.
17. Stephen H. Sosnick, "Toward a Concrete Concept of Effective Competition," *Am. J. Agr. Econ.* 50 (1968): 827–53.
18. William H. Nicholls, *A Theoretical Analysis of Imperfect Competition with Special Application to the Agricultural Industries* (Ames: Iowa State College Press, 1941).
19. A. C. Hoffman, *Large-Scale Organization in the Food Industries,* Temporary National Economic Committee Monograph No. 35 (Washington: U.S. Govt. Printing Office, 1940), p. 84.
20. John Kenneth Galbraith, *American Capitalism: The Concept of Countervailing Power,* 2d ed. (Boston: Houghton Mifflin, 1956).
21. V. James Rhodes, "Supply Management, Market Power, and the Derived Demand for Farm Products," Univ. of Missouri-Columbia, Dept. of Agr. Econ., 1961, unpublished, p. 85.
22. Ronald D. Knutson, "Buyer Strategy in Bilateral Oligopoly," *Am. J. Agr. Econ.* 50 (1968): 1507–11.
23. C. R. Handy and D. I. Padberg, "A Model of Competitive Behavior in Food Industries," *Am. J. Agr. Econ.* 53 (1971): 182–90.
24. William H. Nicholls, "Imperfect Competition in Agricultural Processing and Distributing Industries," *Canadian J. Econ. and Pol. Sci.* 10 (1944): 150–64.
25. Ronald L. Mighell and Lawrence A. Jones, *Vertical Coordination in Agriculture,* U.S. Dept. of Agr., Econ. Res. Serv., Agr. Econ. Report No. 19, 1963.
26. Rafael Trifon, "Guides for Speculation about the Vertical Integration of Agriculture with Allied Industries," *J. Farm Econ.* 41 (1959): 734–46.
27. Brown Shoe Co., Inc., v. United States, *U.S. Reports,* vol. 370 (Washington: U.S. Govt. Printing Office, 1962).
28. A. C. Hoffman, "The Economic Rationale for Conglomerate Growth from a Management Perspective," in *Economics of Conglomerate Growth,* Leon Garoian, ed. (Corvallis: Oregon State Univ., Agricultural Research Foundation, 1969). See also other articles in the report.
29. James J. Eppenauer, "Financial Practices of Conglomerates: Their Effects upon Agriculture and Agribusiness," Univ. of Missouri-Columbia, Dept. of Agr. Econ., master's thesis, 1974.
30. John Maurice Clark, *Competition as a Dynamic Process* (Washington: Brookings Institution, 1961), p. 145.

CHAPTER FIVE **DIMENSIONS AND STRUCTURE OF MARKETING**

1. National Commission on Food Marketing, *Food from Farmer to Consumer* (Washington: U.S. Govt. Printing Office, 1966), p. 107.
2. Forrest E. Scott, Jeannette Findlay, and Leland W. Southard, "Farm Food Marketing Bill Statistics," *Agricultural Marketing Costs and Charges,* vol. 4 of

Major Statistical Series of the U.S. Department of Agriculture, U.S. Dept. of Agr., Handbook 365, 1970, p. 18.

3. Terry L. Crawford and Andrew Weiser, "The Bill for Marketing Farm-food Products," *Marketing and Transportation Situation,* U.S. Dept. Agr., Econ. Res. Serv., Aug. 1975, pp. 13–36. Further explanatory information is in Scott, Findlay, and Southard, pp. 24–32.

4. Michael G. Van Dress, *The Foodservice Industry: Type, Quantity, and Value of Foods Used,* U.S. Dept. of Agr., Stat. Bulletin No. 476, 1971.

5. Crawford and Weiser, pp. 17, 22.

6. Ibid., p. 24.

7. T. Q. Hutchinson, "U.S. Railroad Performance Indicators, 1958–67," *Marketing and Transportation Situation,* U.S. Dept. of Agr., Econ. Res. Serv., May 1970, pp. 24–30.

8. Crawford and Weiser, p. 23.

9. Leo V. Blakley, "Domestic Food Costs," A.E. paper 4410, Okla. State Univ., Dept. of Agr. Econ., Aug. 1974 (mimeographed).

10. See Forrest E. Scott and Henry T. Badger, "Farm Food Market Basket Statistics," *Agricultural Marketing Costs and Charges,* vol. 4, *Major Statistical Series of the U.S. Department of Agriculture,* U.S. Dept. of Agr., Handbook 365, 1970. Also two reports of the National Commission on Food Marketing, *Food from Farmer to Consumer,* and *Cost Components of Farm-retail Price Spreads for Foods* (Washington: U.S. Govt. Printing Office, 1966).

11. National Commission on Food Marketing, *Organization and Competition in Food Retailing* (Washington: U.S. Govt. Printing Office, June 1966), pp. 24–25.

12. Willard F. Mueller, "Statement . . . before the Committee on the Judiciary, Subcommittee on Monopolies and Commerce, House of Representatives, Concerning the Structure and Performance of the Food Industries, July 19, 1973," Univ. of Wisconsin, Dept. of Agr. Econ., p. 69.

13. Harold F. Breimyer, "Do the Poor Pay More for Food?" Univ. of Missouri-Columbia, Dept. of Agr. Econ., Nov. 1, 1969. See also, Donald E. Sexton, Jr., "Comparing the Cost of Food to Blacks and to Whites—a Survey," *J. Marketing* 35 (1971): 40–46; and *Society and Marketing,* Norman Kangan, ed. (New York: Harper & Row, 1972), section 3.

14. National Commission on Food Marketing, *Organization and Competition in Food Retailing* (Washington: U.S. Govt. Printing Office, June 1966), p. 73.

15. C. R. Handy and D. I. Padberg, "A Model of Competitive Behavior in Food Industries," *Am. J. Agr. Econ.* 53 (1971): 182–90; and Daniel I. Padberg, *Economics of Food Retailing* (Ithaca: Cornell University Food Distribution Program, 1968).

16. Ronald D. Knutson, "Buyer Strategy in Bilateral Oligopoly," *Am. J. Agr. Econ.* 50 (1968): 1507–11.

17. National Commission on Food Marketing, *Studies of Organization and Competition in Grocery Manufacturing* (Washington: U.S. Govt. Printing Office, 1966), p. 17.

18. Ibid., pp. 16–18.

19. See John R. Moore, "The Fluid Milk Industry," and Richard G. Walsh and Bert M. Evans, "The Baking Industry," in *Market Structure of the Agricultural Industries,* John R. Moore and Richard G. Walsh, eds. (Ames: Iowa State Univ. Press, 1966).

20. U.S. Department of Agriculture, *Agricultural Markets in Change,* Agr. Econ. Report No. 95, 1966.

21. U.S. Department of Agriculture, Economic Research Service, *Market Structure of the Food Industries,* Marketing Research Report No. 971, 1972.

22. Donn A. Reimund, *Farming and Agribusiness Activities of Large Multiunit Firms,* U.S. Dept. of Agr. Econ. Res. Serv. ERS-591, 1975.

23. Frederick Lundy Thomsen and Richard Jay Foote, *Agricultural prices* (New York: McGraw-Hill, 1952), p. 119.

24. William G. Tomek and Kenneth L. Robinson, *Agricultural Product Prices* (Ithaca: Cornell University Press, 1972), p. 215.

25. George B. Rogers, "Pricing Systems and Agricultural Marketing Research," *Agricultural Economics Research,* U.S. Dept. Agr., Econ. Res. Serv., Jan. 1970.

26. George B. Rogers and Leonard A. Voss, eds., *Readings on Egg Pricing*, Univ. of Missouri-Columbia, College of Agr., 1971.

27. Tomek and Robinson, pp. 215–32.

28. V. James Rhodes, "Pricing Systems—Old, New and Options for the Future," *Bargaining in Agriculture: Potentials and Pitfalls in Collective Action*, Harold F. Breimyer, ed., Univ. of Missouri Ext. Div., C911, June 1971, pp. 8–13.

29. Ibid., pp. 12–13.

30. Tibor Scitovsky, *Welfare and Competition*, rev. ed. (Homewood, Ill.: Richard D. Irwin, 1971).

31. Roger W. Gray and David J. S. Rutledge, "The Economics of Commodity Futures Markets: A Survey," *Review of Marketing and Agricultural Economics* 39 (1971): 57–108.

32. Tomek and Robinson, pp. 233–76.

33. Allen B. Paul, "The Role of Competitive Market Institutions," *Agricultural Economics Research*, U.S. Dept. of Agr., Econ. Res. Serv. 26 (1974): 41–48.

34. Olan D. Forker, "Agricultural Prices in the 1970's: How Will Value be Established?" *Southern J. Agr. Econ.* 6 (July 1974): 27–32.

35. Ralph D. Johnson, *An Economic Evaluation of Alternative Marketing Methods for Fed Cattle*, Univ. of Nebraska-Lincoln, College of Agr. SB 520, 1972.

36. L. F. Schrader, Richard G. Heifner, and Henry E. Larzelere, "The Electronic Egg Exchange: An Alternative System for Trading Shell Eggs," Mich. State Univ., Agr. Econ. Report No. 119, 1968.

37. The Thor-Goldberg thesis stated in Ray A. Goldberg, "Profitable Partnerships: Industry and Farmer Co-ops," *Harvard Business Review* 50 (1972): 108–21.

38. See Harold F. Breimyer, "The Problem and Its Setting," in *Bargaining in Agriculture, Potentials and Pitfalls in Collective Action*, Harold F. Breimyer, ed., Univ. of Missouri, Ext. Div., C 911, June 1971, pp. 3–7; also other chapters in the report.

39. Peter G. Helmberger and Sidney Hoos, "Economic Theory of Bargaining in Agriculture," *J. Farm Econ.* 45 (1963): 1272–80.

40. Ibid.

41. E. M. Babb, S. A. Belden, and C. R. Saathoff, "An Analysis of Cooperative Bargaining in the Processing Tomato Industry," *Am. J. Agr. Econ.* 51 (1969): 13–25.

42. See George W. Ladd, *Agricultural Bargaining Power* (Ames: Iowa State Univ. Press, 1964).

CHAPTER SIX ROLE OF MARKETING RESEARCH

1. United States Congress, *Agricultural Marketing Act of 1946* (7 U.S.C. 1621–27), sec. 1621.

2. Frederick V. Waugh, ed. *Readings on Agricultural Marketing* (Ames: Iowa State College Press, 1954).

3. Public Law 88–354, 89th Congress.

4. Bruce W. Marion and Charles R. Handy, *Market Performance: Concepts and Measures*, U.S. Dept. of Agr., Econ. Res. Serv., Agr. Econ. Report No. 244, 1973.

5. John W. Kendrick, *Productivity Trends in the United States* (Princeton: Princeton Univ. Press, 1961).

6. Marion and Handy, pp. 28–29, 90–96.

7. For a tableau of goal specification at successive levels of aggregation see "Underlying Objectives of Marketing Efficiency Programs," report of Work Group I, in *Marketing Efficiency in a Changing Economy*, report of the National Workshop on Agricultural Marketing, June 17–24, 1955, U.S. Dept. of Agr., Agr. Marketing Service, AMS-60, pp. 179–92.

8. Tibor Scitovsky, *Welfare and Competition*, rev. ed. (Homewood, Ill.: Richard D. Irwin, 1971).

9. U.S. Department of Agriculture, *Marketing Margins and Efficiency*, report of Marketing Research Workshop, July 9–19, 1950, Agr. Res. Admin., 1950.

10. Ben C. French, "The Analysis of Productive Efficiency in Agricultural

Marketing—Models, Methods, and Progress," Univ. of California-Davis, Dept. of Agr. Econ., manuscript for publication by Am. Agr. Econ. Assn.

11. Marion and Handy, p. 115.

12. Ibid., p. 87.

13. William H. Waldorf, "The Demand for and Supply of Food Marketing Services: An Aggregate View," *J. Farm Econ.* 48 (1966): 42–60.

14. See Rolando Polli, "A Review of the 'Market Basket' and 'Farm Food Marketing Bill' Statistics as Measures of Market Performance," Marketing Science Institute, unpublished working paper, March 1969, cited by Marion and Handy.

15. Louis W. Stern, "Market Structure as a Measure of Market Performance," Marketing Science Institute, working paper, Feb. 1970, cited by Marion and Handy.

16. Marion and Handy, pp. 37–45.

17. See also Willard F. Mueller, *A Primer on Monopoly and Competition* (New York: Random House, 1970).

18. Marion and Handy, p. 57.

19. Louis W. Stern, *Distribution Channels: Behavioral Dimensions* (Boston: Houghton-Mifflin, 1969).

20. Marion and Handy, p. 108.

21. Ibid., p. 109.

22. Henry Schultz, *The Theory and Measurement of Demand* (Chicago: Univ. of Chicago Press, 1938).

23. Reported in reports of "Household Food Consumption Survey 1965–66" series, U.S. Dept. of Agr., Agr. Res. Serv., 1972, 1973.

24. See Harold F. Breimyer, *Demand and Prices for Meat,* U.S. Dept. of Agr. Tech. Bul. No. 1253, 1961, pp. 81–83.

25. See G. G. Quackenbush and J. D. Shaffer, *Collecting Food Purchase Data by Consumer Panel,* Mich. State Univ., Agr. Exp. Station, Tech. Bul. 279, 1960. See other individual studies such as J. D. Shaffer and G. G. Quackenbush, "Consumer Purchases of Peaches: M.S.U. Consumer Panel 1953–1955," *Quarterly Bulletin,* Mich. State Univ., Agr. Exp. Station, 40 (1957): 162–71; H. F. Wang and G. G. Quackenbush, "Distribution of Expenditures for Various Foods, 1955–57, M.S.U. Consumer Panel," *Quarterly Bulletin,* Mich. State Univ., Agr. Exp. Station, 42 (1960): 886–912; Anthony Y. C. Koo, "An Empirical Test of Revealed Preference Theory," *Econometrica* 31 (1963): 646–64.

26. A series of reports by individual commodities has been released by the Georgia Experiment Station, Experiment, Georgia. Among summary articles is J. C. Purcell and Robert Raunikar, "Quantity-income Elasticities for Foods by Level of Income," *J. Farm Econ.* 49 (1967): 1410–14.

27. A reference on market studies for new products is James W. Taylor, John J. Houlahan, and Alan C. Gabriel, "The Purchase Intention Question in New Product Development: A Field Test," *J. Marketing* 39 (1975): 90–92.

28. See Peter L. Henderson, James F. Hind, and Sidney E. Brown, *Promotional Programs for Lamb and Their Effect on Sales,* U.S. Dept. of Agr., Marketing Research Report 522, 1962.

29. Wendell E. Clement, Peter L. Henderson, and Cleveland P. Eley, *The Effect of Different Levels of Promotional Expenditures on Sales of Fluid Milk,* U.S. Dept. of Agr., ERS-259, 1965.

30. R. G. Bressler, Jr., "Research Determination of Economies of Scale," *J. Farm Econ.* 27 (1945): 526–39; and Social Science Research Council, *Efficiency in the Production of Marketing Services,* Economic Efficiency Series (Chicago: Univ. of Chicago Press, 1950).

31. Robert W. Rudd, "Research in Marketing Efficiency," in *Marketing Efficiency in a Changing Economy,* Report of the National Workshop on Agricultural Marketing, June 17–24, 1955, U.S. Dept. of Agr., Agr. Marketing Service, AMS-60, p. 64. (The article remains an excellent review of the concept of efficiency in relation to marketing research.)

32. John M. Brewster, *Comparative Economies of Different Types of Cottonseed Oil Mills and Their Effects on Oil Supplies, Prices, and Returns to Growers,* U.S. Dept. of Agr., Marketing Research Report No. 54, Feb. 1954.

33. See William C. Crow, *Wholesale Markets for Fruits and Vegetables in 40 Cities,* U.S. Dept. of Agr., Circular No. 463, Feb. 1938.

34. French, "The Analysis of Productive Efficiency," p. 7.

35. Ibid., pp. 28–33.

36. Ibid., pp. 47, 66, 76–80, 193–97.

37. Ibid., pp. 84–86.

38. Ibid., p. 37.

39. George B. Rogers and Earl H. Rinear, *Costs and Economies of Scale in Turkey Processing Plants,* U.S. Dept. of Agr., Marketing Research Report 726, Sept. 1963.

40. R. Kenneth DeHaven, "Conjunctive Effects of Economies of Scale and Rate Structures in Establishing the Geographical Milk Supply Area of the Plant," *J. Econ. Theory* 3(1971): 199–206.

41. Paul L. Farris, "The Pricing Structure for Wheat at the Country Elevator Level," *J. Farm Econ.* 40 (1958): 607–24.

42. R. R. Newberg, *Livestock Marketing in the North Central Region,* Ohio Agr. Exp. Station Bull. 846, 1959.

43. Willard F. Mueller and Leon Garoian, *Changes in the Market Structure of Grocery Retailing* (Madison: Univ. of Wisconsin Press, 1961).

44. Bob R. Holdren, "Competition in Food Retailing," *J. Farm Econ.* 47 (1965): 1323–31; and Holdren, *The Structure of a Retail Market and the Market Behavior of Retail Units* (Englewood Cliffs: Prentice-Hall, 1960).

45. Daniel I. Padberg, *Economics of Food Retailing* (Ithaca: Cornell University Food Distribution Program, 1968); also Daniel I. Padberg, *Today's Food Broker: Vital Link in the Distribution Cycle* (New York: Chain Store Age Books, 1971).

46. John R. Moore and Richard G. Walsh, eds. *Market Structure of the Agricultural Industries* (Ames: Iowa State Univ. Press, 1966).

47. Sheldon W. Williams, David A. Vose, Charles E. French, Hugh L. Cook, and Alden C. Manchester, *Organization and Competition in the Midwest Dairy Industries* (Ames: Iowa State Univ. Press, 1970).

48. National Commission on Food Marketing, *Food from Farmer to Consumer* (Washington: U.S. Govt. Printing Office, 1966); and 10 individual reports.

49. Examples for reference are a now-classic source on market news: Kenneth J. McCallister, "The Role of Market News in Marketing and Some Problems," *J. Farm Econ.* 32 (1950): 958–68; and W. F. Williams, E. K. Bowen, and F. C. Genovese, *Economic Effects of U.S. Grades for Beef,* U.S. Dept. of Agr., Agr. Marketing Res. Report 298, 1959.

50. J. Patrick Madden and Marion D. Yoder, *Program Evaluation: Food Stamps and Commodity Distribution in Rural Areas of Central Pennsylvania,* Pennsylvania State Univ., Agr. Exp. Station, Bull. 780, June 1972.

51. J. Gerald Feaster and Gary B. Perkins, *Families in the Expanded Food and Nutrition Education Program: Comparison of Food Stamp and Food Distribution Program Participants and Non-participants,* U.S. Dept. of Agr., Econ. Res. Service, Agr. Econ. Report 246, 1973.

52. Harold F. Breimyer and Harold G. Love, *Supplemental Food Programs,* Univ. of Missouri-Columbia, Col. of Agr., Ext. Div. MP 200, 1970.

53. John A. Jamison, "Marketing Orders and Public Policy for the Fruit and Vegetable Industries," *Studies in Agricultural Economics, Trade, and Development,* Stanford Univ., Food Research Inst. 10 (1971): 223–392.

54. Carl E. Shafer, "The Effect of a Marketing Order on Winter Carrot Prices," *Am. J. Agr. Econ.* 50 (1968): 879–87.

55. W. D. Dobson, "A Model for Evaluating Consequences of Changes in Federal Milk Order Pricing Policies," *Am. J. Agr. Econ.* 52 (1970): 599–602.

CHAPTER SEVEN **GOVERNMENTAL POLICIES IN MARKETING**

1. Martin Pfaff, *The Grants Economy: Unilateral Transfers in the U.S. and International Economic Systems* (East Lansing: Institute for Social Science Research, Michigan State Univ., 1968), p. 20.

2. Don Paarlberg, "Statement . . . before the Department Operations Subcommittee, Committee on Agriculture, House of Representatives, Nov. 1, 1971," U.S. Dept. of Agr., 1971.

3. For a brief history of federal marketing services see Harold F. Breimyer, "Fifty Years of Federal Marketing Programs," *J. Farm Econ.* 45 (1963): 749–58.

4. National Commission on Food Marketing, *Food from Farmer to Consumer* (Washington: U.S. Govt. Printing Office, 1966), p. 111.

5. Brown Shoe Co., Inc., v. United States, *U.S. Reports,* vol. 370 (Washington: U.S. Govt. Printing Office, 1962).

6. See Randall E. Torgerson, *Producer Power at the Bargaining Table* (Columbia: Univ. of Missouri Press, 1970).

7. U.S. Department of Agriculture, press release 3478-74.

8. Data from press releases of the U.S. Department of Agriculture.

9. Articles published at the time included Frederick V. Waugh, E. L. Burtis, and A. F. Wolf, "The Controlled Distribution of a Crop Among Independent Markets," *Quar. J. Econ.* 51 (1936): 1–41; and Frederick V. Waugh, "Market Prorates and Social Welfare," *J. Farm Econ.* 20 (1938): 403–16.

10. See the series of reports, *Legal Phases of Farmer Cooperatives,* published by the Farmer Cooperative Service, U.S. Dept. of Agr.; and Joseph G. Knapp, *Capper-Volstead Impact on Cooperative Structure,* U.S. Dept. of Agr., Farmer Cooperative Service, FCS Information 97, 1975.

11. Torgerson, *Producer Power.*

12. See U.S. Department of Agriculture, *Questions and Answers on Federal Milk Marketing Orders,* AMS-559, 1975; and U.S. Department of Agriculture, *Marketing Agreements and Orders for Fruits and Vegetables,* Program Aid No. 1095, 1975.

13. Farmer Cooperative Service, *Price Impacts of Federal Market Order Programs,* Special Report 12, 1975.

CHAPTER EIGHT ECONOMICS OF TRANSPORTATION

1. Terry L. Crawford, "The Bill for Marketing Farm-food Products," *Marketing and Transportation Situation,* U.S. Dept. of Agr., Econ. Res. Serv. Aug. 1974, p. 25.

2. Jules Dupuit, "La Mesure de l'Utilité des Travaux Publics," *Annales des Pont et Chaussées,* Paris, 1844. Reproduced in Frederick V. Waugh, ed., *Readings on Agricultural Marketing* (Ames: Iowa State College Press, 1954), pp. 285–87. (Selection translated by F. V. Waugh, letter to Harold F. Breimyer, Jan. 18, 1969.)

3. William J. Baumol, Burton N. Behling, James C. Bonbright, Yale Brozen, Joel Dean, Ford K. Edwards, Calvin B. Hoover, Dudley F. Pegrum, Merrill J. Roberts, and Ernest W. Williams, Jr., "The Role of Cost in the Minimum Pricing of Railroad Services," *J. Business* 35 (1962): 358–66. Also published, slightly modified, in Donald S. Watson, ed., *Price Theory in Action* (New York: Houghton-Mifflin, 1965), pp. 259–69. Quotations are from former source.

4. Ibid., p. 358.

5. Ibid., p. 360.

6. Ibid., p. 361.

7. Ibid., p. 363.

8. One statement is John Richard Felton, "Commodity Rate Discrimination in Railroad Transport," *Transportation Problems and Policies in the Trans-Missouri West,* Jack R. Davidson and Howard W. Ottoson, eds. (Lincoln: University of Nebraska Press, 1967), pp. 58–80.

9. Baumol et al., p. 361.

10. Ibid., p. 364.

11. Ibid., pp. 365–66. Reprinted by permission of the University of Chicago Press. Copyright 1962 by the University of Chicago.

12. James H. Lauth and Edward F. Heitz, "Rate Making Procedures and Rate Structures," paper delivered at National Extension Transportation Workshop, Univ. of Missouri-Columbia, May 21, 1965, U.S. Dept. of Agr., Agr. Marketing Service, 1965 (mimeographed), p. 22.

13. Ibid., p. 20.

14. See Richard N. Farmer, "The Case for Unregulated Truck Transportation,"

J. Farm Econ. 46 (1964): 398–409; W. Miklius and D. B. DeLoach, "A Further Case for Unregulated Truck Transportation," *J. Farm Econ.* 47 (1965): 933–47; and John C. Spychalski, "Two Cases for Unregulated Truck Transportation: Comment," *J. Farm Econ.* 48 (1966): 124–26.

15. For a brief summary of "the basic transportation cost equation" see Forrest Baker, "The Role of Transportation in Population Distribution," *Increasing Understanding of Public Problems and Policies—1971*, National Public Policy Education Committee (Chicago: Farm Foundation, 1971), pp. 75–81.

16. A reference piece on the "growing crisis" in rural transportation is *Prelude to Legislation to Solve the Growing Crisis in Rural Transportation*, Parts I and II, Committee Print, U.S. Senate, Committee on Agriculture and Forestry, 94th Congress, 1st Session, 1975.

CHAPTER NINE LOCATION AND COMPETITIVE STRUCTURE

1. Johann Heinrich von Thünen, *Der isolierte Staat* (Berlin: Verlag von Wiegandt, Hempel and Parey, 1875).

2. Martin T. Katzman, "The Von Thuenen Paradigm, the Industrial-Urban Hypothesis, and the Spatial Structure of Agriculture," *Am. J. Agr. Econ.* 56 (1974): 683–96.

3. Ibid., p. 694.

4. Kenneth DeHaven, "Conjunctive Effects of Economies of Scale and Rate Structures in Establishing the Geographical Milk Supply Area of the Plant," *J. Econ. Theory* 3 (1971): 199–206.

5. Many references on location theory are available. A few are William Alonso, "Location Theory" in *Regional Development and Planning—A Reader*, John Friedmann and William Alonso, eds., (Cambridge: MIT Press, 1964), pp. 78–106; Melvin Greenhut, *Plant Location in Theory and Practice* (Chapel Hill: Univ. of North Carolina Press, 1956), Chapters 11 and 12; Leon Moses, "Location and the Theory of Production," *Quar. J. Econ.* 72 (1958): 259–72; Claude C. Haren, "Rural Industrial Growth in the 1960's," *Am. J. Agr. Econ.* 52 (1970): 431–37.

CHAPTER TEN MARKETING IN ECONOMIC DEVELOPMENT

1. Harold F. Breimyer, "Influences of Rural Institutions on the Economic Development of Agriculture in Less Developed Countries: Product Markets," in *Institutions in Agricultural Development*, Melvin G. Blase, ed. (Ames: Iowa State Univ. Press, 1971), Ch. 4.

2. Cyril S. Belshaw, *Traditional Exchange and Modern Markets* (Englewood Cliffs: Prentice-Hall, 1965), p. 110.

3. See W. David Hopper, "Discussion: The Role of Agriculture in the World Economy," *J. Farm Econ.* 43 (1961): 345–47.

4. John Abbott, *Marketing Problems and Improvement Programs*, FAO Marketing Guide No. 1, Food and Agriculture Organization of the United Nations, 1958; and Abbott, "The Role of Marketing in the Development of Backward Agricultural Economies," *J. Farm Econ.* 44 (1962): 349–62.

5. Theodore W. Schultz, "Economic Growth from Traditional Agriculture," *Agricultural Sciences for the Developing Nations* (Washington: American Academy for the Advancement of Science, 1964), pp. 185–205.

6. Norman R. Collins and Richard H. Holton, "Programming Changes in Marketing in Planned Economic Development," *Kyklos* 16 (1963): 123–37.

7. James D. Shaffer, "On Institutional Obsolescence and Innovation—Background for Professional Dialogue on Public Policy," *Am. J. Agr. Econ.* 51 (1969): 245–67.

8. Martin Kriesberg, "Introductory Statement," *The Marketing Challenge: Distributing Increased Production in Developing Nations*, U.S. Dept. of Agr., For. Agr. Econ. Report No. 96, 1970, p. 5.

9. Gunnar Myrdal, *Beyond the Welfare State* (New Haven: Yale Univ. Press, 1960), pp. 134–35.

10. Harold F. Breimyer, "The Three Economies of Agriculture," *J. Farm Econ.* 44 (1962): 679–99.

11. Bruce F. Johnston and John W. Mellor, "The Role of Agriculture in Economic Development," *Am. Econ. Rev.* 51 (1961): 566–93.

12. Richard H. Holton, "Marketing Structure and Economic Development," *Quar. J. Econ.* 57 (1953): 344–61.

13. R. M. Lawson, "The Markets for Foods in Ghana," in *Readings in the Applied Economics of Africa, Vol. I: Microeconomics,* Edith Whethan and Jean Currie, eds. (Cambridge: Cambridge Univ. Press, 1967), pp. 173–92.

14. Herman M. Haag and German Rioseco, *Marketing of Grains and Other Farm Products in the Yaqui Valley, Sonora, Mexico,* Southern Ill. Univ., School of Agr., Publication No. 21, Aug. 1965.

15. Kenneth E. Boulding and Pritam Singh, "The Role of the Price Structure in Economic Development," *Am. Econ. Rev.* 52 (1962): 28–38.

16. Hugh L. Cook, "Market Structures and Economic Development in the Philippines," *J. Farm Econ.* 41 (1959): 1316–22.

17. Collins and Holton, p. 134.

18. See Cook, "Market Structures and Economic Development," for observation on cartelization, integration, and restraint upon growth in lieu of satisfactory institutional structure.

19. Cook, p. 1322.

20. Philip M. Raup, "Some Interrelations Between Public Administration and Agricultural Development," *Public Policy,* Harvard Univ., John Fitzgerald Kennedy School of Government, 1967, pp. 29–58.

21. Martin Kriesberg, "Miracle Seeds and Market Economies," *Columbia J. World Business* 4 (Mar.-Apr. 1969): 55–62.

22. Clifton R. Wharton, Jr., "The Green Revolution: Cornucopia or Pandora's Box?" *Foreign Affairs* 47 (1969): 464–76.

23. Boulding and Singh, p. 35.

24. Lee R. Martin, "Some Marketing Problems in Pakistan and India," *J. Farm Econ.* 41 (1959): 1323–26.

GLOSSARY OF TERMS AND CONCEPTS

Collective bargaining (p. 114): negotiation between two or more opposing groups or organizations conducted in an attempt to arrive at price and/or other terms of trade including terms of contracts.

Conglomerate firm (p. 85): a firm that engages in marketing in two or more different industries.

Function (pp. 9–10): a particular activity (process or service) performed in marketing.

Interpersonal comparison of utility (p. 25): comparison of the psychic appreciation (positive or negative) of productive effort or of consumption as sensed by two or more individuals.

Market clearing price versus administered price (p. 114): the former is a price arrived at ("made" or "discovered") under conditions in which the total quantity offered for sale must be sold; the latter is a price affixed by seller or buyer without a requirement that a particular quantity be sold or bought.

Marketing institution (p. 12): narrow definition, a business entity in marketing (including an individual); broad definition, the business entities, rules, laws, and conventions involved in marketing.

Marketing's dual missions (p. 15): the physical or operational mission of getting product from producer to consumer, and the direction-giving or coordinative mission of motivating, directing, and coordinating the process.

Organizational versus competitive structure of the marketing system: both structures are empirical but they differ in orientation. Organizational structure (pp. 8–12), an anatomical term, relates to how institutions and functions link to comprise the marketing system. Competitive structure (pp. 63–87) pertains to the particular characteristics of the system that affect the competitive behavior of institutions.

Price competition versus nonprice competition (p. 67): price competition is confined to competing for sale or purchase of a product on the basis of its price alone. Contrariwise, the price of a product affects only its sale or purchase. Nonprice competition introduces means other than price in the sale or purchase of a product.

Price-making or price-discovery versus supply and demand analysis of prices (pp. 113–23): the former applies to the actual mechanics of arriving at a price; the latter assesses the underlying economic forces.

Stage (pp. 9–10): a point, or an interruption, in the sequential movement of product from producer to consumer at which functions are performed.

Standard versus differentiated product (p. 58): a standard product is one in which all items are essentially homogeneous and sharply distinguished from other products. A differentiated product bears a close resemblance to another product. It sometimes is a modification of a more basic or typical form.

Stratification of the market (p. 69): division of a market so that a standard product can be sold or bought at different prices, or varying qualities of a product can be sold or bought at the same price. The principle can be extended to stratified differentiation, in which nominal differentiation is employed as a means to stratify the market.

Structure-conduct-performance (p. 80): in this approach attributed to Bain, structure relates to the characteristics of an industry (which may extend to an entire system) defined as "competitive structure" above. Conduct pertains to the discretionary actions taken by a firm or other institution, including especially the competitive tactics employed. Performance refers to the aggregate results, usually viewed in terms of an industry or the marketing system.

Vertical integration (p. 82): exercise by a single firm of control over a product at two or more contiguous stages in marketing.

Workable or effective competition (p. 81): standards of market conduct and/or performance that are both attainable and socially acceptable.

INDEX